**Residential Spatial
Structure**

Residential Spatial Structure

Michael C. Romanos
University of Illinois at
Urbana-Champaign

Lexington Books
D.C. Heath and Company
Lexington, Massachusetts
Toronto   London

Library of Congress Cataloging in Publication Data

Romanos, Michael C.
    Residential spatial structure.

    Includes bibliographical references.
    1. Housing—Mathematical models. 2. Cities and towns—
Mathematical models. 3. Land—Mathematical models. I. Title.
HD7287.5.R59   301.5'4   75-37469
ISBN 0-669-00490-1

Copyright © 1976 by D.C. Heath and Company

Published simultaneously in Canada

Printed in the United States of America

International Standard Book Number: 0-669-00490-1

Library of Congress Catalog Card Number: 75-37469

To Vasso

Contents

List of Figures and Table

Table

Foreword

The work of Professor Michael Romanos is the newest addition to the Regional Science Monograph Series of Lexington Books. In some respects it differs from the other volumes which have appeared over the past four years. It attacks boldly a topic of great current interest and one in which our underlying theories are particularly deficient. In its careful analysis of the state of the arts in this crucial area, classification of existing theories and models, discussion of underlying assumptions, conclusions, and testing procedures, this book is unique to the literature.

Of the many restrictive, often unrealistic assumptions beclouding the issue of spatial structure of residential areas, the existence of a single center upon which all urban functions are focusing is perhaps the most damaging. Almost without exception, the numerous theories and models dealing with the subject either assume explicitly a monocentric city or simply multiply the centers without changing the basic assumptions concerning the behavior of households in urban space. Professor Romanos goes beyond this simplistic postulate. The multi-center framework he adopted and the rigorous demonstration of the spatial consequences to which it leads represent a significant contribution. His work exposes one of the causes of the lack of agreement between predictions based on elaborate and mathematically elegant models and observed spatial patterns. He shows the intensity of land uses and the values of land in the areas between two urban centers to be considerably higher than those of the older theories.

In many ways the work of Romanos represents the final word in this line of modeling urban structures, clearing the way for other approaches. Future work, intimated in the present volume, may go beyond the assumed desire of households to minimize broadly conceived traveling costs and involve such factors as the changing social composition of neighborhoods, the incidence of violent crime, or the quality of schools. Yet, our ability to incorporate these considerations into models of urban structure is obviously predicated on substantial progress in wide areas of the social sciences which may be far away.

Professor Romanos does not claim to have solved the involved issues of social motivation in decision-making processes of households, but he does provide some new exciting insights. Because of the comprehensive review of the field of urban residential structure and of the new ideas presented, this work richly deserves to be read by students of urban problems.

Stan Czamanski

xiii

Preface

This volume is the result of two years of intensive thinking and theorizing on the state of the art and on problems in the area of intra-urban residential location. The final word in the analysis of household behavior has still not been written, yet new analytical efforts add to our understanding of locational decisions within the urban area. It is with that hope that this book is published.

This study was begun while the author was a resident scholar at the General Motors Research Laboratories, and was completed at Cornell University under partial support by the Cornell Western Societies Program. The findings, opinions, conclusions and recommendations in this report are those of the author and it should not be implied that they represent the views of either the General Motors Research Laboratories or the Cornell Western Societies Program.

A number of individuals deserve credit for their help and assistance in making this study a reality. I am grateful, especially, to Professor Stan Czamanski for introducing me to the new and dynamic field of Regional Science, and for stimulating my interest in intra-metropolitan problems. His incisive comments and suggestions were crucial in the development of this study. Thanks are also due to Professor Walter Isard for his constructive criticism and advice, and to Professor Robert Frank for his creative suggestions in the early stages of this work.

I am most grateful to Mr. David Edelman, a doctoral student in City and Regional Planning at Cornell University, for his continuous editing assistance and his helpful comments on earlier drafts of the study. I also wish to express my gratitude to Mrs. Renee Pierce who competently typed the final draft during long, sleepless nights.

Finally, to my wife Vasso, whose love and support were a continuous source of strength and encouragement throughout the long months of preparation, I would like to express my deep appreciation. Her faith and her devotion gave me confidence needed to complete this work. I gratefully dedicate this book to her.

**Part I
Review of Residential
Location Literature**

1 Introduction

The Character of Urban Phenomena

The problems with which our society is faced are of such complexity that it is becoming increasingly difficult to deal with them successfully. Very often the dimensions of this complexity are not immediately obvious due to the limited available information regarding a phenomenon. However, our efforts to understand such problems through research and analysis continually uncover additional aspects which indicate they are even more complex than we originally thought.

Urban phenomena are among the most difficult to cope with, not only because of their variability and the frequency with which they occur, but also because of the great number of people directly or indirectly affected by them. Two categories of urban phenomena can be identified: phenomena of *socioeconomic* interaction which concern the social and/or economic characteristics and objectives of groups or individuals; and phenomena of *spatial* interaction in which these individuals and/or groups act with reference to the physical and man-made environment. This classification is not discrete, and most phenomena share both types of interaction. And while the sources of urban problems will be found, for the most part, within the first type, it is usually through the second that such interactions become obvious and their effects recognized. Thus, while urban poverty, for example, is caused by an inadequate and malfunctioning market mechanism and by class discrimination, its physical manifestation, the slum, is seen as a problem of "spatial form" or "urban appearance."

It becomes obvious, then, that urban spatial problems should be analyzed not only within their spatial or environmental context, but primarily within their social and economic setting. In this way the underlying causes of the spatial phenomomenon will be revealed, confronted and dealt with. To accomplish this difficult task, however, urban analysis must borrow tools from the social sciences and adjust them to take into account the peculiarities of the urban entity and its components.

That need, in addition to the introduction of "spatial" concepts into the social sciences and the attempts to deal with the traditionally neglected interactions of political, social, and economic forces which cut across the orthodox social science disciplines, necessitated the development of a

3

distinct body of theory dealing with such phenomena, namely, the field of regional science. According to Isard and Reiner, regional science:

> . . . as any social science . . . has three facets which, in any one study, may merge: (1) the normative, (2) the descriptive, and (3) the deductive. Thus, the distribution of a system of urban places in a region, such as a nation or a part of a nation, can be approached *normatively* as in the evaluation of conditions in many developing nations with high concentrations of population in the capital metropolitan areas, *descriptively* (or behavioristically) as in the analysis of existing distributions of hierarchies or rankings of urban centers, and *deductively,* as in the development of a theory of regional urban structure from positions of personal demand functions, distances between consumers, economies of scale, and transport rates.[1]

But regional science is more than just the field which provides the theoretical basis and justification for the use of particular models in planning. As Walter Isard noted in defending the new field at the second national meeting of the Regional Science Association in 1956, the broader scope of regional science is "the study of the full array of the . . . direct and indirect implications [of the physical environment] . . ."[2]

Purpose and Scope of the Study

In keeping with these underlying principles, this study attempts to improve the present state of the art concerning the residential location decision-making behavior of urban households.

Residential land is the largest single component of urban land use, averaging some 40 percent of the total developed land and roughly 80 percent of the land area in all private uses in urban communities.[3] A significant portion of all other uses, such as streets and shopping centers, is closely related to dwelling use. As a result, residential land use is an area of considerable interest. Furthermore, because it is the generator of most types of urban traffic, including the journey to work, shopping, personal business, school, and recreation, and because it contains almost the entire labor force of the city, residential land is one of the major determinants of urban structure. Increasing our predictive skills in defining the nature of the demand for urban space by the household sector will also improve our ability to predict its land requirements, as well as urban growth and change, and emerging patterns of urban transportation.

Because of the importance of residential location problems, considerable interest has been shown and effort expended by sociologists, economists, and urban planners to explain and predict individual locational behavior. Despite this concern, however, the existing theories of residential location have not been very successful in explaining actual locational patterns. This is due to the fact that while the locational decision is quite a complex one, the theories offered have had to rely heavily upon highly abstracting and simplifying assumptions. Although there is obviously a great need for such theories, it is also apparent that the relationships which research has detected within the urban structure must be articulated so that models may be constructed to take into account as many special features and peculiarities of the locational process as possible. However, this has not been done very often, and as a result, there exists a gap between the theoretical concepts and the empirical work which attempts to test them.

Theories of residential location have usually developed a mathematical model using the generally accepted assumptions listed below:

1. There exists only one center of economic activity, the Central Business District, where all employment is concentrated;
2. The rest of the urban area is devoted to residential uses;
3. There exists an isotropically distributed radial road network, so that transport costs are the same in all directions;
4. The home-to-work journey is the determinant of accessibility; and
5. All households have identical tastes and preferences.

Any attempt to relax one of these assumptions usually occurs after the model has been completely developed. Furthermore, the rest of the basic assumptions remain unaltered. But such an approach accepts the initial structure of the model—i.e., the set of axioms on which the model is built—as correct, and shows how *this model* is capable of dealing with certain phenomena when some of its assumptions are modified. This does not, however, mean that the modified model is indeed capable of explaining all the dimensions of the actual phenomenon. Thus, the model may distort reality since relaxing just one, or even more than one, of the assumptions at a time does not necessarily make the model's approach any more pragmatic.

One of the most critical assumptions found in most theoretical treatments of residential location is the assumption of a single center of economic activity for an urban area. This is where all employment is concentrated, and where all journey-to-work is channeled by means of the isotropic transportation network. This assumption alone largely determines the form of the urban area as well as its patterns of growth and outward expansion. Its value for the analysis of urban characteristics has been considerable indeed, but often its users have not completely realized the limitations which the assumption imposes.[4] Thus, most models of residential location begin with the assumption of monocentricity, although some later attempt to modify it by considering urban areas containing more than one center.[5] The attempts are either intuitively[6] stated or rigorously formatulated (as in the case of Muth[7]). The problem in most of these cases is still that the model keeps certain basic attributes unchanged despite the "reality" introduced with the acceptance of additional urban centers. A notable exception to this practice is the analysis performed by Quigley.[8] "Urban center" or "urban economic center" is taken here to mean the locus of concentration of a variety of economic activities as opposed to those activities dispersed in the urban area around it. These activities are considered to be all services, retail and business transactions, entertainment, etc.

One such simplified model concerns the attitudes and behavior of households. They are assumed in this instance to remain the same regardless of the number of urban centers in their immediate area. Thus, in the multiple-center case, each household is still assumed to depend upon only one center—*its* center—for employment and shopping, so that the presence of other centers will not affect its residential location choice. This, however, is not necessarily true. First, there may be more than one working member in a household, and if so, they are not necessarily employed in the same urban center. Second, even if only one member of the household is working, he does not commit himself permanently to one center because he knows that there are employment opportunities in the remaining centers, and he wants to keep his options open. Third, employment centers are also shopping places, business transaction places, recreational centers etc., so that individuals and households are also attracted there for reasons other than employment.

Theses of the Study

In the light of the above discussion, the major thesis of this study is that in urban areas containing more than one center of economic activity, a household will take into account the location and the magnitude of *all* these centers, and not only of the one where the head of the household is employed. In addition, this study argues that in the presence of several urban centers, the distribution of values of certain important urban variables such as the prices of land and housing will be drastically different than what has been suggested by earlier studies.

This is due to the aggregate effect of these centers which differs for the various residential locations within the urban area. For example, in a city of two urban centers, it is argued that the price of housing will generally be higher in the area between the two centers than in the areas towards the urban periphery, and that this is because the locations between the two centers have the more advantageous total accessibility to places of employment, shopping, etc.

The difference between the usual approach and the thesis being offered

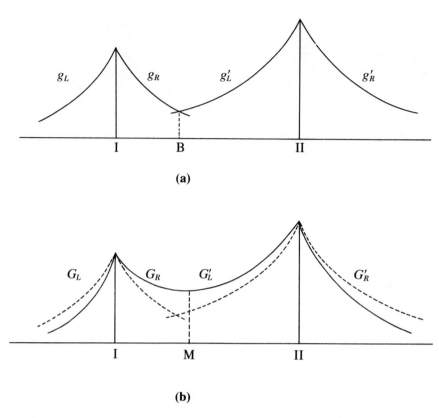

Figure 1-1. Modification of Urban Gradients When Multiple Centers Are Considered Simultaneously

is shown in figure 1-1. Figure 1-1a shows the rent gradients for a linear city with two centers, I and II, under most existing theories. The gradients g_L and g_R, g_L' and g_R', are identical since it is assumed that at equal distances from the center of activity, accessibility is the same, and thus the land, housing and rent values are also the same. In figure 1-1b, the same city is presented, but now the gradients G_L and G_R, G_L' and G_R' are quite different from each other. This is because the locations between centers I and II have greater accessibility advantages, and thus higher values of the aforementioned variables. In other words, the higher demand for say, housing, in the area between I and II will greatly alter the balance of housing prices in the whole urban area.

Furthermore, the boundary B of figure 1-1a between the two "markets" for the urban center goods and services is meaningless in figure 1-1b. The point M now corresponds to the location of the lowest value of the variable—be it land value, or housing value, etc.—but there is no actual boundary to the area of each center users. Since every household living in the area has the option and the possibility of using *both* centers, it will not want to confine itself within any one market area boundary.

This comparison of the two gradient configurations is based on a set of assumptions which are generally employed in the development of the monocentric models. It is thus assumed that nonresidential activity is concentrated at the urban centers so that the rest of the urban area is devoted to residential use alone; that the whole urban area expands on a land surface with undifferentiated physical features so that no location is more desirable than any other location because of such characteristics; and finally, that the market analyzed is a perfectly competitive one so that prices are not determined as a result of speculation or other market mis-functions.

The concept of the "market area," which has been widely used in rural areas, is not as clearly and easily defined in the case of densely populated areas. Since William J. Reilly developed his laws of "retail gravitation" in the early 1930s,[9] there have been numerous efforts to define the "break-ing-point" between market areas. There have even been some recent works, notably Richard Muth's attempt which is discussed in Chapter 4 of this study (pp. 75-78). The search for breaking-points is, of course, a consequence of the deterministic approach followed by most models of location. Within metropolitan regions, however, there is no such thing as an absolute breaking-point. As Brian Berry states:

In densely built-up areas consumers have considerable business centers of differing attractiveness available within the maximum distances they are willing to travel. They will visit none exclusively, but each at some time and some probability.[10]

This study attempts to develop a model of household residential loca-tion incorporating some of the key variables in the locational decision choice, while relaxing two basic assumptions concerning the spatial pattern of the urban area and the behavior of the individual household. The two assumptions relaxed concern (i) the monocentric city pattern, and (ii) the exclusive use of only one urban center by each household.

The model follows an approach used by other theorists of household location to determine equilibrium in the market for consumers and produc-ers of housing. The model is a spatial microeconomic one, focusing on the individual household as representative of the urban group analyzed, and using a set of assumptions similar to the ones used in previous similar locational studies. The main difference, then, between this and previous studies lies in the relaxation of the two important assumptions mentioned above. In this way, the locational attitudes of households in the presence of many urban centers of economic activity may be taken into account.

This study does not pretend to be a complete analysis of the household residential location choice, if only because the analysis performed here basically concerns accessibility considerations. It presents, however, a complete model of the decision process in the setting of the contemporary metropolis, and confronts it with analogous monocentric theories. Thus, it identifies and brings to the fore the points of divergence of the generalized monocentric model and the simultaneous polycentric model developed herein. And since the primary purpose of the study is to show the variation of the variable values caused by the presence of many urban centers, as well as the changing individual attitudes in the presence of these centers, the view taken here is considered to be justified.

Variables of primary interest to the study are the ones which best indicate the desirability of particular locations to households, and which are primarily responsible for the over all urban residential structure. Their equilibrium spatial distribution within the metropolis is the problem with which this study is concerned. These variables are:

1. The price per unit of housing, an index of the desirability of a particular housing bundle by households. A housing bundle is composed of the land, the physical structure, and all the auxiliaries necessary to provide the complete range of what is usually called "housing services";
2. The residential land rent, an indicator of the relative desirability of the various locations due to their particular locational advantages;
3. The quantity of housing per unit of land, a variable considered to represent the building densities in the various areas of the city; and
4. The quantity of housing consumed per household, a variable indicating the distribution of households in relation to the prevailing urban densities.

About Theory and Models

In order for complex phenomena to be understood and analyzed so that useful decisions can be made, there is a need for abstraction to reduce the many complex components of the problem to its essentials. While such abstractions necessarily reduce both the degree of detail and the level of reality of the problem, it is only through them that exercises of great magnitude and complexity can be undertaken. This, then, is the use of that level of abstraction of reality which we call "theory."

More precisely, a theory constitutes "an integrated body of definitions, assumptions, and general propositions covering a given subject from which a comprehensive and consistent set of specific and testable hypotheses can be deduced logically."[11] These hypotheses must also take a form permitting causal explanation and prediction. Of these two characteristics, the former is present when a "causal" relationship is hypothesized between some program or activity and some desired effect. This concept is perceived as a chain or nexus of events usually related along a time continuum. As formulated by Chapin, "cause and effect, or causality as a system of ideas, is an explanation of successive events by a set of assumed antecedent-consequent relationships . . ."[12] On the other hand, the latter, that of prediction, characterizes a particular theory when the hypotheses deduced give value to some property not immediately observed. Therefore a prediction in this context is actually equivalent to a generalization.[13]

However, causality and prediction alone do not sufficiently explain the uses and advantages of theoretical development. The two attributes in fact may be included in scientific research that does not even involve theory. What gives a special role to theory, then, is the consistency of its definitions, assumptions, and propositions with previous research findings and current observations; the minimum number of such definitions, assumptions, and general propositions contained in the body of the theory; the ability to give testable form to its deduced hypotheses; and its success in having these hypotheses verified empirically.[14]

Based on the above sequence, it is useful to consider theory as an axiomatic system composed of three types of statements: definitions, axioms, and theorems. Definitions are the self-evident, precise statements of the essential nature of a phenomenon, while axioms are generally accepted propositions which are taken to be true during the course of the theoretical argument. These axioms or postulates are the requirements necessary for the development of the theory, and serve to define its structure. Every other statement in the theory is proved from the axioms and/or other statements already proven in a logical and precise way. Such statements are referred to as theorems. Theorems, then, are propositions demonstrable by reasoning using a body of definitions and axioms.[15]

Because of these characteristics, theory is extremely valuable as the starting point for empirical research. It not only provides testable hypotheses, but also permits cumulative research and allows a systematic research procedure. On the other hand, the fact that theory facilitates the research process can allow it to be misused. Historically this has caused many wasted years of work and generated some very famous scientific debates.[16]

In discussing the numerous theories constituting the state of the art pertaining to residential location, the axiomatic approach just described will be followed. Although the theorists who will be discussed seldom use it explicitly, it is considered a very useful system of reference for two important reasons. First, it forces an explicit description of the assumptions and postulates used in the theoretical development, and second, it allows the deduction of both obvious and obscure implications of these a priori postulates.

Within the context of the social sciences, theory attempts to identify single variables or more complex factors, and trace their role and the ways in which they interact with the social environment in forming social phenomena. These variables and their relationships are then recorded in symbolic form creating sets of mathematically expressed functions called "mathematical models." As long as these variables can be measured, or at least ordered, such expressions are possible to formulate.

There are cases where models may not be mathematical. Basically, one can distinguish between two types of models, the *physical* and the *conceptual,* according to the way in which they represent the real world. There are also two types of physical models, *analogue* models and *iconic* models:

a. The *analogue models* use one physical entity to represent another. Such models are often used for simulation purposes, particularly in traffic studies;

b. The *iconic models* constitute a scale representation of the real world. Maps, and architectural and engineering models are examples of this type.

Conceptual models can also be classified further into *verbal* models and *symbolic* models.

c. The *verbal models* are descriptions of reality in logical terms and use spoken words. Their value for predicting or precisely specifying the state of a system is limited;

d. The *symbolic models,* the most significant type of model, are usually expressed in mathematical terms. In this type of model, functions among mathematical symbols express real world relationships and phenomena.

The two terms "theory" and "model," however, are not interchangeable, although there is a tendency among writers to use them as such. In a discussion of this tendency, Czamanski states:

. . . in theory the emphasis is on logical coherence and generality, while a model is bound by data availability. Hence, a model has to be explicit where a theory directed towards a vigorous derivation of logical and relevant propositions from parsimonious postulates can afford to be more vague.[17]

Thus, a model consists of a number of observable and measurable variables interconnected through a set of mathematical formulae. (From this point on in the book, the word "model" is taken to mean "symbolic" or "mathematical" model.) The nature of these variables and their roles and positions within the model essentially define the type of model with which we deal. Tinbergen's classification of types of variables, adopted by Czamanski, distinguishes five main categories based upon the role of the variables within the model. These are:

1. *Target variables*—i.e., those in whose behavior we are interested;
2. *Intermediate variables*—which are involved in the description and operation of the model, but are themselves of no immediate interest;
3. *Instrument variables*—which can be influenced by policy makers;
4. *Data variables*—which are exogenously determined, and independent of the model; and
5. *Lagged endogenous variables*—which may be intermediate and/or target variables considered endogenous because they enter the model with time lags.[18]

Furthermore, depending on whether the various types of variables are treated as inputs or outputs, four types of social science models may be distinguished.[19] They are:

1. *Analytical or Descriptive models*, which simply reduce the complexity of the described phenomenon by aggregating its most relevant features;
2. *Forecasting models*, in which the causal relationships endogenous to the phenomenon are made explicit. In this type of model the data and instrument variables are used as inputs while the intermediate and target variables are the outputs;
3. *Conditional models*, which constitute an "if . . . then . . ." variation of the forecasting models when no definite future values can be assigned to some of the input variables; and
4. *Planning models*, which are the inverse of the forecasting models since the data target variables become inputs while the instrument variables are outputs. The difference between planning and forecasting models lies in the type of problems to which they address themselves. Thus, a forecasting model will give the future value of a target variable when the future values of the instrument and data variables are given by the operation of the model alone, while a planning model will try to determine the future values of the instrument variables so that the data and target variables will have certain specified future values.

Models have been used in the social sciences for a long time, although initially their use was quite fragmentary.[a] As long as the problems dealt with were relatively simple and easy to comprehend, such use was satisfactory. However, as social scientists gradually became involved in more

---

[a] In economics in particular, Cournot, Marshall, Edgeworth, Walras and Keynes, among others, all relied heavily on mathematical models of economic systems, although some of them, particularly Marshall, detailed a largely nonmathematical exposition.

complex problems, the need for more general and consistent theoretical treatments of social phenomena became apparent. This awareness has been particularly obvious in the treatment of residential location problems where a variety of different approaches has been applied to the analysis and description of the decision process and its resulting urban configurations. Thus, it is necessary to precede the development of the multi-center model of residential location with an analysis and critique of the literature and the various approaches to the problem contained therein.

Study Format

The review of residential location literature is the subject of the first part of the study and consists of Chapters 2 to 4. The analysis performed attempts to (1) classify the various theories and models of residential location primarily on the basis of their fundamental underlying assumptions, and (2) present the most characteristic examples of each of these categories. Thus, while the literature search was as exhaustive as possible, not every single scholarly work on residential location is discussed here. Such an effort would be a major undertaking in its own right. The studies thoroughly presented are the ones considered to be path-breaking efforts that have contributed significantly to our understanding of the urban residential location phenomenon. In addition, studies which have added important elements to the above structure, or have corrected or clarified basic issues, are also mentioned.

Thus, Chapter 2 is a presentation of descriptive models containing basically the land use modeling and land allocation efforts with their applications in major land use and transportation studies, as well as the applications and limitations of the density gradient, gravity, and potential types of models. Chapter 3 then discusses explanatory theories and models which follow a macro-spatial approach to analysis. The two orientations discussed are those of the urban land and real estate school and the human ecological school. Finally, Chapter 4 presents the more behavioral, microeconomic models in which the individual household, rather than the population group, constitutes the unit of analysis. Within this context, models are distinguished as either operational or theoretical and the various approaches to each of the two categories are discussed. The chapter ends with a more in-depth analysis of the equilibrium monocentric model. Its weaknesses and its applicability to the simulation of the residential location process in the multi-center metropolis are discussed.

The second part of the study deals with the development of such a model. Chapter 5 describes the locational decision of households in a linear, one-dimensional city with two or more centers of economic activities and employment. The target variables are derived mathematically on the basis of exogenously determined data variables, and suggestions are made for modifications and additional refinements in the treatment of the problem. Chapter 6 then generalizes the model for a two-dimensional urban area with several urban centers. Alternative paths to the development of such a model are suggested, and the end distributions of certain variables are discussed. Finally, Chapter 7 summarizes the effort presented in this book and discusses its contribution to the existing state of the art. It further suggests ways in which this effort can be improved upon and thereby become useful as a planning and policy tool.

2

Macro-Spatial Models of Residential Land Allocation

State of the Art

The fundamental importance of the location of residences to the spatial arrangement of activities in urban areas and the extent to which urban land is taken up by residential uses have stimulated a considerable number of theoretical and applied studies. However, the direction a particular study has taken has usually depended upon the purpose of the study and the field or discipline within which it originated. Thus, researchers have analyzed the patterns of residential location and/or the behavior of the locating households in a variety of ways.

Although there are no clear distinctions among the different orientations, several basic categories of studies can be identified. These are based upon the principal approach followed in developing the theory or model of residential location. The literature will therefore be organized for review and analysis into four groupings presented in ascending order of the degree of sophistication in assumptions used and procedures followed:

1. Efforts using an "assignment" approach in dealing with the land distribution in a specific area;
2. Models based on a gravity or potential type assumption in allocating residential land;
3. Theories following the human ecology approach in exploring patterns of residential land distribution; and
4. Theories and models using behavioral postulates in simulating individual or group residential location decisions.[1]

The first two categories deal with the problem of distributing new households among the zones of an urban area, while the latter two classifications attempt to analyze the physical, social, and economic factors entering the decision process of the locating new households.

In this chapter, there are two types of models dealt with: land allocation studies of the "assignment" category, based on observed regularities and mainly used in the early land use-transportation studies, and models of spatial interaction—the gravity and potential formulations.

15

The "Assignment" Approach

Early metropolitan transportation studies, such as the Detroit Area Traffic Study and the Chicago Area Transportation Study, dealt broadly with residential location as part of their overall land use analysis and forecasting. The individuals who conducted these studies realized the importance of understanding residential location patterns for the development of their trip generation models. Their traffic and origin-destination surveys revealed important associations between the volumes of generated traffic and the various types of land use. Residential land use in particular was found to be most important. For instance, it generated approximately 53 percent of all the daily traffic in the Chicago area.[2] These transportation studies attempted to describe and predict traffic flows as a function of residential and nonresidential acreage, densities, and location.

Since the early transportation studies did not utilize automatic equipment as extensively as subsequent ones, their efforts were limited to describing observed regularities in the patterns of land uses. That is, they did not explain the reasons for the occurrence of such patterns and can therefore be classified as *ad hoc* attempts.

Studies of this category generally use a technique involving three major operations. The first is to determine the proportions of land in each sub-area of the urban area studied to be set aside for housing and related uses. Next is to determine the densities at which residential land uses will be built up, and the computation of a "holding capacity"[3] for each sub-area (i.e., the maximum number of dwelling units for each sub-area that can be accommodated in the available vacant and renewable land in accordance with the zoning and density standards). Finally, the last step involves the allocation of the estimated total of new households among housing and density types, and then among the zones or sub-areas according to local trends, conditions, population, and income factors, etc.

This method was used in the Detroit Area Traffic Study by J. Douglas Carroll and his associates in the early fifties.[4] The assumptions on which it was based were that: (1) the cost of a site is higher the more accessible the site is, (2) high site costs result in high intensity of land use, (3) the central business district is the point of highest accessibility, and (4) with increasing distance from the CBD, supply more nearly equals demand so that site costs are reduced and less intensive development results.

These macro-level assumptions concern the urban area as a whole, and provide the framework for the application of the previously presented allocational model. Considering the state of the art at the time, this assignment process was a contribution in the right direction. As a pioneering effort, it identified the assumptions related to the patterns of urban growth and expansion, noted the importance of accessibility to location, and applied the holding capacity technique to allocate future land uses by zone. An improved version of the "assignment" approach was used in the Chicago Area Transportation Study by Carroll and Hamburg, who were already experienced in the Detroit techniques. The part of the study dealing with residential land use is most relevant here in that it employed the notion of the density-saturation gradient.[5]

The density-saturation gradient was an observed regularity obtained through land use and population analysis. In forecasting land use, the procedures developed were to be objective, systematic, sufficiently mechanical, and able to detect quantified regularities in the organization of land use. These procedures were based on certain axioms concerning urban structure and growth, namely that: (1) various activities compete for available sites so that the most desirable sites receive the highest bid; (2) higher site costs in turn result in more intensive use of the site; (3) site is more "desirable" if it is more accessible to other sites; and (4) the central business district is taken as the location of highest accessibility while peripheral sites are considered less accessible.

In order to allocate future city residents among sub-areas, the population holding capacity by zone was obtained by multiplying the net acreages of designated residential land by estimated residential densities for each zone, and by adding the product to current population. Next, the ratio of the existing population to population capacity was obtained. Plotting that ratio indicated a considerable regularity in the density distribution as shown in figure 2-1.

It was observed that the curve of figure 2-1 reached a peak of 96 percent at 7 miles from the central business district (the density-saturation point), and that the peak was moving away from the center at a rate of 1.6 miles per decade. Both the peak and the rate of peak movement were assumed to remain constant during the forecast period. Consequently, the future percentage of holding capacity for each zone was determined and was multiplied by its estimated capacity in order to obtain estimates of future population allocation by zone. These estimates were then subjectively adjusted for proximity to expressways and city services, and for other spatial peculiarities.

The modified assignment procedure used in the Chicago study does not constitute a "model" of residential location. However, it approximates a predictive model in that it hypothesizes a certain growth process rather than rely upon arbitrary judgement in distributing residences among zones. This growth process is viewed as an essentially concentric expansion of densities about an inner zone. Nevertheless, it says little about the forces causing the observed distribution in the urban area.

There are several objections to the assumptions concerning urban spatial pattern and growth processes. First, the theory places too much em-

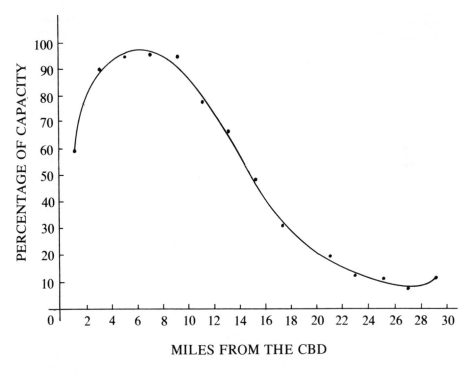

Source: J.R. Hamburg and R.L. Creighton, "Predicting Chicago's Land Use Pattern," *Journal of the American Institute of Planners* 25, 2 (May 1959).

Figure 2-1. Chicago Area Transportation Study—1956 Population as a Percentage of Population Capacity

phasis on site accessibility; a site exhibits a value not only because of its location relative to the city center, but also because of the particular functions and characteristics of the site. Second, the central business district is not the only center in a metropolitan area; there are additional centers, the accessibility to which should also be considered. Finally, there is no real justification for the adoption of the density gradient for forecasting purposes.

As far as the process itself is concerned, only one of the four stated objectives, systematization, was actually achieved. Furthermore, the procedure itself was neither objective nor machine-processing-amenable since there were several subjective decisions made by the study team, one example being the determination of the various zonal densities. In addition, since there was no real use of quantitative analysis at any stage of the procedure, one might challenge the extent to which it used quantifiable regularities of land use.

While the Chicago Study made a considerable effort to operationalize a set of explicit hypotheses concerning urban spatial patterns, there were other parallel efforts to improve the conceptualization of the urban growth process and construct a reliable theory of land use changes. A major such contributor was Ernest Jurkat.[6] Jurkat's studies for the Philadelphia-Southern New Jersey Transportation Region and the St. Louis Metropolitan Area provided a more sophisticated analysis of the relationship between traffic generation rates and both residential and nonresidential land uses. In conceptualizing the residential location problem, Jurkat suggested a distance-density distribution of class where, "for all practical purposes, class differentiation can be basically reduced to income differentiation . . ."[7] More precisely, both distance and density were associated with particular costs of a residence; and the balancing of the distance and density costs with the income potential (opportunity) of individual residents would produce the "locational equilibrium." Thus,

If (income) potential . . . increases, locational equilibrium is sought at a higher level of density cost or distance cost or both. If density and/or distance cost decrease, locational equilibrium can be achieved with lower yields of opportunity.[8]

Jurkat's proposal also included a dynamic gravity model based on the above balance assumption. Thus, the effort is a transitional one and belongs between the two classes of models rather than in the group of "assignment" studies. In his own words:

The principal aspect a dynamic gravity model has to define and explain is the geographical distribution of change in residential and non-residential densities that will be compatible with uniform locational equilibrium ratios throughout the metropolitan area. This can be accomplished by relating the distributions of density change to the distributions of the factors that have been recognized as the generators of change.[9]

These generators of change are considered to be the expansion of population, economic activity and productivity, the improvement of both public and private transportation facilities, the decrease in travel distance/time, and institutional arrangements as taxation, zoning, etc.

In summary, the land use allocations analyzed thus far use a simplified theory of the pattern and growth of cities. Accessibility to central services is taken to determine the intensity of land use and, consequently, its density. This in turn determines the type and extent of land use based upon the user's ability to pay for the particular site costs. Thus, the two determinants of residential land use, "accessibility" and "density," are of interest here. While accessibility is used by the majority of the approaches to be analyzed later and will therefore be discussed again, density as a crucial element in all descriptive studies (as the density gradient) requires more analysis at this point.

Density Models

To begin, with one major urban center as the point of optimum total access and the focus of activities affected by the same kind of attraction—accessibility—density peaks at the center and falls off in all directions with increasing distance. This regularity then, was fundamental to all the assignment models. Furthermore, it became the pivotal element for a subclass of models called "density models."

The first analytic formulation of the density gradient was given by Colin Clark,[10] who based his formulation on two assumptions:

1. Residential densities are high in the interior of the city and progressively decline towards the outer suburbs; and

2. In most cities, high inner densities tend to fall, and low outer-suburban densities tend to rise over time.

Empirical analysis has provided evidence that the density gradient is given by a negative exponential equation of the form:

$$d_r = d_o e^{-br}, \tag{2.1}$$

where d_r = density of resident population at radial distance r from the center,

d_o = the peak density at the center of the city,

b = a slope factor, and

e = the base of natural logarithms.

In this formulation, the coefficient b of the exponent measures the steepness of the gradient. A high value of b indicates a sharply declining density with distance, while a low value means a slowly declining density.

Although Clark's formulation appeared to be a good fit to his own sample data, as well as to data used by other researchers,[11] it failed to provide a theoretical rationale for the equation. Such an explanation was provided later by Berry, Simmons, and Tennant,[12] and others to be discussed in the behavioral models section. But several studies of the density gradient showed that it followed almost identical patterns over the past half-century, and gave support to the "crest of the wave" theory of urban growth. Hans Blumenfeld, among others, correlated these density patterns and the pace with which they shift away from the center over time with future population distribution in the Toronto area.[13] The results of his and other similar studies indicate that the practical application of population trends analysis has several limitations. First, such formulae are based on observed past trends which are assumed to continue unaltered;[14] although, in reality, they may change in the future. Second, the analysis is applicable only to certain rings where suburban growth occurs, and it is not adequate for the rest of the urban area. Finally, while the conclusions may be valid for an urban concentric ring as a whole, they yield no information on densities within the various segments of the ring.[15]

Discussion and criticism of the density gradient has stimulated efforts to detect the major factors influencing the levels and shape of urban densities. Some of these factors are the age of the city,[16] the size of the SMSA and the proportion of manufacturing outside the central city,[17] and distortion of the shape of the urban area.[18] However, the multiple regression models employed in these analyses have not been as satisfactory as the negative exponential function in describing the density gradient itself.

The Gravity and Potential Concepts

The use of the gravity model in studies of residential land allocation is an improvement over the empirical allocations analyzed above. While in the "assignment" approach a simplified technique was devised and tailored to a particular city at a certain time, the gravity model incorporates the interactions among the forces shaping urban pattern and land use. The gravity concept basically postulates that interaction between two centers of population concentration is determined by two counteractive forces, an attracting force created by the population masses of the two centers, and a friction against interaction caused by the distance between them. Thus "interaction between the two centers of population concentration varies directly with some function of the population size of the two centers and inversely with some function of the distance between them."[19] The postulate is based on the following axioms:

1. Interaction is produced because individuals are in direct or indirect communication with each other;
2. Any individual generates the same amount of interaction as any other individual in the group;
3. The probable frequency of interaction generated by an individual at a given location is inversely proportional to the difficulty of communicating with that location; and
4. The friction against this communication is directly proportional to the physical distance between the individual and the given location.[20]

Although not explicitly spelled out in the axioms, it is obvious that the term "communication" refers to some form of movement over space. This can be either the physical motion of an individual or the movement of relevant information. In locational studies such as the present one, "communication" is replaced by "transportation," and the friction against it is measured either directly by the physical distance involved, or indirectly by the commuting time required to overcome this distance. Therefore, the general equation giving the amount of interaction between two places i and j is,

$$I_{ij} = K\frac{(w_i P_i^\beta)(w_j P_j^\gamma)}{w_D D_{ij}^\alpha}, \qquad (2.2)$$

where K = a constant of proportionality;

P_i = population of place i;

P_j = population of place j;

w_i, w_j, w_D = weights applied to the masses and to the distance variable;[21]

D_{ij} = the distance between i and j;

α = an exponent of distance;[22] and

β, γ = exponents of individual population elements;[23]

For a set of n places, the total potential W_i of a place i created by all other places is,

$$W_i = K \sum_{j=1}^{n} \frac{w_j P_j^\beta}{w_D D_{ij}^\alpha} \qquad (2.3)$$

Both the gravity and potential formulations present a number of weaknesses concerning urban residential location. First, and foremost is the thoeretical justification of the model as it applies to residence location choice. This issue is of course the primary element of controversy over every application of the gravity model.[24] Because of the individualistic character of the residential choice of households, and due to the variety of factors other than accessibility which influence this choice, the application of the gravity formulation to such studies is questionable.

Second, the formulation assumes that the coefficients α, β, and γ remain constant over time. This implies both that the relative conditions in the urban area remain constant over time, and that the way in which households perceive these conditions does not change. But since the general social, economic, political and, consequently, spatial conditions in urban areas are far from being stable, the exponents themselves cannot be expected to remain constant, but rather to fluctuate.

A third argument against the gravity concept is its aggregation. The assumption that the "group" contains individuals with identical perceptions of attractiveness is clearly false since zones are not necessarily homogeneous, and groups with differing characteristics exhibit different perceptions. The effect of this assumption can be especially important. It suggests future urban configurations very distant from the actual ones arising from the differences between groups.

A final weakness of the gravity model is the way in which it treats the supply of residences. In its initial applications, the housing supply is assumed as homogeneous over the entire urban area, a consideration which obviously does not reflect reality. This assumption was first introduced by Hansen,[25] but was later successfully relaxed by Stouffer.[26]

The first application of the concept to residential distribution is attributed to J. Douglas Carroll, Jr., who studied the journey-to-work patterns in a number of major urban areas and concluded that, "forces are constantly at work tending to minimize the home-work separation."[27] However, Walter Hansen first proposed the model for population distribution among residential sub-areas.[28] On the assumption that, "the more accessible an area is to the various activities in a community, the greater its growth potential,"[29] the forecast growth G_i for a zone i of an urban area of total growth $G_t = \Sigma_i \, G_i$ is given as a function of "accessibility" as,

$$G_i = G_t \frac{A_i^\alpha V_i}{\sum_i A_i^\alpha V_i} , \qquad (2.4)$$

where A_i = an accessibility index for zone i;

V_i = the vacant land in some i; and

α = an empirically determined constant.

The index of accessibility A_i is computed from

$$A_i = \sum_j \frac{S_j}{T_{ij}^x} , \qquad (2.5)$$

where S_j = the size of activity in zone j (i.e., number of jobs);

T_{ij} = the travel time between zones i and j; and

x = an exponent describing the impact of travel time between zones.

Although Hansen proposed this model for the distribution of small increments of growth, he also claimed that it could be used in long-range forecasts through successive applications taking into account changes in accessibility occuring over time. But attempts to apply the model in the Washington, D.C., metropolitan area, as well as in the Hartford Area

Traffic Study, revealed considerable variations in comparison to actual values.[30]

The assumption concerning the equal desirability of the total supply of housing to all households independent of income levels, employment type etc., was modified by Stouffer through the stratification of residence types. Thus, housing submarkets constituted the total supply of residences. Stouffer's model [31] postulated that the number of individuals (or families) G_r going a given distance r is directly proportional to the number of opportunities Q_r (residences) at that distance, and inversely proportional to the number of "intervening opportunities" Q. The mathematical formulation is

$$G_r = K \frac{Q_r}{Q}, \qquad (2.6)$$

where K = proportionality constant assuming that activities allocated equal the number that need allocation.

A weakness of the gravity-potential approach for residential land use application is that the population growth, i.e., the number of new families which constitutes demand, is estimated outside the model. In addition, the same problem arises on the supply side since prior knowledge of the number of "intervening" residences is required at each interval. Therefore, the whole process is merely distributional. Consequently, it can be applied either for simple forecasting where existing trends are followed, or for planning where interference from the planner occurs. In neither case does the model explain the actual individual residential location process. This is because there is no consideration of the distribution of locational rents in the urban area as a whole. The social status of a particular location, the availability and cost of the various utilities and amenities, etc., are also not considered.

An improvement over the two previous formulations is the Schneider opportunity-accessibility model.[32] This was proposed by Lathrop and Hamburg to allocate population growth to residential areas.[33] In the Schneider model, the distribution of population growth (the activity) is a continuing evaluation of potential dwelling units which are rank-ordered from an urban center serving as the location of employment. These potential dwelling units are the opportunities, and are obtained from the product of vacant land available for residential development times the appropriate population density. Its formulation is

$$A_j = A[e^{-lQ} - e^{-l(Q+Q_j)}], \qquad (2.7)$$

where A_j = the amount of activity (number of families) to be allocated to zone j;

A = the total number of families to be allocated within the urban area;

l = the probability of a unit of activity (family) being sited at a given opportunity (residence);

Q = the opportunity for siting a unit of activity rank ordered by access value and preceding zone j; and

Q_j = the opportunities in zone j.

The formulation uses negative exponential functions. This assumes that the settlement rate per unit of opportunity is highest at the point of maximum accessibility. Similar to the Stouffer model, this formulation describes an allocation of households by starting their search at the center of the city, and moving across rings containing the opportunities.

As with the previous forms of the gravity model, this formulation includes a parameter l which must be borrowed from a similar case or be assumed constant and be calibrated. However, the probabilities of a site being selected are different for different households so that l cannot, in fact, be constant. (In fact, the model itself was applied to two areas, Greensboro, North Carolina, and the Eastern Massachusetts Regional Planning Project; and in both of them it was found that l varies.) Later models belonging to the behavioral group introduce differences in preference. For example, they consider the preference for residences away from the central city over those near the center.

The most comprehensive and best documented gravity model was constructed by Ira Lowry for use in the Pittsburgh region.[34] The model assigns urban activities to sub-areas of a region. The space-consuming activities are of three types: basic (industry, business, and administration), retail and residential. Of these, the employment levels and locations of basic sectors are assumed to be determined outside the model, while the employment levels and locations of the retail sector are assumed to be determined endogenously. Finally, the household sector depends on the total level of available employment in both basic and retail sectors, while it influences the size and location of the retail sector. Thus, there are two innovations in this model: First, both the population size and the population distribution are determined within the model; and second, there is a feedback between service and residential uses. None of these characteristics appeared in any of the earlier models being examined.

Lowry's underlying theory of spatial structure is that basic activities directly determine the amount and location of residential activity and indirectly determine the amount and location of retailing activity. Thus, there is a sequence of residential location, service location, and then residential location again which moves towards spatial equilibrium without a time constraint.[35] The process uses total, basic and vacant land, as well as basic employment in each square mile tract as inputs, and then allocates residential and service land uses. More specifically, the number of households A_j in each tract j is a function of the tract's accessibility to places of employment:

$$A_j = K \sum_{i=1}^{n} \frac{E_i}{T_{ij}}, \qquad (2.8)$$

where E_i =   total employment in tract i;

T_{ij} =   index of trip distribution increasing with distance between i and j,[a] and

K =   a constant used as a scale factor, equating the total number of households to the total number of jobs available, that is:

$$K \sum_{j=1}^{n} \sum_{i=1}^{n} \frac{E_i}{T_{ij}} = A, \qquad (2.9)$$

where A =   total number of households.

Solving equation (2.9) for K and substituting for it in equation (2.8) we obtain,

$$A_j = \frac{A \sum_{i=1}^{n} \frac{E_i}{T_{ij}}}{\sum_{j=1}^{n} \sum_{i=1}^{n} \frac{E_i}{T_{ij}}}, \qquad (2.10)$$

which is the potential submodel used to allocate population to each urban zone.

Given the residential space available, the number of households which can be assigned to a specific tract is limited by a maximum-density constraint derived from the land use accounting system, although residential densities are not predetermined as in the Chicago study for example. Thus, residential density is generated by the model and varies directly with the accessibility of the tract to places of employment. This constraint is given by,

$$A_j = Z_j^H V_j^H, \qquad (2.11)$$

---

[a] T_{ij} can be simply the distance or the travel time between i and j as in the models discussed previously. However, Lowry determined it on the basis of data available from the Pittsburgh Area Transportation Study, as

$$T = 43.90 \, r^{-1.33}, \qquad (2.8a)$$

where r = distance from residence in miles.

where Z_j^H = a maximum-density constraint in sub-area j for the household sector (H); and

V_j^H = the area of vacant land available in sub-area j.

Lowry used the same limiting value for all the sub-areas, but each zone can have its own value. The maximum density constraint insures that when a zone becomes "saturated," the excess population is distributed among all other zones in proportion to their population potentials.

Although Lowry meant his effort to be an experimental one, it has had a serious influence on later urban land use modeling. The interaction among activities introduced by the model seemed to represent quite accurately the actual spatial distributions in the areas where it was tested.

A Critique of the Gravity-Potential Concept

The notion of the accessibility of residences to employment has been emphasized in the spatial interaction type formulations, often with quite satisfactory results. There remains, however, the question of the adequacy of the gravity postulate to explain residential location. As a descriptive device, the gravity concept has very few rivals. However, its behavioral interpretation is very ambiguous. Thus, if we consider the gravity model simply as a construct, it is useful only in describing the decline of interaction between activities as their distance increases. At the other extreme, however, the gravity model could be considered simply as the mathematical formulation which only happens to describe the behavioral relationships which we have observed among the activities. The criticism of the gravity model, therefore, depends not on the formulation itself, but primarily upon the assumptions and the theory which underlie the model and its use.[36]

A second problem is that of aggregation which is present in all gravity formulations. It has been observed that while it is difficult to predict the behavior of a particular individual, it is conceivable to describe and, to a certain extent, predict the behavior of groups of individuals. It is therefore desirable to aggregate groups in modeling interactions such as the gravity approach. On the other hand, excessive aggregation eliminated most useful information and reduces the potential of the model for prediction. In the Lowry model, for example, the trip distribution index of equation (2.8a) was derived for all households within the zone, independent of occupation. However, when Lowry disaggregated by occupation, he obtained results which clearly indicate that distance has different effects upon different groups. The results are presented in table 2-1. As the results in table 2-1 indicate, the trip index varies regularly with occupation, and the higher

Table 2-1
Trip Distribution Index Used in Lowry's Residential Allocation Model

All occupations	$T = 43.90 \ r^{-1.330}$
Managers, professional etc.	$T = 35.69 \ r^{-1.080}$
Clerical, sales etc.	$T = 37.16 \ r^{-1.125}$
Craftsmen, operatives etc.	$T = 48.47 \ r^{-1.470}$
Laborers, domestic and service workers	$T = 60.08 \ r^{-1.850}$

Source: Ira Lowry, *A Model of Metropolis* (Santa Monica, Calif.: The RAND Corporation, August 1964).

status types show less response to the length of the journey-to-work than the lower status ones. This raises the question of how much disaggregation could be attempted before the properties of the model itself begin to become invalid.

A final criticism refers to the degree of detail offered by the model.[37] This relates to the previous criticism since it depends on the degree of aggregation used. It is also a general criticism of all allocational models, and refers to the fact that only information concerning a tract of land—in this case equal to one square mile—is provided. Thus, more about the spatial distribution of residences within the tract is not known.

In concluding this section, certain essential points related to the characteristics of the gravity-potential concept itself should be noted. To begin with, the formulation used in the social sciences is analogous to that used in Newtonian physics to describe interactions among groups of molecules. But, unlike humans, molecules are not capable of making individual decisions concerning their actions. Thus, it is not known to what extent the probability used in predicting the behavior of molecular groups can be used for groups of humans.

A second point is that the use of the gravity-potential concept yields only a suggested pattern of the movement of people in response to an existing set of choices of work places (if more than one) and residential areas. The distribution of households throughout the urban area is given as the interaction of both demand (in terms of quantity demanded *only*) and supply (in terms of quantity supplied *only*). But this is not an allocation based on proper demand functions for the housing good in relation to its quantity, quality and location.

Yet a third point having to do with the gravity model's assumptions merits consideration. To the extent that access and the cost of space determine residential location, each group of people, business people and workers alike, should be concentrated in the parts of the urban area that present the highest comparative advantage of access. However, as Lowry's analysis of Pittsburgh indicated, the business executive tends to value accessibility less than the worker, and this alone shows that there are important factors omitted from consideration in the gravity formula. Factors like imposed residential segregation (the urban ghetto), neighborhood amenity, and other individual or group characteristics are a few.[38]

Finally, the main weakness of all the descriptive models which have been dealt with so far should be repeated. This is the fact that such models may not capture real cause-and-effect relationships, and that the impacts of these relationships may change over time. This, of course, suggests that attention should be directed towards analyzing the behavior of decision-making units, be they single individuals or entire social groups. Such attempts will be discussed in the following pages.

Against this background of negative attributes and problem areas, the advantage of the gravity formulation over the simple descriptive "assignment" applications should also be stressed. In the first place, the gravity-potential postulate introduces *some* behavioral content to the analysis. After all, households *do* consider seriously both accessibility and cost during their locational decision. Second, it does not predetermine the output of the modeling process, but is basically neutral to it. (For example, the gravity formulation lets the model determine the residential densities,[39] instead of preconceiving them through the shape of the density gradient as in the Chicago study.)

In addition, the gravity-potential postulate considers external effects such as the impact of the transportation system (in computing time-distance and accessibility) and the distribution of basic employment. This latter point relates to the hypothesized form of the urban area itself in that the assignment method assumes a monocentric area, while the gravity formulation allows for several urban centers. Moreover, the incremental character of the application of the gravity model includes a dynamic quality, even though the result is generally some kind of spatial equilibrium. Finally it can be considered from all the literature on gravity models that as long as the behavioral models are not operational, and formulations for empirical applications are needed, the gravity and potential type models remain the best available alternative.

However, in addition to the simple assignment and gravity types of formulations, more theoretically based approaches have been developed to deal with the residential location process. In most cases these are nonoperational theories and explanatory models ranging from the completely non-quantifiable macro-spatial approach to the most analytic microeconomic efforts. The presentation and discussion of these theories and models is the subject of the following two chapters.

3

Behavioral Theories of Residential Location: The Macro-Approach

Economic and Sociological Approaches

The previous chapters have shown that assignment and gravity models of spatial interaction adopt a simplified set of assumptions regarding urban structure without attempting to explain either why this structure appears as it does, or what the reasons for the observed peculiarities are. These models, then, lack explanatory behavioral elements in their structure. Such elements, however, are provided by theories grounded in economics and sociology; and they will therefore be the subject of the rest of this analysis.

We can distinguish two trends followed by behavioral theories. One deals with the urban area as a whole, and attempts to develop hypotheses concerning the patterns and growth of cities. From this viewpoint, residential land location is but one element of the system. On the other hand, the second trend deals specifically with the residential location problem; and the rest of the system is either considered to be completely exogenous or is analyzed only to the degree necessary to develop the theoretical argument.

The former approach will be considered first. While it still maintains a holistic view of the city, it is nevertheless a significant improvement over the approaches discussed in Chapter 2. This category includes theories which draw from economics as well as from sociology. Furthermore, the two are so interwoven that presenting each approach by itself would do injustice to the other and would leave the exposition incomplete. Thus, while economics provides the general direction of this study, and economic analysis is applied to the development of the multi-center city model, sociological theories of urban residential structure will also be discussed.

The two "schools" to be analyzed here are the urban land and real estate school and the human ecological school. The former considers how the spatial organization of cities and towns is determined by the economics of land, while the latter addresses how this spatial structure is explained by the urban population distributions of social variables such as race, income, ethnic character, and education.

The Economics of Land

These theories of urban spatial structure and residential location are concerned primarily with land values and their distribution within the urban

31

area. In fact, the first attempts to deal with land values appeared among the physiocrats of the eighteenth century and were oriented mainly towards agricultural land. Although land value analysis has been an important part of economic thought ever since, the analysis of agricultural land continued to dominate the scientific inquiry until the later part of the nineteenth century.[1] Actually, it was not until the beginning of the twentieth century that essays devoted exclusively to urban land economics appeared.[2]

The Concept of Land Rent

However, during the period when economists dealt solely with agricultural land, they had considerable analytical difficulty conceptualizing how land could command a price when no resources had been committed to its production, and how some land could command a higher price than other land.[3]

The concept, then, which dominated the economists' early studies of land value was land rent. In the same way as the wage rate is the price of labor services,[a] land rent is taken as the price of the services yielded by land during a specific time period.[4] Assuming that factor and product markets are perfectly competitive, (i.e., each participant can buy and sell unlimited quantities of goods and services without affecting the prices set by the market), and that people own productive land and capital only because of the returns they yield, (so that they will seek to use their assets in the most productive way), then, in equilibrium, all equally productive land commands the same price or rent.

The nineteenth century economic world was dominated by two conflicting views of land rent. The first was expressed by Ricardo as early as 1817, while the second was formulated by Wicksteed late in the century. Ricardo's treatment, considered fundamental until just recently, is based on the notion of land fertility. The most fertile land is put to use first since it requires the least land and the smallest amount of nonland input relative to output. The less productive land is then used as the demand for the agricultural product increases. Consequently, land rent at any fertility level is proportionate to the excess of the productivity of land at that level over the productivity of the least productive land in use,[5] and land rent is a residual equal to the excess of revenues from the sales of produced goods over remunerations for nonland factors used in production. The analysis then, is devoted primarily to fertility differentials. Since at that time agriculture was still the principal economic activity, this kind of analysis was

---

[a] Most urban uses of land require both land and capital (structures) as well as other factors of production. "Improved land value" refers to the price of land and the structure on it, whereas "unimproved land value" refers to the price of land without structures. When the terms "land value" and "land rent" are used here, they refer to the prices and rents of unimproved land.

justified. However, its application to urban land is of little relevance because what makes urban land valuable is certainly not ferility.

To that end, it is more useful to consider the theory of location differential rent developed by Johann Heinrich von Thünen a few years later.[6] In von Thünen's formulation, a city is surrounded by a plain of uniform fertility in which the city's food is grown. Since an isotropic transportation network is assumed, food can be shipped straight to the city from any point on the plain. Transportation cost per mile is constant so that the land farthest from the city brought into production commands rent of zero, and the rent increases with land located closer to the city. All the land at a given distance from the city commands the same rent. This is given by a linear function of a slope proportionate to the ton mile, as shown in figure 3-1.

The rent of any point of the plain is the value of the point's product minus the production and transportation costs incurred at that point. The rent, then, determines the agricultural land uses around the market city since products of higher value can bid higher prices for the use of land which is assigned to the highest bidder. This causes a number of concentric rings to be formed around the market. Each such ring is devoted to the production of a particular good; and they occur in decreasing order of unit prices with increasing distance from the market. This is shown in figure 3-2.

In figure 3-2, four farming activities compete for land around the market city 0. Each of the four activities has a rent function given by:

$$R_i(d) = G_i(p_i - w_i - td), \qquad (3.1)$$

where $\qquad d =$ distance from the market;

$R_i(d) =$ land rent per acre at distance d from the market;

$G_i =$ the output in tons per acre per year;

$p_i =$ the price per ton of product G_i in the market;

$w_i =$ the cost of nonland inputs per ton per year; and

$t =$ the transportation cost per ton-mile.

Equation (3.1) represents the rent that a farmer of product i can pay at each distance d from the market. Obviously, for distances $d<d_1$, farmer 1 can offer a higher rent than any other farmer. Therefore, land between d_1 and the city is allocated to user 1. Similarly, for distances between d_1 and d_2, farmer 2 outbids all others, and so on. Thus, the final curve of rents around the city is indicated by 1, 2, 3, 4, which is the envelope of the prevailing segments of the individual rent-offer functions.[7]

The Ricardo/von Thünen model of agricultural production became the basis of the voluminous literature of urban land values and spatial structure, and is best represented by the Alonso study mentioned earlier. It will

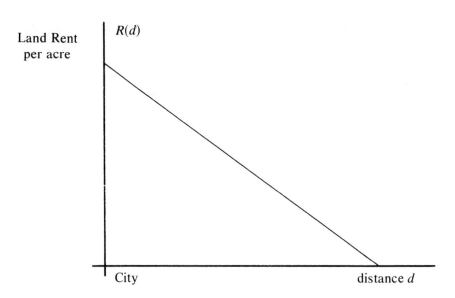

Figure 3-1. The von Thünen Land Rent Function

be discussed extensively in the following chapter. Considering how old this model is it is amazing how little our knowledge and imagination has advanced over the years. In fact, even today, the monocentric city hypothesis is almost always the starting point for scientific inquiries in urban economics.

The development of neoclassical theory, however, provided marginal productivity theory as a new tool of microeconomic analysis. This led to a different view of land rent. The marginal product (*MP*) of a factor of production is the change in production resulting from a small change in the amount of an input used. The value of that marginal product (*VMP*) is the price of output multiplied by the marginal product of the input, and shows the change in revenue resulting from a small change in the employment of a factor (with all other inputs kept constant). Accordingly land rent, as the remuneration for the land factor of production, is also determined by the value of its marginal product. The factor price (P_F) on the other hand, shows the change in cost which results from a one-unit change in the employment of the factor. As long as the factor price is less than the *VMP*, profit to the activity can increase with the employment of additional units of the input. However, when P_F is larger than *VMP*, profit would increase with decreasing factor employment since cost would be reduced more than revenue. It then follows that profit is at a maximum when an amount of the factor is used that allows its marginal product to equal its marginal cost.

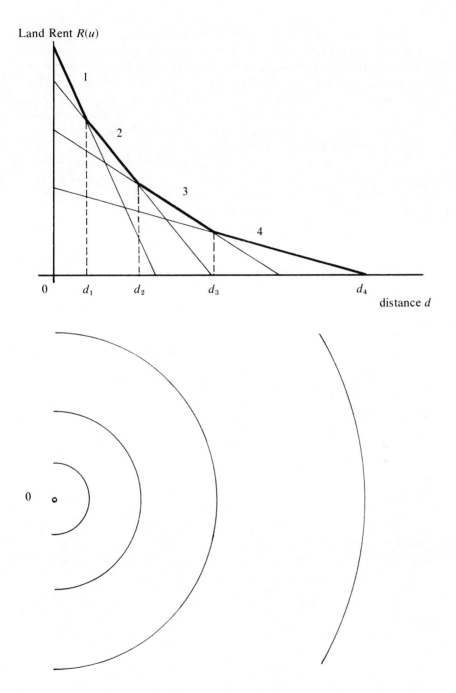

Figure 3-2. Ring Formation Around the Market

Nevertheless, at the level of the firm, factor prices are fixed because they are determined by supply and demand interaction at the industry level. But at the industry level, the factor-demand schedule is downward sloping, as is the firm's *VMP* schedule. The factor supply curve, on the other hand, is normally upward-sloping for the industry; and the equality of demand and supply determines the factor price in the market. Land rent is similarly determined except that the land supply is fixed. The supply-demand interaction for land is shown in figure 3-3.

In figure 3-3, the vertical schedule S_L represents the industry supply of land, fixed at level L, while the curve D_L is the industry demand for land. R, then, is the level of land rent the industry will have to pay for the amount L of land, and is equal to the value of its marginal product.

The question now arises as to what extent the two theories are really dissimilar. Although the analytical approach to land rent is different for each theory, it has been shown that under certain conditions, the two theories merge into one. The first to take note of this was Philip Wicksteed who proved that, (1) if the production function has constant returns to scale, and (2) if input and output markets are competitive, then land rents both exhaust marginal revenues and satisfy the criterion of fertility differentials.[8]

The limited case proved by Wicksteed, however, is not the only situation in which the two theories are equivalent. This was demonstrated by Kunt Wicksell years later in a rigorous proof and generalization of Wicksteed's argument. Wicksell proved that even when the production function does not have constant returns to scale, Wicksteed's theorem still holds.[9] He argues that if, with competitive input and output markets, the production function and fixed competitive factor prices give a U-shaped long-run average cost curve as shown in figure 3-4, then p is the long-run equilibrium price for the industry and x is the long-run equilibrium output for the firm. This is given by the intersection of the average cost curve (LAC) with the marginal cost curve (LMC). But at this point, price equals average cost so that factor payments exhaust revenues. Although this continues to be a limited case and does not exhaust the problem, Wicksell's contribution goes as far as anyone has yet gone in comparing classical and neoclassical land rent theory.[10]

But while this limited exposition of land rent provides a basic analytical framework for the study of the economics of land, the question remains as to how it is applied to the urban land situation. Actually, urban areas are places where market activity results in much more intensive land uses than in nonurban areas. The theory of rent, however, is not constrained by the intensity of land use, and can therefore be used to analyze land in either the rural or urban context. The difference in the two procedures lies in the nature of the activities performed upon the land, and in the fact that, due to

Land Rent

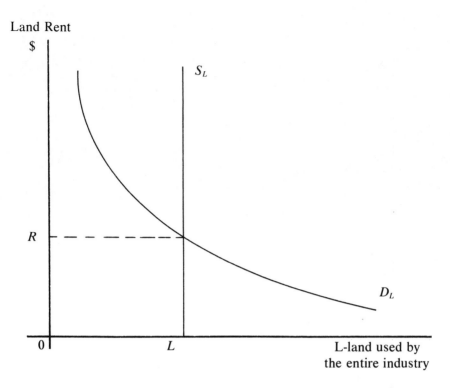

Figure 3-3   Land Rent Determination in the Neoclassical Theory

the intensity of uses in the urban areas, and due to factors generally not present in rural areas (e.g., agglomeration economies, supplementary activities location, ethnic groups confinement within particular urban sectors), irregularities in the pattern of rings appear more often about the center of the city. The application of the theory to urban areas and consideration of the irregularities that occur in the actual allocation of land to particular uses will occupy the rest of this chapter.

Urban Land Use and Real Estate Theories

The first study devoted exclusively to urban land values appeared in 1903 when Richard Hurd, "searching in vain for books on the science of city real estate . . .," decided to publish his *Principles of City Land Values*.[11] Hurd, following closely von Thünen's theory for agricultural land, attempted to outline a theory of urban land values and urban structure. In his treatment, utilities compete for locations in the city and land goes to the

38

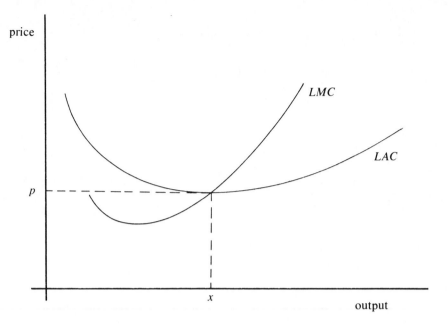

Figure 3-4 Wicksell's Generalization of Wicksteed's Theorem

highest bidder.[12] Fertility differential is replaced by a desirability differential among grades of city land. This produces economic rent in higher grade locations. The value of urban land is determined by "nearness" to the center of the city or the necessary infrastructure, and the size of the site is not considered important. This concept of accessibility implies a treatment of economic activities alone, with accessibility considered to provide an advantage in transportation costs to the center. Residential land, however, is bypassed altogether since:

> The basis of residence values is social and not economic—although the land goes to the highest bidder—the rich selecting the locations which please them, those of moderate means living as near by as possible, and so on down the scale of wealth . . .[13]

Thus, Hurd's analysis, while a starting point for twentieth century real estate economics, did not contribute much to the study of residential land and its location.

A large body of literature on land economics appeared after the 1920s but it was left to Robert M. Haig to organize and develop it into a theory of urban land values.[14] Haig's general principle followed those of Marshall and Hurd; but he also introduced the new concept of the complementarity of land rent and transport costs. To Haig, site rentals and transport costs represent the costs of the "friction of space" which transportation is designed to overcome. This complementarity principle in turn contributes towards determining the layout of the metropolis: "It may be suggested as an hypothesis that the layout of a metropolis—the assignment of activities to areas—tends to be determined by a principle which may be termed the minimizing of the costs of friction."[15] The minimization of the costs of friction is, by itself, a weak explanation of urban patterns. Even if each firm and household behaved in such a manner, there is no reason to believe that the aggregate costs throughout the city would also be minimized. For instance, consideration of the lot size could increase or decrease these costs irrespective of where the lot is located. However, because of the theory's assumption of perfect competition, the minimization approach might be reasonable with regard to agriculture and manufacturing location when transportation costs are the major consideration. In the case of retail services, though, Alonso points out that: "The volume of sales of a retail store will vary with its location, and the firm must weigh the costs of friction against this factor."[16]

Of further importance is the fact that Haig's theory is the first to consider residential land. The choice of residence is based on the estimation of site rent, time value, and transport costs. Lot size is not important and is not considered. This treatment of households, however, is highly unsatisfactory. Since they are noneconomic units, households should be considered to maximize satisfaction rather than minimize the costs of friction. Thus, cost minimization does not consider the possibility of a household trading the size of its lot for more accessibility, or vice versa. As Richardson observes, were the friction of space the only household locational force, dwellings would tend to be clustered about the center of the city at very high densities.[17]

In addition, this theory assumes that the location of *all* households occurs instantly so that the total supply of residential land is allocated simultaneously among households. However, since household occupancy lasts for a period of time, once a residence is occupied, newly locating households must search elsewhere for houses even if this will not minimize their costs of friction. While Haig's theory provides a good analysis of the role of costs of friction in urban locational decisions, it is nonetheless insufficient to completely explain such decisions. This is especially so with regard to residential land use.

Although residential land use did not attract much attention during the early years of the development of urban economics, it began to appear more frequently as the subject for empirical studies which had been stimulated by land theories. These studies provided very valuable insights into urban structure and the land requirements of various uses. Harland Bartholomew's studies are among those most often mentioned because he accumulated a wealth of information on land uses in American cities.[18] However, Bartholomew's tabulated information is not related to the location of these activities. Thus, a review of his work merely yields the amounts and percentages of land uses of various categories.

Homer Hoyt, on the other hand, traced the development of land uses in Chicago over a period of one hundred years.[19] However, he also analyzed the particular relationships of these values to their land uses; and residential land use was given major attention. By tracing the growth and expansion of the various income groups initial locations, Hoyt gave a realistic dimension to the influence of land values in determining land uses. He conceived of the "residential developer" as an economic man who makes decisions to satisfy the demand for particular residence types, as well as to maximize returns on his investment. This line of thinking was later extended by Ratcliff, who states that:

If (the developer) assumes that so many dollars must be invested in the buildings and land improvements, the calculated net worth less this sum will represent what he would be justified in paying for the land. But if he assumes an acquisition cost for the land, the balance of the net worth after deducting land cost will represent what he would be justified in paying for building and improvements. His decision to proceed with the investment in the enterprise will depend upon the relationship of the hypothetical initial net worth of the proposed land development and the necessary or actual total capital cost of acquiring the land and erecting the buildings.[20]

Hoyt's work provided the first systematic empirical evidence that spatial variations in land values within the urban area actually bear a close relationship to its land use patterns, that these land use patterns change over time as a result of land value patterns, that the patterns of values change in turn because of the new land uses, and that the intensity of uses changes over time following changes in land values.

In a similar systematic analysis of thirty American cities, Hoyt first presented the well-known theory of radial sectors of urban spatial structure, which will be discussed further in the section on "Spatial Organization Concepts."[21] Here, however, it is important to note that the theory developed partly as the result of observed regularities and trends appearing in American cities, and partly as a criticism of the Burgess theory of concentric zones (also to be discussed in the section on spatial organization). Although Hoyt introduced a more realistic picture of the city than the familiar concentric pattern dating from the time of von Thünen and Hurd, his theory included arguments characteristic of the classical real estate school which have been attacked often by both later land economists and the human ecologists. These arguments are, first, that there is one single core for the city where all economic activity is concentrated, and, second, that transportation costs are decisive for location decisions. The first argument is unrealistic for modern metropolitan areas, while the second simply overemphasizes the importance of both accessibility and transportation. Both criticisms appear throughout the early literature of urban economics. These two concepts do not exhaust Hoyt's theory of sectors. Actually, the major factor in the radial sector development of a city appears to be the location and direction of the expansion of high income areas. This subject will be discussed more thoroughly in the section on "Spatial Organization". Here, however, we are dealing with the assumptions common to all urban land economics theories of the early 1900s.

Not all urban land economists attempted to explain urban patterns solely by these two assumptions. Richard Ratcliff, for instance, discusses the location of households in a different light.[22] His position is that, ". . . to break down the residential areas for more refined structural analysis, there are many physical, social, and economic characteristics which form individual geographical patterns and which might be used as a basis for delineating residential sub-areas."[23] Ratcliff suggests further that there may be more than one cluster of blocks where the rent is the highest in the city, and that there appears to be a decline through successively lower rent levels until the meanest housing and lowest rents are reached. The residential areas of the high income groups are clustered around these high rent poles when the size of the city is small, but tend to be found at the periphery of larger and more dynamic communities. As far as the lower income areas are concerned:

Immediately surrounding the high-rent areas or sectors, which are necessarily small in extent, are the zones of intermediate housing. In some cases, there will be additional intermediate-rent areas at the periphery of the city at a point removed from any high-rent district. The low-rent areas of the community usually may be found both at the center and at the edge of the developed area . . . The traditional association of the lowest rent districts and the central portions of the community is too limited a view. The crowded slums of the older, central districts have their counterparts in the shack towns of the outlying districts.[24]

Thus, Ratcliff does not offer a formal, geometric representation of the city, but instead presents a realistic set of observations similar to both the human ecologists' sociological explanation and those offered by the multi-nuclei city hypothesis. Those alternative directions are examined in the next section.

Land economists did little during the fifties and the sixties to explain urban residential patterns. Nevertheless, the elements presented by the real estate theories such as accessibility and the friction-of-space costs, have been widely used ever since. One interesting modification of the accessibility concept was suggested by Guttenberg, who sees the "community effort to overcome distance" as the organizing principle of urban spatial structure.[25] His system includes three components—the "distributed facilities," the "undistributed facilities," and "transportation." If transportation is poor, the urban area assumes a pattern of distributed facilities; but if it is good, the area assumes more concentrated patterns that result in undistributed facilities. Thus, Guttenberg proposes a dynamic system where transportation is the key to the development of urban structure and the way in which growth proceeds. As growth occurs, structural adjustments to overcome distance usually take the form of new centers, improved transportation facilites or both. Although the theory acknowledges that transport efficiency is not the sole variable responsible for the spatial pattern of a city, it nevertheless maintains that (other things remaining constant) accessibility serves to sort activities spatially.

Guttenberg's hypothesis does not belong to the real estate economics school, although it uses the same assumptions and arguments. Instead, it provides a dynamic framework for explaining urban form, while giving no indication of how this framework can be translated into an analytical system capable of being tested. This is why the theory is presented here instead of with the group of analytical models of urban structure.

Actually, the real estate economics school first attempted to explain urban spatial patterns. While its view was limited to the economics of land, and its methods were applied to productive, as opposed to residential, land, it nevertheless provided a solid framework for the spatial analysis of urban phenomena. Later researchers used economic theory and the anlaytical techniques of location theory to test, alter and improve the hypotheses and arguments of the real estate economists. Even today, accessibility to the centers of employment and major urban activities is one of the key factors considered in studies of urban spatial patterns and many analytical models, including that of Chapter 5, use it as a principal explanatory variable for the behavior of households.

The Human Ecological Approach

At the same time the real estate economists were attempting to give satisfactory explanations for the distribution of land values and the location of urban sub-areas, the human ecologists were using a different approach to the same problem. While the land economists were considering the economic point of view and were analyzing land under market conditons, the human ecologists were basing their analyses on sociology and its offspring, human ecology.[26]

There are two explanations of urban structure in the literature of human ecology. The first is that land values determine land uses, and the second is that other factors are more influential than land values themselves. The former approach is found in the writings of Robert Park, Ernest Burgess, Roderick McKenzie, D. Bogue, James Quinn, and Amos Hawley,[27] among others, while the chief representative of the latter approach is Walter Firey.[28]

Although the ecologists correlate land values with land uses, they seem to reverse the dependency function by arguing that, "Land values are the chief determining influence in the segregation of local areas and in the determination of the uses to which an area is to be put. Land values also determine the type of building that is to be erected in a given area . . ."[29] This explanation is the opposite of that given by the land economists. They argue that the various uses, by bidding for the most advantageous sites, will establish the land prices. Park[30] and Burgess[31] indicate that land values are the most significant of all indexes used in studying the social life and problems of the metropolitan community, while Quinn suggests that land price, "reflects in a simple, quantified form the combined effect of a complex of factors that operated in the metropolitan area."[32] However, Quinn also asserts that there exists such a variation in the urban land prices due to different times, sites, locations and uses, and that "no single formula can be set up in advance for computing the price of any given parcel of land without knowledge of local conditions."[33]

The economists' theory that the minimization of the costs of friction essentially forms the urban pattern has its counterpart in the ecologists' proposition of "minimum costs" as stated by Quinn, Hawley, and others. The hypothesis states that the spatial distribution of ecological units is the result of their tendencies to minimize total costs in order to gain maximum satisfaction.[34] These costs include transportation and location costs (rent), as well as other measurable and unmeasurable costs such as disutility. A corollary of the hypothesis of minimum costs is that of "minimum ecological distance." This states that "if other factors are constant within an area, ecological units tend to distribute themselves throughout it so that the total ecological distance traversed in adjusting to limited environmental factors, including other ecological and social units, is reduced to the minimum."[35] This refers only to transportation costs, and deals with interactions among men in a fashion similar to that of the gravity and intervening opportunities formulation discussed in Chapter 2.

The above two hypotheses reject in principle the land economists' explanation of the urban spatial pattern. However, to what extent their theory explains reality is unknown since the nonrigorous method of presentation and the highly abstract and nonquantifiable nature of the variables make the theory untestable.

The human ecologists have been particularly interested in residential location because of the social dimensions and issues involved. The essentials of their residential location theory were presented by Hawley. He suggested that the reason for residential differentiation is to be found in the rental value of residential land.[36] This rental value is a combination of three factors—land values, the location of other activities, and the time and money costs of transportation to urban activity centers. Since households cannot compete successfully with the more intensive land uses such as business and industry, they are relegated to less accessible sites with lower rental values. Whenever residences are found on high-value land, they are usually in a deteriorated condition. This is because the land is kept in housing only for speculation, i.e., in the expectation of more profitable uses. Such places are occupied by low income households and thus there is the paradox of high income families living on low rent land away from the central city, while low income families occupy high rent lands closer to central locations.

Hawley's theory does have some merit. First, for instance, it partially explains the trend to the outskirts—although it does not consider the household's willing trade-off between access and environmental considerations. Second, the theory also accounts for the existence of gray areas in proximity to the central city. This second explanation, however, is also a partial one in that there are cases where profitability does sustain investment in such low income housing areas.[37] Low maintenance costs, low vacancy rates and consequently little rent loss, and low taxes due to the deteriorated condition of housing are some of the reasons for such profits.

Hawley's explanation of urban residential location depends on urban growth, or its expectation. Growing urban areas expand as new houses which cannot be built within the existing city appear on the cheaper land of the periphery. Yet speculators would not retain their property in the slum areas of transition unless they expected urban growth to change the use demand for their land. Alonso, however, proposes an explanation which does not depend on growth. He states that the size of site is a correlate of income, and that high income households demand more land while they are less interested in accessibility. Hence the phenomenon of wealthy families living in the suburbs while lower income groups that seek accessibility settle closer to the central city.[38]

The interacting analyses of the land economists and human ecologists have resulted in three hypotheses concerning the general shape and spatial organization of the city. These are the concentric zones proposition of Ernest Burgess, the radial sector theory of Homer Hoyt, and Harris and Ullman's multiple nuclei description of the city.[39] These theories will be discussed in detail in the next section, but it is necessary to discuss here the reaction of some human ecologists to these efforts.

A few years after Burgess presented his theory of concentric zones, Maurice Davie attempted to test it by investigating the land use patterns of New Haven.[40] He found twenty-two different areas whose order seemed to defy any generalization. He then studied maps of twenty other cities and reached similar conclusions. His rejection of Burgess' theory in particular and the attempt to formalize urban ecological patterns in general, was definitive. He wrote, "there is no universal pattern, not even an 'ideal' type."[41] Despite the fact that Homer Hoyt's radial sector hypothesis added a considerable degree of reality to the Burgess hypothesis, scholars within the field of human ecology still tended to reject a formal scheme altogether. Characteristic approaches are those of Zorbaugh and Firey.

Harvey Zorbaugh, Paul Hatt, and other authors stressed a concept of "natural areas" which is independent of ring or sector hypotheses.[42] The main argument of the theory is that members of the same racial, religious, national, or cultural group have a tendency to live in the same area. The natural area is thus "a geographical area characterized both by a physical individuality and by the cultural characteristics of the people who live in it."[43] This theory, then, is simply a formalized statement of the concentration and segregation forces in the city, and refers to human nature rather than to actual physical locations within the urban area. But while it explains why there are structural divisions in the city, it does not relate them to the spatial framework. That is, it does not explain why a certain group locates in a particular area.

The strongest criticism of "universal" urban patterns, however, has come from Walter Firey. He rejects any attempt to explain such patterns solely in the economic terms of land values, economic competition, etc.[44] Firey argues that noneconomic factors, mainly cultural values and the social behavior of households, are much more important than economic considerations in the location of households. Thus a group may exhibit a persistent attachment to a particular location because intangible values have been attributed to that location. The theory introduces a "symbol-sentiment" relationship between groups and areas. Space becomes a "symbol" for certain cultural values that have become associated with a certain spatial area and may bear "sentiments" which can significantly influence the locational process. Thus, particular groups resisting locational changes can influence "planning decisions" and "controls," and these in turn can mold the physical pattern of the city.

Firey's objections are certainly valid, and his suggestions concerning the location resistance of social groups have been solidly documented in the case study of Boston. He has, of course, received severe criticism. Later writers have argued that Boston was not a good case for generalized statements because of its very special character and historical position. They have also noted that the theory's theses, though seemingly true, are probably overemphasized in the case of Boston.[45] But Firey's theory opened an entirely new direction to analysts; and he certainly was not the only one to stress the existence of an emotional factor in the selection of location. For instance, similar positions have been taken by Lynd and Lynd[46] and by Hoyt.[47] Nevertheless, Firey extended his analysis beyond the level of observation and description to the level of theory. His theoretical construct suggests the use of a "principle of proportionality" in order to give recognition to the various values which play important roles in urban land use allocation. That is, he proposes that such values be taken into account in proportion to their importance in locational process so that a certain balance is achieved in terms of community goals. He further suggests that this approach allocates land to all end-uses, while allowing none to take up more than its fair share.[48] Firey, in short, assumes a limited supply of urban land. Although we can think of the urbanized area as a continuously expanding one without fixed boundaries, in reality the limitations of distance, legal constraints, local jurisdiction boundaries, etc., make urban land a limited resource.

Firey perceives the urban structure in a very broad sense. He dislikes those approaches which assume that only a single discipline is capable of explaining all the intricate relationships of the contemporary city, and that the "rational man" is actually representative of the random household and its decision behavior. The role of human values and ideals in framing social behavior is indeed fundamental to the contemporary analyst, for social behavior directly influences urban land use patterns. Yet, because of the interdisciplinary approach required, little progress has been achieved since Firey's writings appeared.

Spatial Organization Concepts

It has already been demonstrated that the economic and human ecological analyses of urban structures provide a number of elements explaining the location behavior of households and groups. Moreover, they also present certain formalized "ideal" patterns of urban structure to explain the often random appearance of a city. But these efforts have attracted tremendous criticism from scores of scholars who have been against either the concept of an ideal pattern, or particular aspects of the spatial organization schemes. Such attacks characterized the era when the two "schools" discussed above produced their most brilliant writings, and when scholars still believed that such a theoretical organizational undertaking was both possible and fruitful.

The three most important organizational schemes were proposed by Ernest Burgess,[49] Homer Hoyt,[50] and Harris and Ullman,[51] and are known respectively as the concentric zone concept, the radial sector concept, and the multiple nuclei concept. It is interesting to note that Burgess' hypothesis, the first to appear, was an offspring of the Chicago school of urban sociology. Hoyt's theory, on the other hand, was suggested as an improvement to the first and came from the land economists. Finally, the multiple nuclei hypothesis was the result of an "interdisciplinary" attempt to explain urban structure. This sequence of appearances is similar to the sequence which produced Firey's writings; and just as with Firey's writings, the multiple-nuclei hypothesis has received very little improvement and refinement until now.

Ernest Burgess' theory of "concentric zones" initially analyzes the expansion of the city, and then discusses the "processes of urban metabolism and mobility"[52] which are closely related to expansion. The main hypothesis is that the process of expansion can be illustrated best by a series of concentric circles, as shown in figure 3-5.

The circular zones show that the influence of a large city center over its surrounding area diminishes with increasing distance. Social differentiation, which is polarized toward the city center, can be demonstrated by comparing the averages of a social indicator such as poverty for all of the circular zones. The trend line of these averages gives a gradient pattern reflecting the spatial structure of land use within the city that is determined by the accessibility needs and preferences of firms and households. Aside from the loop containing the central business district, the rings of the city are characterized by income-level residential land uses. Thus, the second zone, or zone of transition, contains poor and old residential property and run-down areas that have been invaded by business and light manufacturing as the CBD expands. The third zone, that of workingmen's homes, includes residences in close proximity with industrial plants. These homes have the double advantage of low rents and ease of commuting to work. The fourth zone is a high class residential area, while the fifth is one of residential suburbs and satellite development within commuting distance to the central city. As growth occurs, each zone tends to extend its area by invading the next outer zone in an "invasion-succession" sequence. If, on the other hand, there is a decline of population, the outer zones tend to remain stationary while the transitional zone recedes into the loop thereby creating commercial and residential slums.

However, a similar idealized formulation can be derived using economic instead of sociological principles. In fact, the formation of such concentric rings has already been discussed, first as a result of the bid rent function, and then as a consequence of the Haig application to the land within the city. To summarize briefly, land rent is defined as negative transport costs due to accessibility. Moreover, various economic activities derive utility from a piece of land, and the greater this utility is, the higher the rent an activity is willing to pay. Thus, under competitive conditions, each piece of land is allocated ultimately to its highest bidder so that throughout the system rents are maximized. If a city of one central business district is assumed, this rent maximizing pattern causes in concentric rings to form around that center. This occurs because the utility derived from

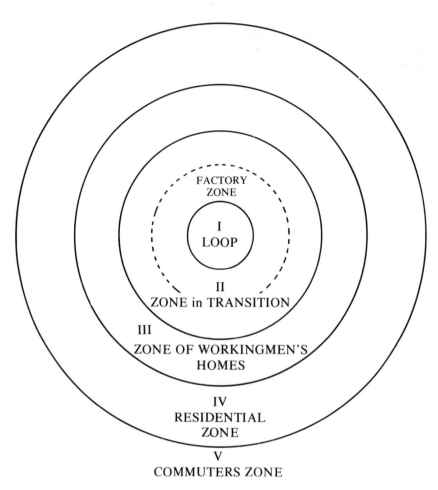

FACTORY
ZONE

I
LOOP

II
ZONE in TRANSITION

III
ZONE OF WORKINGMEN'S
HOMES

IV
RESIDENTIAL
ZONE

V
COMMUTERS ZONE

Source: Robert E. Park, Ernest W. Burgess and Roderick D. McKenzie, *The City* (Chicago: Chicago University Press, 1925) Introduction © 1967 by The University of Chicago.

Figure 3-5 The Growth of the City According to Burgess

land by each activity has a different slope, and the intersection of the utility representing bid rent functions defines the boundaries of each ring. A simplified scheme produced under these assumptions is shown in figure 3-2.[53]

The economic explanation of the concentric zones hypothesis might seem inconsistent with the original Burgess formulation and the particular uses he assigned to each ring. This inconsistency springs from the fact that if there actually is such a bidding process, the land around the central business district should be used by those activities whose demand for central land is high, but which could not pay quite as much as the highest bidders that obtained the central locations. In the Burgess formation, however, the rings around the center are the "transitional" zone occupied by poor housing and deteriorating structures, and the "workers housing" zones where residences and industry are located in close proximity. Yet the inconsistency does not really exist because such areas exhibit high rents while actually being occupied by poor families and blue collar workers. This explanation was first provided by Hawley, and was presented in the previous section. An even more elaborate explanation was provided by Alonso, and will be discussed in the following chapter.

Both approaches to the concentric zone hypothesis hae have been widely criticized. The basic criticisms are well known. First is the assumption of monocentricity which is not valid in the case of large multifoci metropolitan areas. (This criticism gave rise to the next theory to be discussed, that of many "nuclei" existing within the urban area.) Next is the argument of McKenzie, Hoyt, and Kish, among others, that cities do not actually conform to the concentric pattern, but rather tend to grow unevenly in different parts of a zone creating "sectors" of expansion.[54] (Hence the development of Homer Hoyt's "radial sector" theory that will be discussed next.) Finally, the concentric pattern does not exist where topographical features or the transportation network are taken into consideration. In the latter case, land use and population tend to push out along the main roads distorting the circular shape into a star-like formation. However, as long as the theory is conceived as an underlying principle of spatial organization rather than as a precise representation of urban structure, these criticisms do not invalidate it.

Land economist Homer Hoyt's "radial sector theory" is directly related to the Burgess hypothesis.[55] In fact, Hoyt's theory arose from his criticism of the concentric zone theory's limitations. It concentrates on the areal pattern of and shifts in residential location. The main argument is that different income groups tend to live in distinct areas which, instead of occupying entire rings around the Central Business District, are sectors around it. Thus, there are well-defined, sector-shaped, high income residential areas adjoined on one or both sides by middle income areas. High, medium, and low income households are taken here to correspond to high, medium or low rental (or priced) residential areas. Low income areas, on the other hand, usually occupy completely isolated sectors at the other side of the city. Once the low and middle income sectors are established, they tend to keep their character.[56] High income groups, however, tend to expand outward and gradually abandon the areas adjacent to the core. These are then invaded by lower income groups.[57] Growth occurs along main transportation routes or, in general, along the lines of least resistance. Thus, movement is either towards another existing urban center or towards open country where no barriers to expansion are present. This tendency is strengthened by new retail establishments, banks, etc., which are also moving outward; and it can continue as long as it is not slowed down by the decisions of property developers.[58] The hypothetical structure of a city of radial sector zones is shown in figure 3-6.

The sectors of figure 3-6 correspond to the following uses:

Central Zone 1:	City center;
Sectors 2:	Wholesale and light manufacturing activities;
Sectors 3:	Low income residential areas adjacent to wholesale manufacturing zones;
Sector 3':	Low income residential areas around the city center, possibly territory abandoned by higher income groups;
Sectors 4:	Middle income residential zones adjacent to the high income area;
Sector 5:	High income zone, expanding outward over a narrow sector and leading the general trend of urban expansion.

Viewing the radial sector theory from the residential location point of view, there is, first of all, excessive emphasis given to the high income group's importance in dictating patterns of urban expansion and residential relocation. For example, what if growth occurred due to the influx of large numbers of workers to the urban area in response to new manufacturing activity? Would it then be reasonable to expect this increased demand for low and medium income housing to result in the expansion of high income areas? In addition, the whole approach to the location and spatial connections of different income households is not reliable because it oversimplifies the population distribution within the urban area.[59]

A closer look at the radial sector theory reveals many similarities to the Burgess hypothesis. Not only do both concepts deal with a monocentric city that grows by outward expansion, but they also indicate that the growth proceeds in successive rings.[60] The main difference is that the relatively homogeneous rings of Burgess are diversified by sector in Hoyt. Hoyt's approach, however, is a considerable improvement over Burgess' because it not only allows the location of different activities at equal distances from the center of the city, but also accepts the uneven growth and expansion of different sectors of the city. In addition, it takes into account the existing transportation network, other urban nuclei, and other special attractions such as the location of the homes of prominent citizens.

The above two theories assume that a city has but one dominant center, although the sector hypothesis makes provision for the existence of alternative urban centers. The problem of the monocentric assumption, present

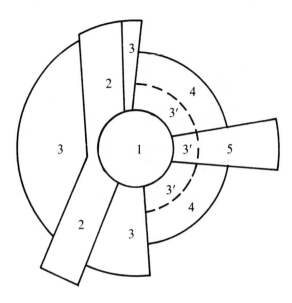

Figure 3-6 Sector Theory of Urban Structure

not only in descriptive studies of the types reviewed thus far, but also in the more elaborate behavioral models which will be considered next, was first handled by Harris and Ullman[61] as suggested by McKenzie.[62] McKenzie observed that there is a series of nuclei present in the pattern of urban land uses rather than only one central core as suggested by Burgess (and later by Hoyt). The concept of multiple nuclei was then expanded by Harris and Ullman. They observed that these nuclei are either preexisting agglomerations which become urban nuclei as the areas between them are filled through urban growth, or new centers emerging from the need for certain types of services as the size of the urban area increases. Furthermore, because of their different origins, the functions performed by these nuclei differ from center to center and from city to city.

The rise of separate nuclei reflects, according to Harris and Ullman, a contribution of four factors. They are the need for specialized facilities by certain activities, the profit from the grouping of certain like activites (for example retail and financial districts), the fact that certain unlike activities are detrimental to each other (e.g., factory and high income residential development), and the inability of certain activities to afford the high rents of the most desirable sites.[63] A paradigm of a city structure representative of the multiple nuclei hypothesis is presented in figure 3-7.

According to this hypothesis, households locate around these urban

52

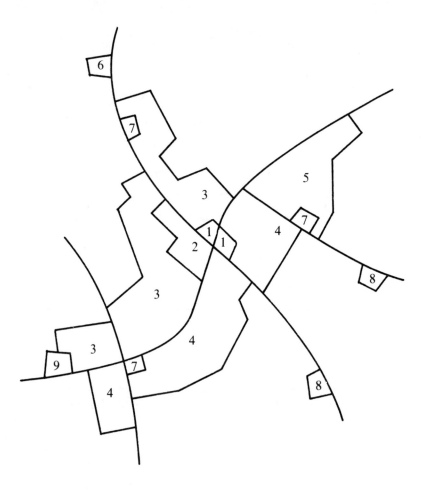

Zone 1: Central Business District
Zone 2: Wholesaling and light manufacturing
Zone 3: Low income residential
Zone 4: Medium income residential
Zone 5: High income residential
Zone 6: Heavy manufacturing
Zone 7: Outlying business and commercial district
Zone 8: Residential suburb
Zone 9: Industrial Suburb

Figure 3-7 A Multiple Nuclei City

nuclei in a fashion similar to that of the radial sector theory. That is, expansion proceeds outward radially as in both the concentric zone and the radial sector hypotheses and households locate so as to minimize the friction costs of transportation. But this theory adds a considerable degree of reality to these other hypotheses of urban structure because it recognizes the existence of several nuclei within the urban area, as well as the variety of reasons which might give rise to any one of them. But is the multiple nuclei theory really a *theory*? It is a more realistic description of a real city, but it is a static description. It says nothing about the forces which contribute to the emergence of the new nuclei, although it does refer to possible reasons for their existence. But how can one predict or anticipate where and when a new center might arise in the urban area? And what would the nature of this center be? How can anything at all be said about the residential location process as long as location for Harris and Ullman depends upon the various nuclei? It is obvious that while the descriptive part of the hypothesis is superior to the previous two hypotheses, its theoretical explanatory arguments do not stand up to criticism. What is needed is an approach which will introduce a dynamic element to the hypothesis so that it becomes operational and offers predictive potential. Although the dynamic element was not present in the original formulation, it is possible to introduce it as Guttenberg has suggested.[64]

The above discussion of the real estate and human ecology schools' approaches to urban residential location reveals that both have contributed significantly to the understanding of this urban phenomenon. The economic and social aspects of human behavior were analyzed and used to explain why people choose particular areas of the city to live in, and why there is such a deviation from the patterns theoretically suggested. But even though both schools provided explanations for the various location trends, regularities, and deviations, they nevertheless failed to provide quantitative or quantifiable measures to make empirical testing possible. Thus, while the explanatory power of these theories is clearly superior to the ad hoc and gravity-potential approaches, they largely lack the operational capabilities of these other types.

The explanation for this limitation is twofold. On one hand, consideration of behavioral variables needs advanced techniques to measure and quantify them so the theory can be transformed into a mathematical model for empirical testing. On the other hand, too many variables considered simultaneously only result in very complicated formulas. These are likely to be difficult to comprehend and nearly incapable of providing qualitative results. Nonetheless, the analytical work which appeared in the sixties and seventies has proceeded along these lines in attempting to explain urban spatial patterns. The part of this more recent literature that refers to residential location is reviewed in the following chapter.

4

Behavioral Models of Residential Location

Macro- Versus Micro-Approaches to Residential Location

In the two previous chapters, residential location was treated in its macroeconomic context. The theoretical developments presented attempted to answer questions such as "Where do groups of people of some similar characteristics tend to locate within the urban area?" and "How is residential land allocated among those groups?" These are very important questions that need to be answered. Due to their aggregate nature, however, such theories do not provide a clear insight into the forces affecting the individual residential location choice in urban areas. Theories which follow a microeconomic approach, and which are the subject matter of this chapter, are more useful in this context.

The unit of analysis in the microeconomic approach is the individual, or the individual household. And while in models of workplace choice the individual himself is considered as the decision unit, in models of residential location choice the whole household is usually considered the decision unit. Furthermore, in analyzing the household, a common set of axioms constitutes the base of most theories. These are as follows:

1. The household analyzed is taken as the representative, "average" decision unit, the behavior of which can be expected to reflect "reasoned" household behavior;
2. This household has a certain income per unit of time (its budget) and particular needs to satisfy. These can be grossly divided into the need for shelter and the need for all other goods;
3. The household obtains this income by rendering services to an "employer" and is, therefore, associated with one or more workplace. This association is economic as well as spatial since the distance between work location and residential location is decisive for the way in which the household's income is consumed. That is, the distance between these locations necessitates additional transportation expenditure in terms of both dollars and personal time.

Within this set of needs and constraints, the household must decide where to locate. This decision process takes place within the framework of a market mechanism for all households simultaneously. Thus, the household must specify its preferences, identify the part of the available supply

55

which meets its preferences, and then compete with other households in the market for a particular residential location. This complex process is the subject of the microeconomic residential location theories and models discussed in this chapter.

Because of the complex nature of the process, no single approach has been found to be superior to all others. Instead, each approach has some particular merit, and usually addresses itself to only certain aspects of the problem. Thus, some theories try to simplify and abstract from reality in order to develop theorems that are universally applicable, while others try to understand one facet of the problem by relaxing assumptions and then exhaustively analyzing only certain issues. Nevertheless, both approaches deal with the behavioral processes which cause urban spatial patterns. Thus, the advantages of this category of theories over the previously analyzed one is apparent. These not only trace the phenomena by simple description of their resulting spatial patterns, but also analyze the behavior of the participating units so that a set of behavioral explanatory theorems can be deduced.

Within this class of models, two major groups can be distinguished by the form in which they are expressed. These are the operational models and the equilibrium models. The former can actually be used as explanatory and predictive devices in real world applications, while the latter abstract reality with many simplifying assumptions and are consequently of little practical value. The two categories of models are discussed in the following sections.

Operational Models

The earliest attempts at building models with operational potential appeared in response to the land economists of the forties and fifties. Their approach was based on many simplifying assumptions and a tendency to generalize about urban spatial organization. One of the first to suggest the new path was Paul Wendt who, in a series of papers which appeared in the late fifties, attacked the familiar Haig and Ratcliff propositions for giving excessive importance to transportation costs and the monocentric city pattern.[1] Wendt's model deals only with aggregate land values, the secular and cyclical variations of which it tries to predict. Thus, it is not directly related to residential location. Wendt's model is formulated as follows:

$$V = \frac{f_x(P,\ Y,\ S,\ P_u,\ PI) - \Sigma(T + O_c + I_{im} + D_{im})}{f_x(i,\ R,\ C_g)}, \qquad (4.1)$$

where V = aggregate value of urban land;

f_x = expectations;

P = population;

Y = average income;

S = supply of competitive land;

P_u = competitive pull of area;

PI = public investment;

T = local taxes;

O_c = operating costs;

I_{im} = interest on capital invested in improvement;

D_{im} = depreciation on improvements;

i = interest rate;

R = investment risk;

C_g = the possibility of capital gains.[2]

Despite its mathematical formulation, this model is not operational because it is not defined precisely. It is interesting, however, to notice the number of variables considered as exogenously influencing land values. This is in sharp contrast to the limited approach taken by the earlier land economists.

As operational models became more refined, various techniques were used in their development. Some techniques which have produced very promising results are the linear programming and the linear multiple regression analyses. While they are both based on the assumption of linearity, they use different logic in order to formulate the locational model. This is discussed below in more detail.

Linear Programming Models

This technique is used increasingly in urban studies because it considers important behavioral postulates related to the maximization of certain benefits to the household.[3] At the same time, it allows an almost unlimited number of constraints to be present during the unit's decision. Linear programming was initially used in locational problems by Stevens and Coughlin to allocate increments of industrial activity among a number of metropolitan sub-areas.[4] However, it was first applied to the residential location problem by Herbert and Stevens.[5]

The Herbert-Stevens Linear Programming Model

This model was designed to distribute households to residential land in an optimal configuration, and was part of a larger model designed to locate land-using activities for the Penn-Jersey Transportation Study. Despite some shortcomings to be discussed later, the linear programming technique provided a good operationalized—if not operational—form of the microanalytical approach refined at the theoretical level by Alonso.

The Herbert-Stevens model operates iteratively; and the amount of land for residential use and the number of households to be located during the particular iteration are exogenously forecasted. The model, therefore, distributes optimally these new households to the available residential land during the given time period with respect to all previously located activities. The axioms constituting the basis of the model formulation are:

1. The factors considered by a household in choosing its location are its total budget, the items constituting a "market basket" and the costs of obtaining those items. A "market basket" is a unique combination of a residential bundle (which includes a house, an amenity level, a trip set and a site of a particular size) and a bundle of all other commodities consumed annually by a household;
2. For each household group, there exists a set of market baskets among which each household in that group is "indifferent. A "household group" is a collection of households which have similar residential budgets and tastes with respect to residential bundles;
3. The household tends to optimize its situation by selecting from its set of market baskets the one which maximizes the household's "savings." ("Savings" is here defined as the rent-paying ability of the household for a particular site in a particular area.) This allocates households to land in a configuration that is optimal from the point of view of all the households that are to be located.

Thus, the optimal allocation of households is achieved by the maximization of the aggregate rent-paying ability which corresponds to the savings maximized by each household.

The form of the allocation model is the following:

Maximize

$$Z = \sum_{K=1}^{U} \sum_{i=1}^{n} \sum_{h=1}^{m} X_{ih}^{K} (b_{ih} - c_{ih}^{K}) \tag{4.2}$$

Subject to

$$\sum_{i=1}^{n} \sum_{h=1}^{m} s_{ih} X_{ih}^{K} \le L^{K} \tag{4.3}$$

and

$$\sum_{K=1}^{U} \sum_{h=1}^{m} -X_{ih}^K = -N_i, \quad \text{all } X_{ih}^K \geq 0 \qquad (4.4)$$

where U = areas which form an exhaustive subdivision of the region. Areas are indicated by the superscripts $K = 1, 2, \ldots, U$;

n = household groups indicated by subscripts $i = 1, 2, \ldots, n$;

m = residential bundles indicated by subscripts $i = 1, 2, \ldots, m$;

b_{ih} = the residential budget allocated by a household of group i to the purchase of residential bundle h;

c_{ih}^K = the annual cost to a household of group i of the residential bundle h in area K—*exclusive of site cost;*

s_{ih} = the number of acres in the site used by a household of group i if it uses residential bundle h;

L^K = the number of acres of land available for residential use in area K in a particular iteration of the model;

N_i = the number of households of group i that are to be located in the region in a particular iteration;

X_{ih}^K = the number of households of group i using residential bundle h located by the model in area K.[6]

Constraints (4.3) prevent the amount of land allocated in each area from exceeding the available land, while constraints (4.4) insure the location of all households in each group.

An interesting insight to the way in which the model operates is provided by its dual.[a] This is formulated in order to minimize

$$Z' = \sum_{K=1}^{U} r^K L^K + \sum_{i=1}^{n} v_i(-N_i) \qquad (4.5)$$

subject to

$$S_{ih} r^K - v_i \geq b_{ih} - c_{ih}^K \qquad (4.6)$$

$(K = 1, 2, \ldots, U), (i = 1, 2, \ldots, n), (h = 1, 2, \ldots, m)$

$$\text{all } r^K \geq 0 \ (K = 1, 2, \ldots, U)$$

$$v_i \geq 0 \ (i = 1, 2, \ldots, n)$$

---

[a] Every linear programming problem is associated with another linear programming problem called the dual. The relationship between the original problem (called the primal) and its dual formulation is a very intimate and useful one. The dual formulation is developed from the primal by transposing the rows and columns of the constraint coefficients, and by transposing

where r^K = the annual rent per unit of land in area K ($K = 1, 2, \ldots, U$);

v_i = the annual subsidy per household for all households of group i ($i = 1, 2, \ldots, n$).

This formulation suggests that when the optimal solution to the primal problem is achieved (i.e., when bid-rent is maximized) it is exactly equal to the optimal solution of the dual; that is, actual rent paid is minimized.

The Herbert-Stevens formulation has some very useful characteristics. First, by disaggregating households of different socioeconomic characteristics (i.e., similar tastes and budgets), it allows for the recognition of the different behavioral characteristics of these groups, and permits a more realistic allocational process. Second, it simulates the market mechanism and its clearing process with the simple, yet powerful technique of linear programming. Third, it allows for policy constraints to be built into the model through the amount and type of land available at each iteration. Thus, comprehensive plans, land-use regulations, etc. can be effective through the model's use of constraints in the land variables. Finally, the model has an operational form so that its application to real world situation is possible.

At the same time, the Herbert-Stevens model has some disadvantages which are closely related to its good features. The first of these is the linear programming formulation itself which introduces the assumption of linearity to the objective function and constraints. If the objective function and/or any of the constraints are nonlinear, the solution of the linear system will be unreliable. There is also the question of data availability. It is, in general, difficult to obtain reliable data on household tastes, budgets, amenity levels, etc. This shortcoming was a major factor in preventing the model from becoming operational. In addition, there is the problem of disaggregation. That is, while data limitations and computational time suggest little disaggregation of the households unless the household groups are finely defined, the model is unlikely to reflect the full variety of their behavior.[7] Finally, the iterative process only insures the optimal allocation of households within the given iteration, and does not insure that the allocation will be optimal in the aggregate.

The question of how finely to define the various groups of people is also important in the linear programming model solution where there will be only as many nonzero numbers of people of particular types as there are constraints. Thus, if the groups are not very finely defined in terms of housing type, population type, and number of zones, much insight into

the coefficients of the objective function and the right-hand side of the constraints. Consequently, the inequalities are reversed and the problem becomes one of minimizing instead of maximizing. Thus, there is one dual variable for each primal constraint and one dual constraint for each primal variable.

their behavior will be lost. This point was discussed first by Britton Harris and then by Wilson,[8] who attempted to remedy this weakness by developing a corresponding assignment model version. In that version, equations (4.2) to (4.4) are all interpreted as constraints and an entropy maximizing model is derived which would operate iteratively until Z, the aggregate rent-paying ability of households, reaches an upper limit. This method was developed further by Senior and Wilson.[9]

The Southern Wisconsin Regional Plan Model

The technique of linear programming, although providing an excellent operational structure, was not widely adopted in subsequent residential land modeling attempts. The few contributions available usually simplify the form of the equations and inequalities and select variables which do not present many problems of data collection. Despite such efforts, however, the large number of variables involved and the real limitations in data availability still make the linear programming tool largely inapplicable for planning applications.

Nonetheless, using linear programming to allocate urban land to various land use categories was attempted in 1964 by the Southern Wisconsin Regional Planning Commission as part of the Southern Wisconsin Land-Use Transportation Study. A linear programming model was applied to the Waukesha area for the allocation of future land requirements to each zone.[10] Although the objective was much the same as that of the Penn-Jersey Transportation Study, this approach was based on the costs necessary to develop a site for various uses, soil conditions, etc. The model, as described by Schlager,[11] is strictly a design aid, and does not deal with either the personal preferences of families or with any other aspects of human economic and social behavior.

This linear programming formulation has an objective function which minimizes the total cost C_t of developing urban land for a given land use:

$$C_t = C_1X_1 + C_2X_2 + \ldots + C_nX_n, \tag{4.7}$$

where $X_i =$ units of given land use in a given area, and

$C_i =$ the cost of developing a unit of land of the given use in the given area.

There are three constraints included in the problem formulation. They are as follows:

$$\sum_{i=1}^{n} d_iX_i = E_k, \tag{4.8}$$

where E_k = the total land use demand requirement for land use k, and

d_i = service ratio coefficients which provide for supporting service land requirements necessary for primary land use developments, such as streets;

$$\sum_{i=1}^{n} X_i \le F_m , \qquad (4.9)$$

where F_m = the upper limit on land use of a particular category in zone m;

$$X_n \le G X_m , \qquad (4.10)$$

where G = the ratio of land use n allowed relative to land use m with land uses m and n in the same or different zones.

The land use demand equality constraint (4.8) follows a "standardized" format with one equation for each primary land use category. Constraints (4.9) and (4.10) reflect design standards and may take a wide variety of forms.

The simplistic formulation of Schlager's model, while inheriting all the problems of the linear programming approach as well as its data availability and standards selection, does not offer any improvement over the linear programming models examined earlier. On the contrary, much of the detail and ingenuity of the Herbert-Stevens approach is lost; and the whole set of economic nature assumptions regarding individual behavior disappears. For an effort which could have utilized the Herbert-Stevens experience several years after the Penn-Jersey model appeared, the Schlager formulation is not very satisfactory.

Britton Harris' Optimizing Model

Despite the difficulties involved in making the Herbert-Stevens model operational, the clear advantages of linear programming stimulated many scholars to develop the model further. At the University of Pennsylvania, interest was also kept high by Britton Harris and his students since the original model had been developed under his guidance. Harris attempted a modification of the Herbert-Stevens formulation to avoid estimating the desired or actual household budgetary allocations for both housing and nonhousing goods and services.[12] This had been an insurmountable difficulty in operating the original model.

His assumption was that actual consumer behavior could be used to determine a population's housing preference structure. If such a preference function could be estimated (through multiple regression analysis), then it could be used to deduce the budget allocations for each population group. This would produce a situation of indifference among alternative housing bundles. Then the linear programming model could be used to locate the population in the manner suggested by Herbert and Stevens.

In order to construct the preference function, Alonso's theoretical analysis of the housing market was used. This was also the inspiration for the development of the Herbert-Stevens model.[13] Harris envisions a utility function which is simply a more generalized form of the Alonso model, and which specifies a family of indifference surfaces which is the same as those conceptualized by Herbert and Stevens.

But Harris' formulation is not simply that of an allocation model. It also provides a widely praised evaluation mechanism. The housing preference structure of a population is used as the basis for predicting behavior, and for evaluating the relative differences in utility enjoyed by consumers under alternative arrangements of the housing stock. Thus, it does more than merely identify the determinants of residential location. Despite the emphasis given to this aspect of the model, however, there is virtually no theoretical analysis of the housing preferences which constitute the basic criterion of evaluation. There is only the specification of the mathematical form of the preference function, and the empirically unsubstantiated axiom that housing preferences are homogeneous.[14] Aside from this special characteristic of the model, however, its linear programming part is essentially the Herbert-Stevens model discussed previously.

In concluding discussion of the optimizing models which use the linear programming technique, the nature of the linearity assumption should be emphasized. Particular attention should be directed not at the objective function, but rather to the constraint equations or inequalities. While the technique's goal of determining combinations to optimize the whole system through allocation of all needs to the available area seems to make linear programming a very satisfactory tool for the solution of urban location problems (particularly ones of residential location), the frequent presence in the real world of nonlinear constraining situations creates real doubt about the usefulness of the model. Where the constraining relationships are nonlinear, most of the model's usefulness is lost because the linear approximations are very unsatisfactory.

The second basic limitation of the technique is its need for continuous variables while many of the factors entering the linear programming formulation are discrete. Hence, wherever the model contains discrete variables, it will produce an optimum deviating from the actual best solution.

An obvious way to treat these two endogenous difficulties is to use dynamic programming, which can handle both noncontinuous variables and nonlinear relationships. Although the technique is well developed, it has not yet been applied to the solution of the residential location problem.

A third limitation of linear programming stems from the fact that, in the social sciences, it is often necessary to use nonquantifiable variables. Such variables may play a very basic role in the decision process concerning an optimization problem, but their qualitative character prevents them from entering into a linear programming formulation. This is a weakness which is not shared by other model formulations, and arises from the fact that, in linear programming, all the variables have to be measured similarly, i.e., to be expressed in terms of dollars, labor, utility, etc., in order for their aggregate to be optimized.

Econometric Models

The problems faced in the construction and the application of optimizing models in their linear programming form have made researchers turn to simpler and more easily operationalized models. A common approach has been the construction of econometric models in which there is an explanatory rather than an optimizing power to be used and analyzed. The linear multiple regression technique does not present as many operational problems as linear programming. While it also depends on linearity assumptions, nonlinear relationships can be easily transformed into linear ones by various techniques such as taking logarithms. As a tool, the econometric model is much more flexible. Although it is always based on economic theory, the choice of variables is open, and the major emphasis is given to statistical analysis which indicates how reliable the final relationship among the variables is. The general form of the one-equation model is a linear additive relationship of independent (or explanatory) variables which explain the behavioral variations of the dependent (or endogenous) variable. Data on the values of the variables can be taken over a period of time to develop a time series statistical analysis based on trend projection, or drawn at the same time from a number of sub-units to produce a cross-sectional model.

Due to the nature of the econometric model, the linear regression formulation was extensively used in locational studies.[15] The most characteristic application to residential location is probably that of the Penn-Jersey study which was developed to replace the operationally difficult Herbert-Stevens linear programming model.

The Penn-Jersey model constructs a comprehensive picture of the metropolitan economy based on the sequential operation of seven principal sub-models. As presented by Seidman[16] and interpreted by Wilson,[17] the general structure of the model is shown in figure 4-1. The principal sub-models are in the following sequence: residential location, residential land use, manufacturing employment location, manufacturing land use, non-

65

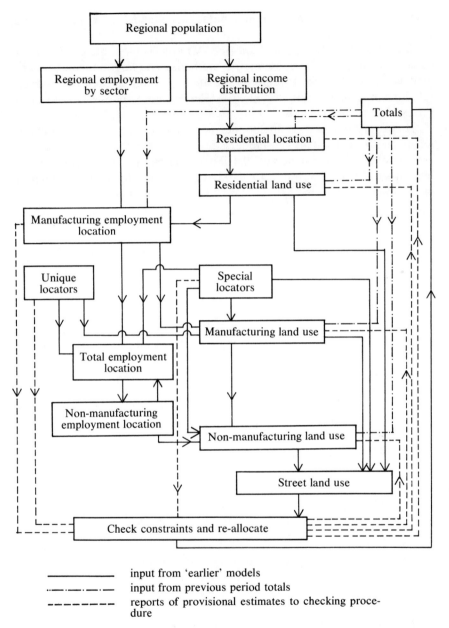

——————— input from 'earlier' models
·—·—·—·— input from previous period totals
———————— reports of provisional estimates to checking procedure

Source: A.G. Wilson, *Urban and Regional Models in Geography and Planning* (London: John Wiley & Sons, 1974). Reprinted with permission.

Figure 4-1. The Structure of the Comprehensive Penn-Jersey Model

manufacturing employment, nonmanufacturing land use, and street land use.

Due to its complexity, the Penn-Jersey model is more than just a set of equations estimated by econometric methods. The large number of sub-models included in the structure of the model, as well as their interwoven relationships, forms this complexity. Furthermore, it operates using a series of five-year periods.

However, the part of the model of concern here is the residential location sub-model. This sub-model is preceded by estimations of regional population and regional income distribution. Population and income information are then used as inputs for estimation of the residential location part of the model. The principal equation to be estimated is

$$U_i^w(t, t + T) = \sum_l a_l^w X_{li}^R, \tag{4.11}$$

where U_i^w = the residential desirability of area i, by households in income group w;

$t, t + T$ = the beginning and the end of the estimation period, the length of which is indicated by $(t, t + T)$;

X_{li}^R = the independent variables (l) used in the residential location model (R), when they determine desirability of area i; and

a_l^w = the coefficient to be estimated.

The actual independent variables used in equation (4.11) are:

$X_{1i}^R(t, t + T)$ = the proportion of population i in the two highest income groups at the beginning of the period;

$X_{2i}^R(t, t + T)$ = the net residential density at the beginning of the period;

$X_{3i}^R(t, t + T)$ = inaccessibility, taken as the weighted sum of different accessibilities at the beginning of the time period;

$X_{4i}^R(t, t + T)$ = the proportion of land available for residential use at the beginning of the period; and

$X_{5i}^R(t, t + T)$ = the proportion of land in "economic" use.

The final form of the model is nonlinear because of the step function introduced in determining migration.[18] The estimation procedures used are nonlinear multiple regression analysis and steepest descent; but many problems arise from the collinearity of many of the variables.

When the residential location model is run, multiplication of the number of households in each zone by the average household size for the zone produces the zonal populations of the end of the period. These outputs are then fed into the residential land use model to determine the amount of residential land consumed per household in each zone.

Even this brief presentation of the Penn-Jersey model indicates its complexity and the difficulties involved in its estimation. Although the econometric form of the models is a part of these difficulties, the development of advanced statistical techniques permits the estimation of the parameters. While complexity springs from the large number of sub-models and variables involved, it is a typical problem of all large scale comprehensive models. For locational and allocational models such as the Penn-Jersey effort, the econometric structure has proven to be an indispensable tool.

Nevertheless, the problem of selecting pertinent variables still exists. As mentioned above, the selection of independent variables in the structure of the residential model has created, among others, serious problems of collinearity. This has caused additional difficulties in the estimation procedures since the variables first had to be rotated using component analysis; then, estimation used regression analysis on these transformed variables; and, finally, the coefficients were transformed back again.

As in the Herbert-Stevens model, the underlying theory is Alonso's locational approach.[19] Here again, net household income (after transportation costs are subtracted) and accessibility are the two major factors in the consumption of residential land. Despite the wide use of these two factors, the concept of accessibility has been severely criticised with regard to both these more advanced operational models and the equilibrium models discussed in the next section. Accessibility has been used especially heavily in residential location models where dependence upon fixed activity centers is obvious, and where the controversy over whether or not accessibility rules the location decision-making process has not discouraged its use. Since econometric models contain several easily obtainable measures of transportation accessibility, complete modeling efforts have been based on it.

Kain's Econometric Model of Residential Location[20]

This econometric model is part of a larger multiple equation recursive model containing seven statistical and two definitional equations. They explain the location and trip-making behavior of workers in terms of four major characteristics: residential space consumption, automobile ownership, modal choice, and length of the journey-to-work. The whole model was tested using data obtained from the Detroit Area Traffic Study's home-interview origin and destination study.

The residential location sub-model uses four separate measures of residential space consumption as dependent variables. They are taken as the key variables determining the form, structure and size of an area. (This breakdown was necessary due to the lack of appropriate data for residential space consumption. Thus, structural type was used as a measure of residential density, and the original equation (4.12) was replaced by three linear statistical and one definitional equation.[21]) The simple axiom on which the model is based is that the worker selects the residential density at which he wishes to reside on the basis of his space preference, his income, and the price per unit he must pay for residential space. The form of the model is

$$R_{ij} = f(F_{ij}, \ Y_{ij}, \ P_j, \ S_{ij}, \ N_{ij}), \qquad\qquad (4.12)$$

where $R_{ij} =$ the residential space consumption of the ith worker employed at the jth workplace;

$F_{ij} =$ the size of the ith worker's family at the jth workplace;

$Y_{ij} =$ the family income of the ith worker at the jth workplace;

$P_j =$ a proxy variable for the price of residential space per unit at the jth workplace;

$S_{ij} =$ the sex of the ith worker employed at the jth workplace; and

$N_{ij} =$ the labor force participation by ij's family, i.e., the number of family members employed.

Despite the simple form of the model, several problems arose during the empirical testing. These were primarily due to the variables used to approximate the above measure and the degree of aggregation used. Nevertheless, empirical results substantiated the selection of determining factors (independent variables). Consequently, this linear model constituted the basis for RAND's more ambitious general comprehensive model of the urban economy and urban transportation.

Summary of Operational Models

Econometric models are becoming increasingly useful tools in the field of location because of their easily testable relationships. However, this occurs at the expense of the more realistic relationships among variables which are sacrificed in favor of linearity. In terms of data limitations, it is probably easier to work with econometric than with linear and dynamic programming models because of the types of variables usually employed. On the other hand, the theoretical advantages of optimizing the locating system are absent. In addition, although econometric models are also based on the prevailing economic location theories, the final testable forms often lose much of the elegance present in the theoretical models.

The limitations of the operational models of residential location behavior are now apparent. In their effort to provide decisionmakers with tools which can use actual information and provide suggested courses of action, they depend heavily upon available data, and use simple forms and relationships which can be tested and estimated with analytical techniques. Their contribution to the development of theory is to indicate the potential use of present-day theoretical developments in real world applications, and to suggest how close to reality our axiom-and-theorem structure really is. In actuality, however, the field of residential location has developed further in other directions where the results, although still highly theoretical, provide increasingly deeper insight into the complexities and peculiarities of the residential location choice. These approaches are based on economic theory and analyze the behavior of individual households as units which seek to maximize their satisfaction (or utility) through rational decisions regarding the purchase of necessary goods and services, including housing.

Economic Equilibrium Models

The approaches analyzed in the subsequent sections will be applications of either general or partial static equilibrium. In contrast to most of the previous macro-spatial models of household location, this category of theoretical developments heavily uses the disaggregated, micro-spatial approach concentrating on the individual household.

Among the behavioral microeconomic models examined here, two trends can be detected; and they will be used to classify the models analyzed. The first approach uses the home-to-work journey as the single most powerful explanatory variable of household location. In practical terms, this approach once again stresses the familiar concept of accessibility. That is, this home-work relationship is reduced to the tendency of households to minimize their transportation costs for the journey-to-work. In relating the transportation factor with the residence factor, these models introduce a trade-off relationship between the transport costs and the housing costs. Most characteristic are the models by Beckmann.[22] Alonso,[23] Wingo,[24] Kain,[25] and Muth.[26] These efforts will henceforth be referred to as "trade-off" approaches.

The second major approach attacks the importance of work location and consequently the importance of home-work accessibility. To such theorists, the costs of journey to work are nothing but constraints upon the final decisions of households. These, then, are primarily concerned with choice of house, selection of residential area, and the environmental con-

siderations in deciding on where to locate. This second approach is represented by Anderson,[27] Ellis,[28] Stegman,[29] and Richardson;[30] and in recent
years it has been gaining more and more ground as trade-off theories have
not been able to eliminate several of their weaknesses.

Trade-off Models

Theoretical developments following a trade-off approach first appeared in
the late fifties and have continued to appear due to the popularity and wide
acceptance of the underlying assumptions. For historic purposes, the
Beckmann model is discussed first,[31] although its shortness and limited
development do not permit a more exhaustive discussion. Two axioms
constitute the frame of the model:

1. Every household chooses its residential location so as to maximize the
   amount of living space that it can occupy for its housing expenditure;
2. The average household expenditure on residence and commuting is a
   well-defined function of income; the commuting costs function being a
   linear one.

Based on these axioms, the Beckmann formulation proves a theorem
which determines the market solution. The theorem states that land rent
and residential density at each location are determined so that higher
income groups tend to locate further from the center of the city, the sole
location of employment. The theorem explains the phenomenon observed
by both the land economists and the human ecologists; that is, poor families
reside in the central city where land generally commands higher prices,
while the wealthier families settle in the city periphery on less expensive
land.

In later refinements of his model,[32] Beckmann still shows that commuting distance rises with income when tastes are assumed equal. In addition,
if a Pareto income distribution is assumed, distance determines the rent,
density and income functions of the monocentric city.[33]

The Beckmann model represents the pioneering equilibrium microeconomic model of residential location. It gives a clear, if not completely analyzed, solution of the rent, density, and income variables, and
partially explains the form of the contemporary city. Its brief formulation
has stimulated discussions in the literature; and it has been heavily used as
a starting point by later writers.

**Advanced Models of Utility Maximization Under a Budget
Constraint**

To an extent Beckmann's model can be considered a special case of
Alonso's theory.[34] Alonso's approach in turn belongs to the same group of

models as the Wingo, Kain, and Muth formulations mentioned earlier. All of these models are static equilibrium, utility maximization ones which incorporate a budget constraint. While the fundamental principles are the same in all of them, certain assumptions regarding the form of the utility and budget functions are different.

Alonso's model is basically an applied refinement of the von Thünen analysis of land rent and land uses.[35] It describes a process through which households and firms compete for particular lots of land in a way that will maximize efficiency and satisfaction for the competitors. This competition for location and size of lot is expressed through a bid-rent function for each household and/or firm. A market equilibrium is achieved when every bidder has maximized his efficiency subject to his available income.

The Alonso model begins with the following axioms:

1. Urban space is continuous, and there is one urban center which serves as the only place of employment;
2. The household's utility depends upon three variables: housing, distance from the city center and a vector of all the other goods;
3. The price of housing and other goods is independent of the quantities purchased. The prices of housing and commuting depend upon distance from the city center.

Using constraint maximization of the household utility with respect to goods, housing and distance, the model determines individual location according to the following theorem:

The household's equilibrium location is determined by the tangency of the household's highest possible bid-price curve with the price structure curve. The former shows the land rent the household could pay at each distance from the center in order to achieve a certain utility level, and the latter gives the market price of land at each distance from the city center.

Unfortunately, this classical economic equilibrium is not sufficient to derive market equilibrium when urban firms are also present. For this purpose firms, households, and farms are represented by families of bid prices, and the slopes differ from establishment to establishment. Consequently, the steepness of the bid function will determine the distance of the establishment from the city center. Thus, the establishments with steeper bid-price curves locate closer to the center.

The next part of the Alonso model is insufficient; and there is no actual solution to the location problem because the bid-prices are not unique but rather members of families of curves. Despite Alonso's attempt to use the von Thünen prototype to explain variations in the urban land market, the absence of the basic assumption of a perfectly competitive market deprives the model of the ability to provide a market solution.

In the Alonso model, if the value of all goods other than housing is fixed, the utility function represents a trade-off between the quantity of land consumed by the household and the distance of this land from the city center. Since commuting cost increases with distance from the center, higher income households consuming larger quantities of land will balance them with greater commuting costs. Since price per unit of land declines as commuting cost increases, households which wish to buy relatively large amounts of land will move out farther than those which wish to buy relatively small amounts.

Alonso's model was developed during the same period as the similar model developed by Lowdon Wingo.[36] Again, this is a static equilibrium model employing a market mechanism through which households minimize their location costs by choosing between the size and accessibility of a site. The preference for each of these is treated as independent parts of the model, while rent and transport costs are assumed to be complementary.[37] Since Alonso treats space and accessibility preferences as interrelated, this is probably the fundamental difference between the Wingo and Alonso models. In addition, the Wingo model gives in-depth treatment to the pivotal factor of transport costs, and this gives a distinctive character to the model. The axioms of Wingo's model are as follows:

1. The urban population is homogeneous with regard to income and preferences for all goods and services;
2. The location of employment is given;
3. The marginal values placed on leisure and on residential space are known;
4. All but the urban land prices are constant;
5. Transport costs are composed of monetary costs, terminal costs at the city center, and commuting time to work priced according to the marginal value of leisure. Transportation costs are therefore a function of home-work distance when all work locations are found in the city center;
6. Rent is dependent upon accessibility alone so that it varies inversely with distance from the city center;
7. Households spend a constant sum of land rent and transport costs. This is equal to the transport costs to the most distant location when the price of land is zero (the budget constraint).

The individual household equilibrium solution is a combination of the rent at the location (which is equal to the savings in transportation costs) and the size of lot (which is derived from the demand function for residential land) at each distance from the city center. The theorem associated with the household equilibrium solution is that the population density gradient in the monocentric city has a continuously declining slope from the city center to its periphery. To attain market equilibrium, the demand for land at each distance from the city center must equal the supply at that location (given the structure of position rents consistent with individual equilibrium) so that the total available land is allocated among households. The market equilibrium solution, then, occurs when the total city population equals the integral of the density of population over the area of the city.

The major shortcomings of the Wingo formulation are the assumption of constant demand as derived from the budget constraint, and the assumption of income equality for all households. This is in sharp contrast to the Alonso approach which, by introducing a third good, or rather a vector of goods, allows variations in spending for housing and transportation. It further allows for variation in the demand curves for the same individual in different locations. In addition, the elasticity of demand for land is less than unity; i.e., a fall in the price of land with an increase in distance from the city center also involves a fall in total household rent payment. In fact, both Mills and Richardson proved that this is a condition for equilibrium.[38] If the elasticity were equal to unity, the household demand function would be a rectangular hyperbola, and there would be no solution. If, on the other hand, the elasticity of demand were larger than unity, equilibrium could be achieved only for individual households, and only if land at the city boundary were more desirable than centrally located land. In such a case, market equilibrium would be impossible since the amount of space consumed by households would decrease with increasing distance. It would then conflict with the supply of land function. Although Wingo does not elaborate on the elasticity of demand, other researchers do. Consequently, there is evidence that Wingo's formulation imposes a restriction on the value of elasticity which is not substantiated by empirical research.[39]

Nevertheless, the Wingo model presents a certain elegance and simplicity, and it develops powerful relationships among key variables. However, the assumptions used have made the application of the model impossible. This is in spite of Wingo's stated intention of developing an operational framework. Yet some improvements of the model have been suggested by Wingo and others. They concern modifications of the basic assumptions to allow for a higher degree of reality. For example, the assumption of identical incomes and tastes for all households can be modified by stratifying households into income-classes and developing separate expenditure and demand functions for each class. The internal consistency of the model, however, is undeniable; and the Wingo formulation ought to be explored further by other researchers.

A similar study from the same period was conducted by John Kain for the RAND Corporation.[40] Again, Kain's model incorporates the general theory of location common to all previous equilibrium models. It also emphasizes transportation in the same fashion as the Wingo model. However, the main axiom on which this model is based is that accessibility (or its inverse, transportation costs) will influence the household's choice of residential location. The model proves by the use of statistical information and tests the theorem that households substitute journey-to-work expenditures for site expenditures, and that this substitution depends primarily on household preferences for low-density rather than high-density residential services.

A number of sub-axioms are used to derive the theorem suggested above. The most important are that:

1. The household's transportation costs increase monotonically with distance between workplace and residential location;
2. The household is an atomistic competitor in the residential space market; that is, there is a market for residential space, and the price per unit of space is given;
3. The household's work place is fixed;
4. The price of a unit of residential space varies from one location to another, and it decreases monotonically with distance from the household's workplace. These different prices are the location rents of the sites;
5. Residential space is not an inferior good and households choose their residential location and residential space consumption by maximizing their utility subject to a certain income;
6. Similar groups of households place the same valuation on time per mile.

The model reaches an equilibrium solution by maximizing the utility of individual households through minimizing the total location costs. However, the constraints imposed upon the solution include not only the income of the household, but also its preferences for residential space and the unit price of residential space. To Kain, equilibrium is achieved, where the incremental savings in location rents obtained by commuting an additional unity of distance per quantity of space equal the incremental increase in transportation costs over this additional distance. At that point:

. . . We have obtained those locations which minimize the household's locational costs for each quantity of residential space. In addition, we have obtained the household's required expenditures for each quantity of residential space. This is all the information we must have to enable us to obtain a unique locational solution for each household.

Total location costs divided by the quantity of residential space is the price the household must pay per unit for residential space. With this price information the household's locational solution is straight forward. Given the price of all other goods and services, the household's preference for residential space, its preference for all other goods and services and its income, the household's consumption of residential space is uniquely determined. Knowing its consumption or residential space, we have uniquely determined its residential location.[41]

This is a static partial equilibrium model which, unlike the previous ones, evaluate the relationship among the model variables through empirical observations rather than mathematical manipulation. The data used were not always sufficient to substantiate the hypotheses tested; but in most cases, they support the model's argument for the importance of accessibility to employment to household location.

The most complete analysis of residential location using the static microeconomic equilibrium approach was presented by Richard Muth in his *Cities and Housing*. Muth's approach differs from Alonso's in two important ways. First, Muth uses "housing services" combining land, size of housing structure, and other dimensions of the value of housing. Alonso, however, primarily considers location and size of the residential lot. Second, unlike Alonso, Muth considers household income as one of the determinants of the transportation expenditures.

Furthermore, while Muth is concerned entirely with the housing market and says very little about the location of other urban activities, his model development rests on three sets of axioms concerning housing services, transportation costs and the centers of nonresidential activity.[42]

The housing market axioms are:

1. The prices of all commodities other than housing and transport are the same everywhere in the city;
2. The price of housing is an index of the prices of all those items which are generally encompassed by housing. These include the services for land and structure;

The transport cost axioms are:

1. The cost per trip consists of a fixed part and a variable part. Fixed costs include total waiting time, parking charges and fixed bus fares; and variable costs contain commuting time and variable transit fares or private automobile expenditures;
2. The variable portion of the transport costs increase at a nonincreasing rate with distance from the CBD or any other center of activity;
3. Time costs are a function of the wage rate;
4. The household makes a fixed number of trips to and from the CBD per unit of time regardless of location or any other consideration;
5. Transport costs are the same in all directions;

The axiom concerning the centers of economic activity is:

1. There exists only one center of economic activity, the Central Business District, where all employment is concentrated.

The Muth model uses a utility function of the general form:

$$U = U(x, q) \tag{4.13}$$

where x = dollars of expenditure on all commodities except housing and transportation but including leisure; and

q = consumption of housing.

Thus, while Muth includes "leisure" in the definition of the "other commodities," unlike Alonso, he excluded commuting distance from the utility function. The budget constraint is given as:

$$y = x + p(k)q + T(k, y), \tag{4.14}$$

where y = household income;

k = distance from the CBD;

$p(k)$ = the price per unit of housing, a function of the distance k; and

T = cost per trip, a function of distance and income.

Household equilibrium is obtained by maximizing utility, subject to the budget constraint, with respect to housing, distance and other commodities as follows:

$$U_x - \lambda = 0 \tag{4.15}$$

$$U_q - \lambda p(k) = 0 \tag{4.16}$$

$$qp_k + T_k = 0 \tag{4.17}$$

$$y - x - p(k)q + T(k, y) = 0$$

(the budget constraint of equation 4.14)

Equations (4.15) and (4.16) together imply that the marginal rate of substitution between housing and other commodities is equal to their price ratio; while equation (4.17) states that in equilibrium location, the household's marginal transport costs will equal its marginal housing savings. The demand function for housing can be derived from equations (4.14) through (4.16), and the slope of the bid price function for a household can be obtained from equation (4.17) as:

$$\frac{\partial p(k)}{\partial k} = \frac{-1}{q} \frac{\partial T(k, y)}{\partial k}, \tag{4.17a}$$

Equation (4.17a) implies that as distance from the CBD increases, the household will bid less for each new location. Analysis of the change in the bid-rent function with respect to income reveals that the sign of the change

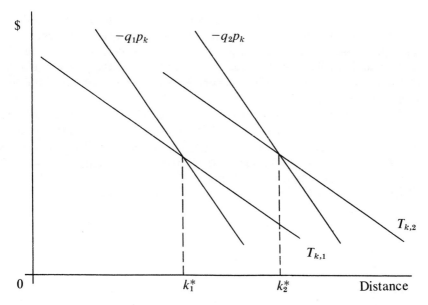

Source: adapted from Richard Muth, *Cities and Housing: The Spatial Pattern of Urban Residential Land Use* (Chicago, Ill.: The University of Chicago Press, 1969).

Figure 4-2. Change in Distance Equilibrium as Income Increases

is positive if the income elasticity of demand for housing space is higher than the elasticity of transport costs. Thus, an increase in income will move the equilibrium distance farther from the center, as shown in figure 4-2. Moreover, household residences will be stratified along radii from the CBD with higher income families residing farther from the center than lower income families.

In his analysis of the supply of housing services, Muth treats land as any other factor of production and does not take into account such characteristics as immobility, indivisibility, durability, etc.[43] The axioms employed in this part of the model are as follows:

1. Firms and households are competitive in both product and factor markets;

2. All firms producing a given commodity (including housing) are identical; that is, they have the same production function and use both land and nonland inputs;

3. Producers employ quantities of land and nonland inputs that maximize profits at each distance;

4. Land rents and housing services are set by the markets so that the profits of housing service producers equal zero everywhere the services are produced.

In differentiating the firm's profit function with respect to land and nonland factors of production, an equation with zero gives the necessary conditions for supply-side profit maximization. The complete model integrating the demand and supply sides is based on the assumption that the urban area extends as far from the CBD as is necessary for the demand to equal the supply of housing services.

Muth's analysis is a landmark contribution to the study of residential location. The analytical part of the study treats a variety of market imperfections, peculiarities of land and housing goods, and the effects of various factors on the demand and supply of housing services. In addition, the empirical work accompanying the model is a major contribution to the field of applied urban research. It is particularly noteworthy for the analysis of income elasticities.

Moreover, Muth was the first residential location analyst to show the conditions under which Clark's hypothesis that urban population densities are given by a negative exponential function of distance from the CBD actually holds. Despite the fact that many writers and several empirical studies have confirmed the basic Clark hypothesis, Muth's work is the first to derive it as a consequence of an equilibrium explanatory model of urban residential structure.[44]

A Discussion of the Monocentric Assumption

In all of the long run, spatial equilibrium models which we have discussed so far, the common, central assumption has been that there is only one center of economic activity, the CBD. This corresponds to the point of highest accessibility where all employment in the urban area is concentrated, and from which travel costs in all directions are the same per unit of distance. This assumption of monocentricity and its corollary, the isotropic transportation network, have decisively shaped the urban structure and form according to these models. The assumption is old, and was originally found in von Thünen's model of agricultural land use.[45] While in von Thünen's analysis the assumption of a sole center is partially justified by the model's concern with a city and its tributary area (i.e., farmland producing for the city), within urban areas the application of the same principle is not as straightforward. Yet all writers from Beckmann to Muth have used the von Thünen analysis as their starting point.

Urban conditions, however, increasingly differ from those of the rural hinterland as the size and degree of diversification and specialization of the city increases. And while monocentricity could be accepted as a starting point in model development, the very strong conclusions offered by the previously mentioned analysts are not justified.

The monocentric assumption has several effects on the urban patterns derived by these models. First, it is clear that with increasing size of the urban area employment is by no means concentrated at one central point. Furthermore, it cannot be assumed, as many models do, that the bulk of employment is centralized, and that the rest is evenly spread throughout the area. On the contrary, there is strong evidence that a continuous decentralization of employment takes place in the larger urban areas of the United States. For instance, studies by Meyer, Kain, and Wohl,[46] and by Kain[47] clearly indicate that there is a postwar trend toward the rapid expansion of manufacturing, commercial, and service activities in the suburban rings of metropolitan areas. At the same time, growth in the central city is minimal and is often negative.[48] Trends in the suburbanization of employment centers are explained by the household's desire for a better quality residential environment and more residential space, the expansion of the urban transportation networks, and the increasing availability of the private automobile. This has caused reduction in total transportation costs, and increased the real incomes of households. However, the suburbanization of population and the suburbanization of employment cannot be considered independently. Since residential location still depends greatly on the location of employment and the length of the journey-to-work, only definite suburbanization patterns in employment location could fully explain the outward movement of households.

By assuming concentrated employment in the CBD, two biases will influence the results of monocentric models:

1. In explaining urban structure and the location of households, the CBD is given more importance than it really deserves; and
2. The analysis of the rest of the urban area becomes inadequate because the homogeneity of residential land is interrupted by the presence of nonresidential uses. Furthermore, the smoothness and continuity of the concave functions representing urban population densities and bid-rent prices disappear; and certain phenomena which take place within the noncentral areas of the city are neglected by the models.

In addition to these weaknesses, monocentricity is a problem in relation of the character and functions attributed to the CBD. As Mills indicated,[49] a reason for the employment importance of the CBD could be the presence of at least some industries with increasing returns to scale at low levels of output. Such increasing returns could induce other industries, vertically related to the original ones, to locate nearby, and an agglomeration focus would then be created. But Mills notes that such agglomeration would be somewhat inconsistent with the Wicksteed-Wicksell theorem discussed in Chapter 2, and consequently with the theory of urban land rent. In addition, industries with major internal scale economies are less frequently observed in central city locations.

Nevertheless, the admission of such increasing returns in the central city contradicts the fundamental assumption of monocentric models with regard to constant returns in the production of central goods and services. Aside from leaving part of the questions of special central functions unanswered, constant returns cannot continue forever in a growing urban area. The increasing need for transportation to the central city, and the diseconomies associated with congestion and land allocated to transportation uses will cause decreasing returns. Therefore, the assumptions of constancy and the continued importance of the central city become invalid.

Several authors have recognized these weaknesses of the monocentric assumption. Some have dealt with the character and functions of the central city, while others have dealt with the presence of additional centers and the modifications required in order for urban residential models to remain relevant.

The location of employment has concerned Mills.[50] In spite of a monocentricity assumption, he does not assume that all workers are employed in the CBD or that all output is produced there. Instead, the whole urban area is considered to be used for the production of a single product with an aggregate production function. This avoids problems of aggregation during the market-clearing process. This urban land use, then, competes with intracity transportation for land. Firms producing output throughout the urban area ship it to the city center where it is sold. Therefore, each unit of output generates a certain demand for transportation to the CBD. In equilibrium, urban land at each distance from the center is exhausted by production and transportation activities. The equilibrium rent distance function has the form:

$$R(u) = R_o e^{-Au}, \qquad (4.18)$$

where R_o = land rent at the city center; and

u = distance from the center.

Thus, as in the previously mentioned Muth model, the familiar negative exponential form is derived from an equilibrium model. The model implies that the negative exponential function can be used to approximate the decline of both land values and the density of land uses as functions of distance from the central city.

The contribution of the Mills formulation is not obviated by the assumption of noncentrality in the employment location, the use of an aggregate production function, and the introduction of the need for land for transportation. But the model explains little regarding residential location and the individual behavior of households. There are no utility functions to indicate household preferences, and no indications of various household characteristics such as family size, income, employment opportunities, and even fixed transportation patterns. Most of the household characteristics discussed in the previously analyzed equilibrium models are absent from Mills.

As Julius Margolis points out in discussing the Mills models of resource allocation,[51] economic models that analyze urban form face the three difficulties of externalities, market imperfection, and the slow pace of the adjustment process. This slow pace is due to the long life of buildings and various forms of technology. While the second and third problems are difficult to handle unless they are considered as deviations from the model's assumptions, the first problem can be dealt with directly in terms of traffic generation and congestion for example.

Major works dealing with traffic generation externalities are the analyses of densities and land uses in a monocentric city by Solow and Vickery[52] and by Solow.[53] In the first of these studies, urban land used for transportation is optimally allocated between traffic generating and traffic carrying uses. The study shows that for cities with a less-than-optimal size the proportion of land allocated to transportation is a decreasing, concave function of distance from the city. The highest proportion of land used for roads is at the center, and no land is allocated to roads at the city limits. However, when the city reaches an optimal size, the optimal road will have a constant width. Of interest here is the analysis of the competitive urban land rent profits. In the equilibrium models analyzed thus far it reflects the highest land desirability and consequently guides the land use decisions in the urban area. On the assumption that no tolls are imposed to control road use and congestion, such a guide could be very misleading and would overallocate land to transportation facilities.[54]

The later work by Solow[55] incorporated residential land. That is, when transportation costs depend not only on distance from the central city but also on traffic congestion, the land is optimally allocated between residential and transportation uses. Moreover, in the initial model formulation, the equilibrium pattern is described in the familiar manner. A decreasing, continuous, and convex rent profile is considered a function of distance from the center, and the richer people live the farther from the city center and consume the most space. However, the introduction of traffic density only allows a general solution of the model for special cases. Even then, congestion alters the urban land value patterns by making the rent profile more convex. It causes the rent per acre to first fall sharply as one leaves the CBD, and then fall less sharply as one approaches the city limits.[56]

Deviations from the standard assumptions of the monocentric models discussed above, and the introduction of new dimensions to urban form such as dispersed employment and traffic densities, contribute much to our understanding of the urban pattern. Such contributions, however, still center on the concept of a single urban center. In many ways, this not only defines the urban structure and configuration, but also introduces a bias in the determination of the spatial distribution of urban variables such as land values, housing rents, and urban densities. It appears that the only way to correct this bias is to relax altogether the assumption of monocentricity.

Attempts to Analyze Multi-Center Areas

The weakness of the monocentric assumption was recognized quite early in the development of urban economic literature. Nevertheless, efforts to develop analytical models incorporating non-monocentric urban patterns were minimal. The first formal recognition of a multi-center urban setting was Harris and Ullman's[57] multiple-nuclei hypothesis of urban structure. Throughout the subsequent literature, the hypothesis was praised for its reality and other merits. But little was done to either test it or improve it due to its static and descriptive, nonexplanatory character.

Considerable work has been done by urban geographers on the location of the urban centers of economic activity, the factors affecting their relative location, and the delimitation of urban "market areas" to which the urban population is allocated.[58] Moreover, the principle of "central place hierarchy" has been applied to urban centers in an effort to detect the urban population's dependency upon a hierarchy of economic centers.[59] But the approach emphasizes the role of the centers in dividing the city into market areas, rather than analyzing the residential location behavior of households in the presence of these centers.

Alonso discusses the possibility of a number of centers in an urban area. In particular he considers the case of two independent centers of either equal or unequal importance.[60] But the consideration is limited to analyzing the shape of the market area boundary when the two centers are competing and individuals have to choose one center that suits them best. While in this case an individual's equilibrium should be possible, Alonso acknowledges that a market equilibrium could be problematical. In any event, he does not attempt to solve either, and his analysis is limited to the descriptive presentation of a series of graphs.

Muth's approach, while quite similar,[61] is more precise and derives the shape of the boundary mathematically. Yet Muth, like Alonso, considers the rent functions of the two centers to be *independent* of each other. Therefore, each household makes a decision on the use of a particular center, which then becomes its *sole* center of economic activity. To Muth, then, the problem is reduced to a search for the boundary between every pair of market areas on the urban plane. Following Launhardt's familiar analysis,[62] the boundary is found to be a branch of a hyperbola, as shown in figure 4-3.

Figure 4-3a shows the variation in housing prices with distance from the

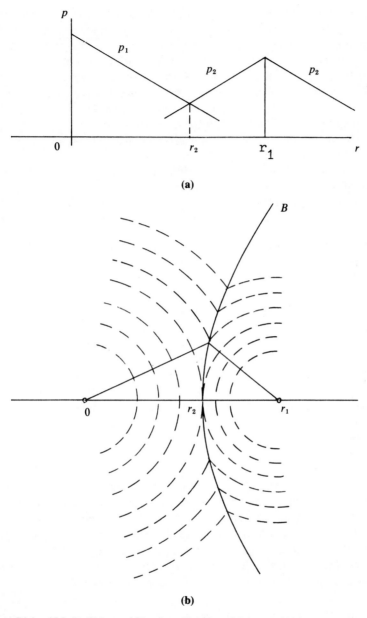

(a)

(b)

Figure 4-3 The Shape of the Boundary Between Two Urban Markets

major center 0 and from a second concentration at distance r_1. These prices decrease with distance from their corresponding centers, due to increasing transport costs. At a distance r_2 from 0, where $p_1 = p_2$, there is a boundary separating the residential areas of workers employed in the two centers. The analysis is carried on in figure 4-3b, where the contours of constant housing prices are shown by dashed lines. These contours are circles with their centers at 0 and r_1; and the locus of their equal price intersections forms the hyperbolic boundary. If the analysis is repeated for every pair of such centers, the final boundary of each urban market sub-area would be a composite of such segments of hyperbolas.

This boundary, of course, is defined as the locus of points on which households are indifferent towards the two centers. Despite the fact that the shape of these independent "market areas" is irregular rather than circular as in the monocentric models presented so far, Quigley states:

In general . . . the existence of multiple workplaces in a city can be "handled" within this classical framework by dividing the urban area into exclusive residence areas around each workplace, each bounded entirely by the locus of points such that workers are indifferent between workplaces (or by the circumference describing the point at which the price of land is equal to its value in 'agriculture') and by applying the monocentric model within each residence/workplace area.[63]

However, while this approach summarizes the literature's treatment of multi-center settings, it does not reflect reality. It first assumes that such a "boundary" actually exists and that an urban area is in fact divided into "exclusive" residential areas. But this is incompatible with the extensive literature on the location of retail centers and their corresponding market areas. Time and again, these studies have abandoned the idea of a boundary. Lakshmanan and Hansen for example, in discussing their delineation of trade area boundaries, assert that the assumption of closed market areas around retail centers is a highly questionable one, and acknowledge the fact that a number of empirical studies have demonstrated a continuum of market orientation of consumers to shopping centers.[64] Actually empirical studies indicate that such "market areas" can only be based on the probabilities that a household will travel to the particular center. Where these probabilities are about equal for two or more centers, a transition zone develops. Here, households are not indifferent between centers but rather tend to use both centers with equal frequency. As Berry states:

Within metropolitan regions . . . ., there is no such thing as an absolute breaking-point. The breaking point formula[65] simply gives the point at which the proportion of consumers located around the breaking-point splits equally between two competing alternatives of differing attractiveness . . . In densely built-up areas consumers have considerable business centers of differing attractiveness available within the maximum distances they are willing to travel. They will visit nonexclusively but each at some time and with some probability.[66]

But if this is so and the households located between two centers use *both*, the rent profiles of the monocentric models which are still used by generalized multi-center models, are altered by the presence of the second center. That is, households located between two centers have certain locational advantages because of their access to the *two*. On the other hand, households with access to only one center have no such advantage. In this light, then, one would expect the rent and land value gradients between the two centers to be distorted when compared with the same gradients for the two centers taken individually, as shown in figure 1-1. The derivation of these new gradients is the subject of the next chapter.

Criticism of Trade-off Models

So far residential location theories and models have been traced according to a sequence proceeding from the simplest to the more advanced. The models discussed first were based on a single concept, that of *accessibility*. It was the critical factor in allocating urban land to various uses, including that of residential land use. Accessibility was discussed in relation to the destination of home-based or activity-based trips. As far as residential location is concerned, accessibility is primarily concerned with the home-to-work journey. In most cases, the desirable destination was a single location in the center of the city (CBD). But if accessibility alone were the critical factor, and households actually aimed at minimizing their transport costs, the high income groups with the most purchasing power would outbid lower income groups and reside close to the city center. In contrast, lower income groups would live on the outskirts. But this directly contradicts both observed urban residential patterns and empirical research. The former shows high income groups residing in the suburbs while lower incomes occupy more central neighborhoods, and the latter indicates that wealthier households prefer to live farther from the city center where densities are lower.[67]

The more advanced theories with which we have dealt also consider the *amount of land desired* as a pivotal factor. Alonso's contribution here was the most decisive, and showed how the two site characteristics compete with each other in the households' locational decision. The trade-off between competition and the individual budget constraints was the focus of the static microeconomic equilibrium models analyzed. The alternative approaches of noneconomists which challenge accessibility as *the* leading factor in the residential location decision have also been discussed. These theories were largely developed by sociologists and human ecologists and were presented in Chapter 3 of this study. They give a clear, if nonquantitative, picture of the various social and environmental factors of importance to households which the land location and allocation models have failed to incorporate.

Because of their qualitative nature, these theories did not develop any further, but remained as isolated efforts from the early decades of the century. The analysis of residential location behavior has been developed primarily by economists who were stimulated by increased interest in urban economics during the sixties.

This development, however, particularly the refining of theories and models incorporating the trade-off principle, stimulated a renewed reaction. Some scholars believed that micro-spatial analysis which had achieved a high degree of sophisitcation and refinement could no longer limit its interests to the purely economic aspects of the problem. Instead, they felt it must also handle other, noneconomic variables. This school of scholars attacked primarily the excessive treatment of the concept of accessibility.

Theodore Anderson,[68] for example, attacks the concept of neighborhood dependence upon a major concentration (CBD). He argues that such concentrations have decreased in importance in recent years, and that no direct relationship exists between the concentration and the characteristics of the residential neighborhood. He also suggests that emphasis should be given to the pattern of social relations among sub-groups, the major residential values held by members of the community and, most important of all, the community power structure.

Britton Harris[69] suggests that such considerations are important because the preferences of the American public: ". . . extend not only, and possibly not primarily to low density, but rather to good housing conditions, neighborhood cleanliness, and possibly to novelty or non-obsolescence of the housing stock.[70] Furthermore, he notes that the tendency of higher income and status groups to segregate themselves socially and geographically may indicate that social preferences are the determining forces in the residential location decisions of such groups. Michael Stegman also questions the preeminence of accessibility in explaining housing consumer behavior.[71] He offers empirical evidence that neighborhood considerations are more important to locating households than accessibility to employment. Such considerations include the quality of housing, amenity, and environmental conditions rather than more residential space. He also acknowledges the fact that the functions attributed to the CBD by trade-off models are no longer present to the same extent as in the past. Thus, basic urban services have become more accessible to suburbanites because of both decentralization of work and shopping activities, and development of urban expressways making the central city more accessible. The result of these changes, it is argued, is that "large numbers of suburban families do not have to trade off accessibility for savings in location rent: they can have both."[72]

The dispersion of employment opportunities is emphasized by Jay Siegel.[73] He concludes that with decentralized job locations urban density patterns are quite unlike those generated by the simple von Thünen-type approach. Siegel attributes the demand for a particular residential location to the socioeconomic characteristics of the neighborhood, the nature and availability of public services and amenities, the site characteristics associated with the location, as well as accessibility to employment. In Siegel's model, a household chooses the residential location that maximizes its utility subject to its budget constraint. The novelties here are that he introduces accessibility to the household utility function, and he does not assume that all jobs are in the CBD. Instead, when location refers both to home and work, household decisions regarding location and housing are determined simultaneously.

It could be concluded then, that trade off models have somehow over-emphasized both accessibility to a major center of employment and the trade-off between accessibility and space. Furthermore, they have underestimated the importance of neighborhood, environmental, and social considerations. To a certain extent, these latter factors can be taken into account in the household's utility function, although there are major problems in defining and quantifying them.[74] But a major weakness of the approach, and one which is inherent in all equilibrium models, is the assumption of freedom of choice for households. It is assumed that the short-run supply of housing is elastic and that the housing market is competitive. However, this freedom of choice may be severely restricted by the household's limited market information as well as by the possibility of a limited supply of the desired housing.

This, of course, relates to the broader issue of the durability of residential capital. Since residential structures are immobile, difficult to modify, and have a long life span, the industry supply of housing curve does not have a smooth and continuous profile. Thus housing prices in the local market are not fixed but will depend on the standing stock.

Quigley provides an excellent discussion of the issue.[75] He introduces the importance of a heterogeneous housing stock and the problems arising from neglecting its durability and inflexibility to change. He states:

The existence of heterogeneous stocks of housing suggests that there may be several more or less distinct submarkets for residential services, and that the surface of location rents may vary between submarkets. Even at the same residential site, the pure location rent for different housing configurations, or submarkets, may vary. In fact, only if the cost of converting units from one submarket to another were zero would we expect identical pure location rents.[76]

If the existence of a heterogeneous housing stock is accepted, and more urban centers of economic activity are also taken into account, the monocentric trade-off model completely collapses. In this case, the supply of a particular housing type in the "exclusive" market area of a center may not be sufficient. Therefore, households employed at the center would have to locate somewhere outside their area. But as soon as households dependent upon this center cross the "boundary" of the market area, the assumption of exclusive areas and the construction of housing rent surfaces are destroyed. The actual rent surfaces may still decline with distance from these centers; but this will occur quite irregularly since quasi-rents and nonrent spaces will be reflected in the rent shape.[77]

The above discussion indicates that trade-off models lead to an impasse due to a number of nonobservable assumptions on market perception and household preference. Among the proposed alternatives, Harry Richardson's "behavioral" model merits attention.[78] He argues that for owner-occupiers, housing preferences (including the desired type of area and quality of the environment) and financial constraints (e.g., household income and the availability of mortgage finance) are the primary factors in a residence location decision. Journey-to-work costs are only a secondary determinant and act as a constraint; i.e., they provide a maximum commuting limit to travel time. Therefore, a household will locate at that site which most satisfactorily meets its environmental and size preferences, and which satisfies the equation:

$$a_i Y_i = p_m q_m, \qquad (4.19)$$

where $Y_i =$ the income of household of class i;

$\quad a_i =$ the maximum mortgage/income ratio that the financing agency is willing to lend to households of income class i;

$\quad q_m =$ the quantity of housing purchased at location m; and

$\quad p_m =$ the unit price of housing purchased at m.

The price is determined by the familiar negative exponential distance function:

$$p_m = J n_m e^{-k d_{om}}, \qquad (4.20)$$

where $\quad n_m =$ an index of environment/quality of the area at location m;

$\quad d_{om} =$ the distance between the city center 0 and location m; and

$\quad J, k =$ constants.

Finally, equation (4.19) is subject to the constraint

$$d_{om} \leq d_x, \qquad (4.21)$$

where $\quad d_x =$ the maximum commuting distance.

However, this model does not eliminate the monocentric assumption.

The locational decision still depends upon a d_{om} distance so that accessibility to a center is again of major importance. In addition, the model adopts an exogenously determined rent function (equation 4.20) and is therefore not dependent on demand. This is clearly a major weakness. In practice it means that in the absence of residential land use demand, the rent gradient is determined by the rest of the economic activities in the urban area. But given the small percentage of urban land consumed by economic activities compared to that consumed by residential land use, this assumption cannot be accepted.

The main contribution of this model is the introduction of the mortgage/income ratio. However, it is considered constant for each income class; and this is questionable since income is only one of the factors a financing agency will consider. Other important factors are the demand for housing mortgages, the prevailing interest rates, the dependability and good name of the borrower, etc. Nevertheless, this factor is certainly important because if we accept the assumptions of the trade-off equilibrium models, it will partially limit the household's choices for residence. If the concept of a trade-off between transport and housing costs is accepted, then households will allocate a larger portion of their income to housing the closer to the center they locate since they can use their savings from transport. This means that their highest bid rent profile could indicate the availability of more money allocated to the purchase of a house. But since equation (4.19) shows that the amount of the mortgage depends on the household's income and not on its location, the mortgage will be constant and will not increase with decreasing distance from the center. Thus, for locations closer to the central city, a household's actual bid prices will be lower than its desirable prices, and the rent gradient will flatten above a certain price level.

Summary

The trade-off, equilibrium, microeconomic models explaining household location behavior offer valuable insight into the problem. They explain a range of locational phenomena that have actually been observed in urban areas. However, it seems that such models explain the nineteenth century city rather than the contemporary metropolis. Indeed, empirical research has indicated that a number of phenomena explained by the trade-off models are of declining importance and magnitude in today's metropolis. Occasionally, they have even been reversed. Such phenomena are the concentration of employment and general economic activity at a single central point, the homogeneity of the housing stock and its short-run elasticity, and the absence of external effects on transportation.

In addition a growing body of literature reveals the interest of many researchers in the social rather than the economic factors of residential location decisions. This trend is strengthened by efforts to quantify and measure individual preferences, and incorporates them in explicit models of human behavior. While it is difficult to abandon the old concept of equilibrium price and its associated axioms, all of these efforts deviate from them at certain points.

In the end, the most recent literature reveals that if we are to understand urban economics more clearly, urban phenomena must be investigated in depth from a different perspective. In particular, the following four problem areas must be considered:

1. The presence of many economic centers in the urban area;
2. The durability and heterogeneity of the housing stock;
3. The presence of externalities; and
4. The imperfect character of the market.

While the modeling efforts in the second, third, and fourth areas have been analyzed, no analytic models tackling the multi-center problem have been found. The only attempts to date have been the moderate efforts to apply monocentric principles to each of a number of urban centers. However, the next chapter will develop a model of residential location in which the demand for household space is shaped in the simultaneous presence of more than one center.

**Part II
Development of a
Residential Location Model**

5

A Model of Residential Location for a Linear Multi-Center City

The Foundation for a Multi-Center Model

In this chapter, a microeconomic equilibrium model of residential location is first developed for a one-dimensional (i.e., linear) urban area; and this linear city is characterized by a number of urban centers of economic activity.

The linear multi-nuclei approach to the analysis of an urban area is adopted for two reasons. First, it facilitates discussion by reducing the space element to a single-distance parameter, and permits the graphic representation of the various curves and gradients. Second, it allows comparisons with the standard monocentric model of residential location, the functions of which are also initially derived.

After the linear model is developed, a generalized two-dimensional model of the city is introduced. The important variables are again described, and the modifications necessary for the progression from a linear to a two-dimensional city are discussed.

Initially, the problem is to derive equations for the variables that describe the equilibrium conditions in a city's residential areas. The important variables are:

1. the price per unit of housing;
2. the residential land rent;
3. the quantity of housing per unit of land (which is considered as a measure of residential density);
4. the quantity of housing consumed per household; and
5. the household income.

Of these, the first four are considered as functions of the distances of households from the centers of economic activity, and of the relative importance of these centers to individual households. Household income, however, is considered as a determinant of these distances.

Initial Assumptions

The basic assumptions employed in the development of the model are summarized as follows:

1. The hypothetical city analyzed is located in a narrow homogeneous von Thünen plain;[1] i.e., a plain of considerable length with undifferentiated physical features in all directions. This narrow plain contains a single large population cluster at some distance from its periphery. In the absence of any specific topographic features, one unit of land differs from another only in its distances from the city centers.

2. All employment, shopping and other activities take place in several defined centers of economic activity which are not necessarily of equal size (see figure 5-1). One of these centers is the Central Business District, while the rest are secondary nuclei. The importance of these centers increases with the number and diversity of the activities located there. All of the city labor force works in these centers, but each worker is employed at only one center at a time. However, the city population uses services located in all centers. It is further assumed that the location of employment is determined for each household prior to the residential location choice.[2] While the exact location of a person's work or other activity within these economic districts is ignored, the spatial extent of the central areas is taken into account in considering the extent of the housing market. That is, the centers are not considered as dimensionless points on the urban plain.

3. The cost of commuting to the centers from the rest of the urban area is constant per mile. Thus, it is assumed that there are no negative external effects as one approaches the city centers. Consequently no congestion costs are incurred.

4. All households have the same additive, separable, and logarithmic utility function for the independent variables of housing consumption, leisure time, and consumption of other goods and services.[a] This has the form:

---

[a] A utility function is characterized as "additive" if it can be expressed as a sum of a finite number of utilities. These must be derived individually by the commodities entering the function. The additivity property can be written as:

$$U(x_1, x_2, \ldots, x_n) = U_1(x_1) + U_2(x_2) + \ldots + U_n(x_n),$$

where U represents utility and $U_1(x_1)$ is the utility yielded by the ith good.

This property assumes that the utility obtained from one good is not affected by the rate of consumption of another. This assumption is not acceptable in theoretical discussions of utility theory because utility is shown to require only ordinal measurement (Pareto). However, it is adopted in this model to simplify the computations. A function . is termed "separable" if it can be represented as the sum of several functions (either linear or nonlinear) of a single variable; i.e., if it can be written as:

$$f(X) = \sum_{i=1}^{n} f_i(x_i).$$

In the above case, the utility function used is of the form:

$$U = \sum_{i=1}^{n} a_i \log x_i,$$

and, therefore, it is separable.

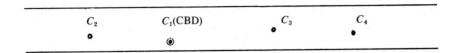

Figure 5-1 Distribution of Centers of Economic Activity in an Urban Area

$$U = \sum_{i=1}^{3} a_i \log x_i.$$

5. In determining housing demand, the preference for housing, leisure, and consumption of all other commodities (goods and services) is assumed identical for all households.

6. The total number of trips to all the centers per unit of time is the same for all households. However, different households have different frequencies of visits to these centers. The money cost of travel is disregarded.

7. The housing supply follows a Cobb-Douglas, first-degree homogeneous function of the inputs of land and capital.[3]

8. The consumption of housing per household is assumed to be independent of r_i, the distance of the housing site from any center i considered by the household.

9. The market for residential land is perfectly competitive. Under this assumption land rent is equal to the landlord's profit per unit area.

Since natural geographic features are not considered, the choice of residence is a function of the distance from the center and the relative importance of these centers to the individual household. The spatial distribution of the previously mentioned variables (i.e., land price and land rent, the quantity of housing per unit land, the housing prices and the quantity of housing consumed per household) is expressed in terms of the distance r_i from the centers C_i, ($i = 1, \ldots, n$), of economic activity.

After the development of the linear city model is completed, some of the initial formulation's very restrictive assumptions are relaxed. The model is then generalized to consider several urban centers along the single dimension. Finally, in Chapter 6, an attempt is made to modify the model in order to analyze a two-dimensional urban area with several urban centers.

Household Equilibrium[4]

According to the fourth of the assumptions stated earlier, the common utility function of households could be written as

$$U = U(s, t, c), \tag{5.1}$$

where s = the consumption of housing in square feet of floor space (either purchased or rented) per unit of time;

t = leisure time; and

c = the consumption of goods and services other than housing, including transportation.

Such general forms of the utility function have been used conventionally, and therefore the results produced have been conventional.[5] Therefore, a more specific form is adopted here, although it too has been widely used in previous studies. However, it allows the forms of the derived functions to be compared.[6] Thus, the household's utility function is assumed to have the form:

$$U = a_1 \log s + a_2 \log t + a_3 \log c, \quad s > 0, t > 0, c > 0, \quad (5.2)$$

where a_i = the coefficients of "attraction," indicating the relative weight given to each of the i factors considered.[b]

As mentioned previously in the summary of assumptions, this is an additive and separable function. It is also an ordinal one since any such function of the form

$$U = f(a_1 \log s + a_2 \log t + a_3 \log s) \quad (5.2a)$$

where f is a monotonically increasing function, could also be used. Functions of this form generate demand functions of income and price elasticities equal to one. This is shown below.

In order to proceed with the derivation of the model, it is first necessary to distinguish among the three locational possibilities shown in figure 5-2. These are:

Case 1—location of households between the centers I and II (A);

Case 2—location to the left of center I (B); and

Case 3—location to the right of center II (C).

The demand functions for housing are then derived separately for each case.

First Case. Households located between centers I and II. (Some functions for this case will use the subscript A.)

For a household located between the two centers, $k_1 r$ is the time

---

[b] If the utility of equation (5.1) were taken as a power function, it would have the form:

$$U' = s^{a_1} t^{a_2} c^{a_3}. \quad (5.1a)$$

But utility is arbitrary to monotonic transformations such as logarithmic transformation. Therefore it can be assumed that utility is a linear combination of the logarithms of quantities. The term "relative weight" refers to standardized coefficients.

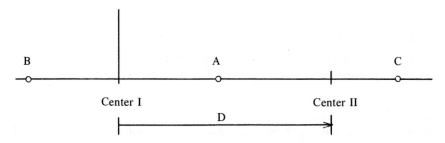

Figure 5-2 The Three Cases of Household Location

consumed by trips to the center I, while $k_2(D - r)$ is the time consumed by trips to the center II, where:

$D =$ the distance between the city centers I and II;

$r =$ the distance of the household location from city center I, $(0 \leq r \leq D)$; and

$k_i =$ the number of trips to center i divided by the velocity of travel. (The velocity of travel is considered constant and equal to the distance traveled per unit of time.) Since the total number of trips to the two centers is fixed and velocity is a constant,

$$k_1 + k_2 = \text{constant} \qquad (5.3)$$

for all households. Therefore, the location of the household depends on the combination of k_1 and k_2 which satisfies condition (5.3).

The distances D and r are always measured from center I, the origin of the system in all cases. The time spent by households at the central location is considered as part of their work and personal business time. It follows that if T is the household's total disposable time, that is the total time available to households minus working and personal business hours, then

$$t_A = T - k_1 r - k_2(D - r) = T - (k_1 - k_2)r - k_2 D, \qquad (5.4)$$

will be the total leisure time remaining after the trips to the two centers. Equation (5.4) is a time constraint for the locating household. Here it is necessary to state the consistency conditions for k_1 and k_2. From (5.4):

$$t_A \geq 0,$$

or

$$T - (k_1 - k_2)r - k_2 D \geq 0. \qquad (5.4a)$$

98

Thus, the following cases exist:

a. $k_1 > k_2$; condition (5.4a) holds for $k_1 \leq T/D$;
b. $k_1 < k_2$; condition (5.4a) holds for $k_2 \leq T/D$;
c. $k_1 = k_2$; condition (5.4a) holds for $k_1 = k_2 \leq T/D.$[c]

In the first two cases, where $k_1 \neq k_2$, the maximum possible household location distance from center I occurs when all available time is exhausted in travel, and leisure time t_A becomes equal to zero. Equation (5.4) then gives

$$ r_{max} = \frac{T - k_2 D}{k_1 - k_2} . \tag{5.5} $$

In the third case, $k_1 - k_2 = 0$, equation (5.4) becomes:

$$ t_A = T - k_2 D . \tag{5.4b} $$

Equation (5.4b) is independent of r, the distance from center I. This means that household A, which makes an equal number of trips to the two urban centers, can locate anywhere between centers I and II. This is not to say that household location is free between I and II, but merely that it is not more dependent upon either of these two equally important centers.

In addition to the time constraint, the household is subject to a budget constraint:

$$ y = c + ps , \tag{5.6} $$

where $y =$ the mean family income;

$p = p(r)$, the price per unit of housing;

and the price of the composite good (the index of all the prices included in it) is standardized to one. It should be mentioned here that the money cost of travel is ignored in the budget constraint, while the time cost is taken into account in the household's time constraint. That is, it is assumed either that public transportation is available and free for everybody, or that the transportation expenditure is very small compared to the housing expenditure.

The utility function (5.2), after the incorporation of the time and budget constraints (equations (5.4) and (5.6)), becomes

$$ U_A = a_1 \log s + a_2 \log [T - (k_1 - k_2)r - k_2 D] + a_3 \log (y - ps) . \tag{5.7} $$

In other words, it is presumed that households take into account both constraints in their efforts to maximize their utility. The combination of the three goods in the utility function yielding the highest utility will determine the equilibrium of the household.

In order to achieve maximum utility, the first partial derivatives of

[c] For a derivation of these consistency conditions, see Appendix A.

equation (5.7) with respect to the consumption of housing s and the distance r from the center I must be equal to zero.[d] These derivatives are:

$$\frac{\partial U_A}{\partial s} = \frac{a_1}{s} - \frac{a_3 p}{y - ps} = 0,\tag{5.8}$$

$$\frac{\partial U_A}{r} = -\frac{a_2(k_1 - k_2)}{T - (k_1 - k_2)r - k_2 D} - \frac{a_3 s}{y - ps}\frac{dp}{dr} = 0.\tag{5.9}$$

After rearranging terms, (5.8) gives

$$s = \frac{a_1}{a_1 + a_3}\frac{y}{p(r)},\tag{5.10}$$

which is the demand function for housing.[e] This is a very simple, well-known form of demand, and tells us that the housing expenditure $p(r)s$ of a household is a fixed percentage of its income. This agrees with empirical observation[7] and is the consequence of using a constant-elasticity utility function. Using equation (5.10) gives:

$$y - ps = y - p\frac{a_1}{a_1 + a_3}\frac{y}{p}$$

$$= \left(1 - \frac{a_1}{a_1 + a_3}\right)y$$

$$= \frac{a_3}{a_1 + a_3}y.\tag{5.11}$$

Then, substitution of (5.10) and (5.11) in (5.9) yields:

$$-\frac{a_2(k_1 - k_2)}{T - (k_1 - k_2)r - k_2 D} - \frac{a_3\left(\dfrac{a_1}{a_1 + a_3}\right)\dfrac{y}{p}\dfrac{dp}{dr}}{\dfrac{a_3}{a_1 + a_3}y} = 0$$

---

[d] The study postulates throughout a spatial continuity; and the relevant variables are assumed to possess all the properties necessary for differentiation and integration. Thus, the first order conditions serve as equilibrium conditions provided that the second order conditions pose no sign problems.

[e] As was mentioned when the utility function was first introduced, such demand functions have unit elasticities with respect to income and price. Indeed, equation (5.10) would have an elasticity with respect to income equal to:

$$e_y = \frac{\partial s}{\partial y}\frac{y}{s} = \frac{a_1}{a_1 + a_3}\frac{1}{p}y\frac{a_1 + a_3}{a_1}\frac{p}{y} = 1,$$

and an elasticity with respect to price equal to:

$$e_p = \frac{\partial s}{\partial p}\frac{p}{s} = \frac{a_1}{a_1 + a_3}\frac{y}{p^2}p\frac{a_1 + a_3}{a_1}\frac{p}{y} = 1.$$

The demand function for c, the composite good, is symmetrical to equation (5.10).

or

$$-\frac{a_2(k_1 - k_2)}{T - (k_1 - k_2)r - k_2D} = \frac{a_1}{p}\frac{dp}{dr}. \qquad (5.12)$$

Since equation (5.12) contains only the variables p and r, it must hold at all distances r and for all households, regardless of the levels of income y and consumption of housing s.

Solving the differential equation (5.12) yields,

$$\frac{1}{p}\frac{dp}{dr} = \frac{a_2}{a_1}(k_1 - k_2)\frac{1}{T - (k_1 - k_2)r - k_2D},$$

and

$$\int\frac{1}{p}\frac{dp}{dr} = dr\frac{a_2}{a_1}(k_1 - k_2)\int\frac{1}{T - (k_1 - k_2)r - k_2D}dr. \qquad (5.12a)$$

The left side of the differential equation (5.12a) gives:

$$\int\frac{1}{p}dp = \log p + b_1, \qquad (5.12b)$$

where b_1 is a constant of integration.

To evaluate the right side of equation (5.12a), it is first necessary to transform:

$$T - (k_1 - k_2)r - k_2D = u, \qquad (5.12c)$$

when

$$\frac{du}{dr} = -(k_1 - k_2), \qquad (5.12d)$$

and

$$dr = -\frac{du}{k_1 - k_2}. \qquad (5.12e)$$

Substituting (5.12d) and (5.12e) into the right side of equation (5.12a) yields:

$$-\frac{a_2}{a_1}(k_1 - k_2)\int -\frac{1}{k_1 - k_2}\frac{1}{u}du = \frac{a_2}{a_1}\log u + b_2, \qquad (5.12f)$$

where b_2 is a constant of integration. Then substituting u from equation (5.12c) into (5.12f) gives:

$$\frac{a_2}{a_1}\log [T - (k_1 - k_2)r - k_2D] + b_2. \qquad (5.12g)$$

Finally, by equating (5.12b) with (5.12g), the solution to equation (5.10) becomes:

$$\log p = \frac{a_2}{a_1} \log [T - (k_1 - k_2)r - k_2 D] + \log p_o, \qquad (5.13)$$

where $\log p_o = b_2 - b_1$, and where

p_o = the land rent at the boundary point of the area of center I lying between centers I and II.

Taking antilogs, (5.13) can be written:

$$p(r) = p_o [T - (k_1 - k_2)r - k_2 D]^{a_2/a_1}. \qquad (5.14)$$

This gives the equilibrium price of housing as a function of the distance r from the center I, the distance D between the two centers, and the land rent p_o at the boundary of center I lying between the two centers.

The land rent p_o' at the boundary of center II, which again lies between the two centers, is

$$p_o' = p(D) = p_o(T - k_1 D)^{a_2/a_1}. \qquad (5.15)$$

Thus, the function $p(r)$ of equation (5.14) as shown in figure 5-3 has been derived.

The relative rent levels at the two center boundaries depend upon the relative importance of the two centers. Therefore, the following cases occur:

1. $p_o > p_o'$; will be true for $0 < (T - k_1 D)^{a_2/a_1} < 1$, or $k_1 > (T - 1/D)$;
2. $p_o < p_o'$; will be true for $k_1 < (T - 1/D)$;
3. $p_o = p_o'$; will be true for $k_1 = (T - 1/D)$.

Equation (5.14) gives the equilibrium price of housing at each distance r from center I as a function of the single variable "distance from the center I." Thus, location alone determines housing price in the model and this is the only pattern of prices consistent with out utility function. Since it is actually the price of land that changes with the distance from centers I and II, housing price is proportional to the land price at each location. Furthermore, since land rent represents the comparative services yielded by a lot of land due to its particular location in the urban area, the change in land price with distance is equal to the land rent.

The price of housing $p(r)$ is a power function of the leisure time available to households. Therefore, the exponent (a_2/a_1) determines the form of the housing value curve and, consequently, the form of the curves of land rent and land value. This occurs because the three are proportional. The a_i coefficients are indicators of the relative weight given to each of the i

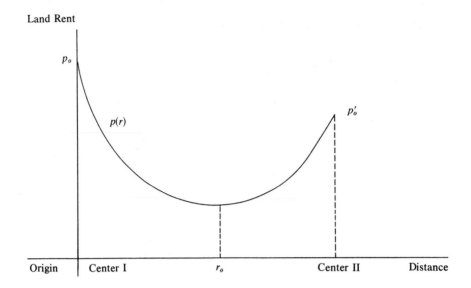

Figure 5-3 Land Rent Function Between Centers I and II

factors so that their magnitudes indicate the relative preferences of the household. It is then feasible to distinguish among three possibilities as follows:

1. $a_2 > a_1$; In this case, time is more important to the household than space, and $p(r)$ will increase with decreasing distance from the centers I and II at an accelerating rate. The curves of housing and land values are then convex downward, as shown in figure 5-4.

For $a_2 > a_1$, equation (5.14) defines a continuous smooth function which has an extreme at point r_0. Differentiating equation (5.14) with respect to distance r, the first order condition for the extreme is:

$$\frac{\partial p}{\partial r} = -p_0 \frac{a_2(k_1 - k_2)}{a_1} \ [T - (k_1 - k_2)r_0 - k_2 D]^{a_2 - a_1/a_1} = 0. \quad (5.16)$$

Solving equation (5.16) for r_0 when $k_1 \neq k_2$,[f] the extreme appears at a distance from center I equal to

$$r_0 = \frac{T - k_2 D}{k_1 - k_2}. \quad (5.17)$$

---

[f] In the event that $k_1 = k_2$, p is actually independent of r, and the household is indifferent as far as a particular location is concerned. It could, therefore, locate anywhere between the two centers, as has already been shown.

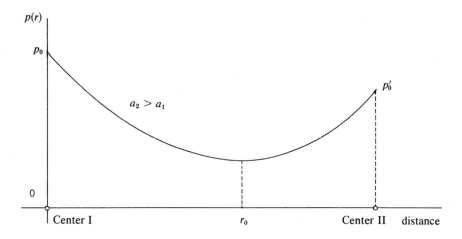

Figure 5-4. Convex Housing and Land Value Curves

From equations (5.14) and (5.16), the second order condition for the identification of the extreme is:

$$\frac{\partial p}{\partial r^2} = p_o \frac{a_2(a_2 - a_1)(k_1 - k_2)^2}{a_1^2} \; [T - (k_1 - k_2)r - k_2 D]^{a_2 - 2a_1/a_1}. \quad (5.18)$$

Since $a_2 > a_1$, the right side of equation (5.18) is always positive, and therefore the extreme at point r_o is a minimum.

2. $a_2 < a_1$; This implies that the household gives more importance to the space factor than the time factor, and therefore that the housing and land values will increase at a decreasing rate towards the center. The rent curve in this case will be concave. Furthermore, equation (5.14) defines a continuous, smooth function which also has an extreme at point r_o. This is given by equation (5.17) obtained through the first order condition (5.16). The second order condition is again given by (5.18), and because $(a_2 - a_1)$ is now negative, the right side of equation (5.18) is always negative. Thus the extreme at r_o is a maximum. This is shown in figure 5-5.

3. $a_2 = a_1$; In this case, the household gives equal importance to the time and space factors. Thus the housing and land value gradients will be straight lines. Equation (5.14) becomes:

$$p(r) = p_o[T - (k_1 - k_2)r - k_2 D]$$

or

$$p(r) = p_o (T - k_2 D) - p_o(k_1 - k_2)r. \quad (5.14a)$$

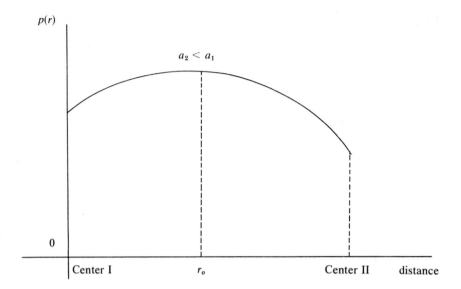

Figure 5-5. Concave Housing and Land Value Curves

The first derivative of (5.14a) is a constant equal to $-p_o(k_1 - k_2)$ so that its value relative to zero is independent of r. Thus, while equation (5.14a) is continuous, it is not a smooth function. That is, it will decrease as long as $k_1 > k_2$ (when the slope $-p_o(k_1 - k_2) < 0$), will be zero for $k_1 = k_2$, and will increase when $k_1 < k_2$. The form of the curve is shown in figure 5-6.

In this case, then, r_o is the "boundary" between the areas served by the two centers.

Second Case. Households located to the left of center I (some functions for this case will have the subscript B—see figure 5-7).

In this case, it is assumed that k_1 must always be $> k_2$ for the household to consider the location. The distane r from center I assumes negative values; and the time consumed in traveling is:

$$-k_1r = \text{ the time consumed by trips to center I, with } r \leq 0; \text{ and}$$

$$k_2(D - r) = -k_2r + k_2D = \text{the time consumed by trips to center II.}$$

Consequently, the time constraint equation is:

$$t_B = T - k_1r - k_2r + k_2D = T - (k_1 + k_2)r + k_2D. \tag{5.19}$$

In order for household B to be located to the left of center I, the time spent on trips to I must be more than the time spent on trips to II. That is,

$$-k_1r > -k_2r + k_2D, \quad r \leq 0,$$

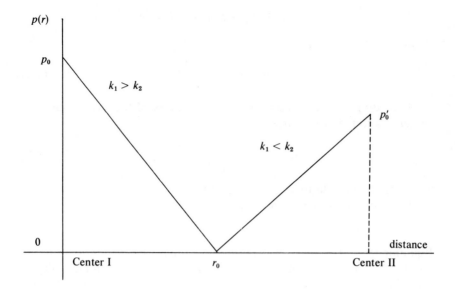

Figure 5-6. Straight Line Housing and Land Value Curves ($a_2 = a_1$)

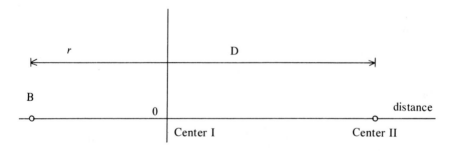

Figure 5-7. Household B, Located to the Left of Center I

or

$$k_1 > k_2 + k_2 \frac{D}{(-r)} \, ,$$

$$\frac{k_1}{k_2} > 1 + \frac{D}{(-r)} \, . \qquad (5.20)$$

If condition (5.20) is met, household B will consider locating to the left of center I; and the range within which its search for a location is confined will be the distance from I constrained by time. Thus,

$$t_B = T + (k_1 + k_2)r - k_2D \geq 0,$$

or

$$|r| = -r \leq \frac{T - k_2D}{k_1 + k_2}. \tag{5.21}$$

According to (5.21), then, the outer boundary of the city to the left of center I is found at distance

$$|r|_{max} = -r = \frac{T - k_2D}{k_1 + k_2}, \tag{5.22}$$

where all disposable time is consumed in transit.

The utility function for household B is

$$U_B = a_1 \log s + a_2 \log [T + (k_1 + k_2)r - k_2D] + a_3 \log (y - ps). \tag{5.23}$$

Equation (5.23) has again incorporated the time constraint (equation 5.19) and the budget constraint (5.6). Thus, the point of maximum utility for household B is obtained by taking the partial derivatives of (5.23) with respect to the consumption of housing s and the distance r from the center I. These are then set equal to zero (first order conditions) as follows:

$$\frac{\partial U_B}{\partial s} = \frac{a_1}{s} - \frac{a_3 p}{y - ps} = 0;$$

(same as equation 5.6)

$$\frac{\partial U_B}{\partial r} = -\frac{a_2(k_1 + k_2)}{T + (k_1 + k_2)r - k_2D} - \frac{a_3 s}{y - ps} \frac{dp}{dr} = 0, \tag{5.24}$$

or

$$-\frac{a_2(k_1 + k_2)}{T + (k_1 + k_2)r - k_2D} = \frac{a_3 s}{y - ps} \frac{dp}{dr} = \frac{a_1}{p} \frac{dp}{dr}. \tag{5.25}$$

Since condition (5.25) again contains only the variables p and r, it holds at all distances r regardless of the levels of y and s.

Following the same procedures as those for equation (5.9), solving the differential equation (5.25) yields:

$$\log p = \frac{a_2}{a_1} \log [T + (k_1 + k_2)r - k_2D] + \log p_1, \tag{5.26}$$

p_1 being the land rent at the left border of the center I area. Taking antilogs in (5.26),

$$p(r)_B = p_1[T + (k_1 + k_2)r - k_2D]^{a_2/a_1}, \tag{5.27}$$

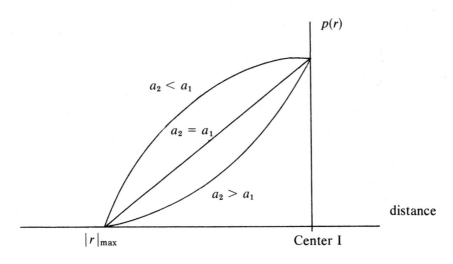

Figure 5-8. Shape of the Housing and Land Value Curves for Household B

gives the equilibrium housing prices for households located to the left of center I as a function of the distance r from the center I.

As in equation (5.14), the price of housing $p(r)$ is a power function of the disposable time available to households. Therefore, the exponent a_2/a_1 again determines the form of the housing value and rent curves and the proportional form of the land value curve. This is shown in figure 5-8.

Thus, for $a_2 > a_1$, the curves are convex;

for $a_2 = a_1$, the curves are straight lines; and

for $a_2 < a_1$, the curves are concave.

Third Case: Households located to the right of center II (when necessary, the subscript C is used in functions of this case—see figure 5-9).

This case is symmetrical to case II, and the development of its functions follows the same logic. Here, it is assumed that $k_2 > k_1$, that is, that household C is more dependent upon center II than center I. Distances D and r are again measured from the origin, and are both positive.

The time constraint is obtained by computing

$k_1 r$ = time consumed by trips to center I

$k_2 r - k_2 D$ = time consumed by trips to center II, $r \geq D$.

Then, the time constraint is given as

$$t_C = T - k_1 r - k_2 r + k_2 D = T - (k_1 + k_2)r + k_2 D. \qquad (5.28)$$

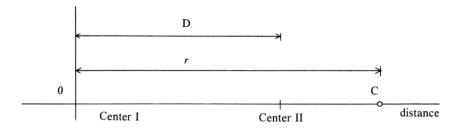

Figure 5-9. Household C, Located to the Right of Center II

Household C locates to the right of center II only if it intends to spend most of its time commuting to center II. That is,

$$k_2 r - k_2 D > k_1 r,$$

or

$$\frac{k_1}{k_2} < 1 - \frac{D}{r} \tag{5.29}$$

(the necessary condition).

In this case, the range within which the household's search for residence takes place is determined by the time constraint. Thus, it must be that:

$$t_C = T - (k_1 + k_2)r + k_2 D \geq 0,$$

or

$$r \leq \frac{T + k_2 D}{k_1 + k_2}. \tag{5.30}$$

At the point where the total disposable time is consumed by transit, the outer boundary of the urban area to the right of center II occurs. That is,

$$r_{max} = \frac{T + k_2 D}{k_1 + k_2}. \tag{5.31}$$

Following the same procedure as above, the first order conditions for household equilibrium are obtained. Thus, the demand function for housing is again given by equation (5.10), and the equilibrium price of housing is

$$p(r)_C = p_2[T - (k_1 + k_2)r + k_2 D]^{a_2/a_1}. \tag{5.32}$$

Again, the relationship of time preference to space preference (that is, the ratio (a_2/a_1) in the exponent of leisure) determines the shape of the curves. This is shown in figure 5-10.

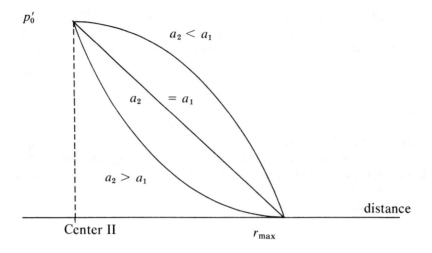

Figure 5-10. Shape of the Housing Land Value Curves for Household C

Evaluation of the Demand Equations

The equations which give the housing and land prices at each point within this linear two-center city have now been derived. But how do these prices relate to the prices that would be obtained if each center were handled individually? In other words, how different is the household demand for residence obtained by considering both centers simultaneously, from the demand given by the monocentric model? The easiest way to determine this is by comparing the price equations derived above to the single equation derived by Beckmann.[8]

Beckmann's housing price function, given in the same notation, is

$$p(r) = p_o \, (T - k_1 r)^{a_2/a_1}. \qquad (5.33)$$

Comparison of his equation with equation (5.14) for households locating between the two centers and having a stronger preference for leisure over housing space, shows that the prices postulated here for any point r between I and II are higher than those postulated by the Beckmann model by

$$p' = (k_1 r + k_2 D) \, p_o^{a_1/a_2}. \qquad (5.34)$$

Since p' is positive as long as either k_1 or k_2 is different from zero, the Beckmann model underestimates the value of land and, consequently, the value of housing in that area. The amount of error depends on the land rent at the boundary of I, the distance between the two centers, and the combination of k_1 and k_2 at each distance r from I.

In addition, comparing equation (5.33) with equation (5.27) for housing prices to the left of center I (again for $a_2 > a_1$), shows that the multi-center model gives prices which differ from the prices of the Beckmann model by

$$p'' = p_0^{a_1/a_2} (2k_1r + k_2r - k_2D). \qquad (5.35)$$

This, of course, assumes the same value of the peak rent p_0. In this case, since $r \leq 0$, the quantity within the parentheses is always negative. Therefore, p'' is always ≤ 0, and the model's price gradient to the left of center I is always below the Beckmann gradient.

Since the Beckmann gradient is higher everywhere to the left of center I, it is obvious that the boundary of the city is farther away from that center in Beckmann's model. In fact, the distance to the city boundary is computed by Beckmann as

$$|r|_{max} = \frac{T}{k_1}, \qquad (5.36)$$

and is larger than the distance computed by the multi-center model by the length

$$|r'| = \frac{K_2 (T + k_1D)}{k_1(k_1 + k_2)} > 0. \qquad (5.37)$$

It can therefore be concluded that the monocentric-city approach distorts the shape of the housing and land value schedules in two ways:

1. It gives lower values in the areas between the centers by disregarding the attraction of the second center; and
2. It yields a wider residential location area towards the outskirts of the city by disregarding the negative effects of limited accessibility to center II from points outside the I-II span.

This distortion is summarized in figure 5-11, which compares the Beckmann gradients to the gradients derived by this model.

An even more interesting result is obtained from the multi-center model when the households exhibit a stronger preference for space than for leisure time (the case when $a_2 < a_1$). In this case, as is shown in figure 5-5, the demand for locations farther away from both centers (but lying between them) is higher than for locations close to them. When the curve of figure 5-5 is compared with the curves of figures 5-8 and 5-10, again for $a_2 < a_1$, it can be observed that while spatial considerations in the outlying areas are not strong enough to overcome the distance factor, they have a powerful effect on the behavior of households when locations between the two centers are considered. This is the case because with increasing distance from one center, locating households are compensated by both more space *and* closer proximity to the second center. Thus, while in the outlying areas of the city any outward move will result in a net loss of leisure time due to

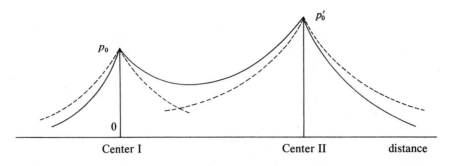

Figure 5-11. Comparison of the Monocentric with the Multicenter Model Gradients for $a_2 > a_1$

increasing travel time, a corresponding move within the I-II distance merely results in the relative change of the k_1 and k_2 parameters. A likely spatial configuration in a city with prevailing space preferences could very well be one of increasingly high housing prices *within* the urban area, and rapidly decreasing prices at a certain distance from the economic centers.

The Supply of Housing

According to the seventh assumption above, the amount of housing available at any distance r from the center I is a first degree homogeneous production function of the inputs of land and capital. It has the form:

$$Q = \gamma K^{\beta} N^{\delta}, \tag{5.38}$$

where $\quad Q =$ housing supply;

$\qquad K =$ input of capital;

$\qquad N =$ input of land;

$\qquad \gamma, \beta, \delta =$ constants, and > 0.

This function has an elasticity of substitution:[9]

$$\sigma = \frac{\dfrac{\partial Q}{\partial K} \dfrac{\partial Q}{\partial N}}{Q \dfrac{\partial^2 Q}{\partial K \partial N}} = \gamma \frac{K^{\beta} N^{\delta}}{Q} = 1,$$

when constant returns to scale are assumed. It gives isoquants of a "normal" convex shape, as shown in 5-12. The function exhibits constant returns to scale when $\beta + \delta = 1$.

N per period

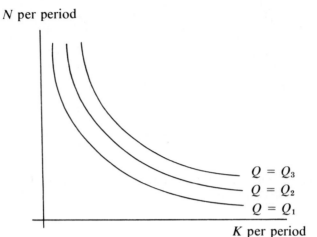

$Q = Q_3$
$Q = Q_2$
$Q = Q_1$

K per period

Figure 5-12   Isoquant Map for a Production Function with Elasticity of Substitution $\sigma = 1$

In this case, equation (5.38) becomes

$$Q = \gamma K^\beta N^{1-\beta},$$

and, dividing by *N*, gives

$$\frac{Q}{N} = \gamma\, K^\beta N^{-\beta}$$

$$= \gamma\left(\frac{K}{N}\right)^\beta.$$

Calling $(Q/N) = h$ and $(K/N) = x$ yields a Cobb-Douglas production function of the form

$$h = \gamma x^\beta, \quad \gamma > 0, \quad 0 < \beta < 1, \tag{5.39}$$

where $h = h(r) = $ the amount of housing per unit of land at distance *r* from the center I;

   $x = x(r) = $ the amount of capital invested on one unit of land; and

   $\gamma, \beta = $ constants.

If *n* is now the annual interest rate plus the annual cost of depreciation of a unit of capital (i.e., the capital annual cost per unit), and is accepted as independent of its locational distance from the centers I and II, then

$$p(r)h - nx = p(r)\gamma x(r)^\beta - nx(r) = q(r). \tag{5.40}$$

This is the profit derived per unit area of land by the owner of the house (i.e., the land rent for that land area), and is a strictly concave function of x because its second derivative with respect to x is always negative.[g] In order for the new owners to maximize housing profits, it is necessary that the first derivative of (5.40) with respect to x be zero. Because of the concavity property, this condition is also sufficient.

Thus,

$$\frac{\partial q}{\partial x} = \beta\gamma p(r)x(r)^{\beta-1} - n = 0, \tag{5.41}$$

and solving for $x(r)$ gives

$$x(r) = \left[\frac{\beta\gamma}{n}p(r)\right]^{1/1-\beta}, \tag{5.42}$$

the maximum amount of capital that can be invested in one unit of land to maximize profits. Substituting in equation (5.39) yields

$$h(r) = \gamma^{1/1-\beta}\left[\frac{\beta}{n}p(r)\right]^{\beta/1-\beta}, \tag{5.43}$$

which is the supply of housing function.

For each of the three cases of household location analyzed above, $p(r)$ is given by equations (5.14), (5.27), and (5.32). Substituting for $p(r)$ from (5.14) into (5.43) gives:

$$h(r) = \gamma^{1/1-\beta}\left(\frac{\beta}{n}\right)^{\beta/1-\beta} p_0^{\beta/1-\beta}\left[T - (k_1 - k_2)r - k_2 D\right]^{(a_2/a_1)(\beta/1-\beta)}, \tag{5.44}$$

which is the amount of housing supplied per unit of land as a function of the distance r from the center I for households A between the two centers. The relative magnitude of the parameters ratio (a_2/a_1) in relation to the ratio $(\beta/1 - \beta)$ will determine the shape of the function (5.44). That is:

---

[g] The proof is straightforward. Taking partial derivatives with respect to x, equation (5.40) gives:

$$\frac{\partial q}{\partial x} = p\gamma\beta x^{\beta-1} - n. \tag{5.40a}$$

The second derivative then has the form:

$$\frac{\partial^2 q}{\partial x^2} = p\gamma\beta(\beta - 1)x^{\beta-2}. \tag{5.40b}$$

But in equation (5.40b), p, γ, β and x are all positive quantities while $(\beta - 1)$ is always negative. Thus the second derivative of equation (5.40) is always a negative quantity and (5.40) is strictly a concave function of x.

if $\quad \dfrac{a_2}{a_1}\dfrac{\beta}{1-\beta} > 1$, or $\quad \dfrac{a_2}{a_1} > \dfrac{1-\beta}{\beta}$

the function will be convex;

if $\quad \dfrac{a_2}{a_1} = \dfrac{1-\beta}{\beta}$, the function will be linear; and

if $\quad \dfrac{a_2}{a_1} < \dfrac{1-\beta}{\beta}$, the function will be concave. $\qquad$ (5.45)

Then substituting $p(r)$ from equations (5.27) and (5.32) into (5.43) yields, correspondingly:

$$h(r) = \gamma^{1/1-\beta}\left(\frac{\beta}{n}\right)^{1/1-\beta} p_1^{\beta/1-\beta}\left[T + (k_1 + k_2)r - k_2 D\right]^{(a_2/a_1)\,(\beta/1-\beta)}, \quad (5.46)$$

and

$$h(r) = \gamma^{1/1-\beta}\left(\frac{\beta}{n}\right)^{\beta/1-\beta} p_2^{\beta/1-\beta}\left[T - (k_1 + k_2)r + k_2 D\right]^{(a_2/a_1)\,(\beta/1-\beta)}, \quad (5.47)$$

the supply of housing function for the areas B (to the left of center I) and C (to the right of center II) respectively.

Then substituting equations (5.42) and (5.14) into (5.40) gives:

$$q(r) = \left(\frac{\beta}{n}\right)^{\beta/1-\beta}\gamma^{1/1-\beta}\,(1-\beta)\,p(r)^{1/1-\beta}$$

$$= \left(\frac{\beta}{n}\right)^{\beta/1-\beta}(1-\beta)(\gamma p_0)^{1/1-\beta}\left[T - (k_1 - k_2)r - k_2 D\right]^{(a_2/a_1)\,(1/1-\beta)}, \quad (5.48)$$

which is the profit derived per unit area of land. In other words, it is the land rent of the site assuming that the market for residential land is competitive (Assumption 9). For the areas B and C, equations (5.27), (5.32) are in the same manner substituted into (5.40), which becomes, correspondingly:

$$q(r) = \left(\frac{\beta}{n}\right)^{\beta/1-\beta}(1-\beta)(\gamma p_1)^{1/1-\beta}\left[T + (k_1 + k_2)r - k_2 D\right]^{(a_2/a_1)\,(1/1-\beta)}, \quad (5.49)$$

and

$$q(r) = \left(\frac{\beta}{n}\right)^{\beta/1-\beta}(1-\beta)(\gamma p_2)^{1/1-\beta}\left[T - (k_1 + k_2)r + k_2 D\right]^{(a_2/a_1)\,(1/1-\beta)}. \quad (5.50)$$

Following the same line of thought as the above analysis yields a land rent function $q(r)$ which is a convex, linear or concave function of distance r from the center of reference. This depends on whether

$$\frac{a_2}{a_1} \gtreqless \frac{1-\beta}{\beta}.$$

Equating Supply and Demand

The maximum profit realized at each site, that is, the maximum site rent, is determined when the local equilibrium of demand and supply is derived for each distance r from the center I (i.e., for each distance $(D-r)$ from the center II).

Within a segment of length dr, it is assumed that there are $m(r)dr$ families residing, where $m(r)$ is the residential density within the segment dr, that is, the number of families per linear unit of land. The aggregate income of these $m(r)dr$ families is $Y(r)$, where $Y(r)$ is the aggregate income per unit land at distance r from the center I (i.e., distance $D-r$ from the center II). Their aggregate demand for housing as given by equation (5.10) is:

$$s(r)dr = \frac{a_1}{a_1 + a_3}\frac{Y(r)}{p(r)}. \tag{5.51}$$

On the other hand, from equation (5.43), the supply of housing within the same segment dr is:

$$h(r)dr = \gamma^{1/1-\beta}\left(\frac{\beta}{n}\right)^{\beta/1-\beta} p(r)^{\beta/1-\beta}\, dr. \tag{5.52}$$

Equating supply and demand gives the family income at each distance r from the center I:

$$Y(r) = \frac{a_1+a_3}{a_1}\gamma^{1/1-\beta}\left(\frac{\beta}{n}\right)^{\beta/1-\beta} p(r)^{1/1-\beta}.$$

Substituting for $p(r)$ from equation (5.14) gives:

$$Y(r)_A = \mu p_0^{1/1-\beta}[T-(k_1-k_2)r-k_2D]^{(a_2/a_1)(1/1-\beta)}, \tag{5.53}$$

the aggregate income of families residing within the segment dr between centers I and II, where,

$$\mu = \frac{a_1+a_3}{a_1}\gamma^{1/1-\beta}\left(\frac{\beta}{n}\right)^{\beta/1-\beta}$$

is a constant.

The corresponding equations for the areas to the left of center I and to the right of center II are derived from equations (5.27) and (5.32). Therefore:

$$Y(r)_B = \mu p_1^{1/1-\beta} [T + (k_1 + k_2)r - k_2 D]^{(a_2/a_1)(1/1-\beta)}, \qquad (5.54)$$

and

$$Y(r)_C = \mu p_2^{1/1-\beta} [T - (k_1 + k_2)r + k_2 D]^{(a_2/a_1)(1/1-\beta)}. \qquad (5.55)$$

Through the equilibrium of supply and demand, equations (5.53) through (5.55) give aggregate family income solely as a function of the distance r. This system, however, does not indicate the composition of the family income that corresponds to this aggregate. This occurs because it was assumed that households have identical tastes and preferences, regardless of income levels, and are therefore indifferent to all locations and neighborhood characteristics. The system shows no instances of income segregation.

The maximum rent at the boundaries of the centers I and II can now be determined by aggregating equations (5.53) through (5.55) over the range of all distances.

Equation (5.53) gives the maximum rents p_o and p_o' at the boundaries of the centers I and II lying between I and II. This occurs when the definite integrals over the distances r_o to r_{max} and r_{max} to r_o' are taken, where r_o and r_o' are the distances of the center boundaries from their corresponding geometric centers-origins of distance measurement. That is:

$$Y_o = Y_{r_o}^{r_{max}} = \mu p_o^{1/1-\beta} \int_{r_o}^{r_{max}} [T - (k_1 - k_2)r - k_2 D]^\delta \, dr, \qquad (5.53a)$$

where Y_o = the total aggregate income of families located between center I and r_{max},

$r_{max} > r_o$, and

$\delta = (a_2/a_1)(1/1-\beta)$.

Using the transformation $T - (k_1 - k_2)r - k_2 D = u$ yields:

$$\frac{du}{dr} = -(k_1 - k_2), \text{ and } dr = -\frac{du}{k_1 - k_2}. \qquad (5.53b)$$

The integral of equation (5.53a) becomes:

$$-\frac{1}{k_1 - k_2} \int u^\delta \, du = -\frac{1}{k_1 - k_2} \frac{1}{\delta + 1} u^{\delta+1} + \text{constant}. \quad (5.53c)$$

Substituting u's transformation from (5.53b) into the integral of (5.53c), and then substituting the whole into (5.53a) gives:

$$Y_o = - \mu p_o^{1/1-\beta} \frac{1}{k_1 - k_2} \frac{1}{\delta + 1} \left[[T - (k_1 - k_2)r - k_2D]^{\delta+1} \right]_{r_0}^{r\max} , \quad (5.53d)$$

where the constant vanishes and $r_{\max} = T - k_2D/k_1 - k_2$, from equation (5.17).

Substituting the two values of r in function (5.53), $r_{\max}$ and r_o successively into the right side of equation (5.53d) and then taking their difference yields:

$$Y_o = \mu p_o^{1/1-\beta} \frac{1}{k_1 - k_2} \frac{1}{\delta + 1} [T - (k_1 - k_2)r_o - k_2D]^{\delta+1}$$

$$p_o = \left[\frac{(k_1 - k_2)(\delta + 1) \, Y_o}{\mu[T - (k_1 - k_2)r_o - k_2D]^{\delta+1}} \right]^{1-\beta} \quad (5.56)$$

For households residing between $r_{\max}$ and center II, the same equation (5.53) will give the maximum boundary rent p'_o in center II at distance r'_o from the origin of center II. Thus, the two limits of integration in this case will be r'_o and $r_{\max}$, where,

$$r'_o \geq r_{\max} .$$

Substituting r'_o and $r_{\max}$ into equation (5.53d) and taking their difference gives:

$$Y'_o = - \mu p_o'^{1/1-\beta} \frac{1}{k_1 - k_2} \frac{1}{\delta + 1} [T - (k_1 - k_2)r'_o - k_2D]^{\delta+1} ,$$

where Y'_o is the total aggregate income of families located between $r_{\max}$ and center II. Then, the maximum rent at r'_o is:

$$p'_o = \left[\frac{-(k_1 - k_2)(\delta + 1)Y'_o}{\mu[T - (k_1 - k_2)r'_o - k_2D]^{\delta+1}} \right]^{1-\beta} . \quad (5.57)$$

The maximum rent p_1 at the boundary of center I and to the left of that center is obtained from equation (5.54) in a similar manner. Thus:

$$Y_1 = \mu p_1^{1/1-\beta} \frac{1}{k_1 - k_2} \frac{1}{\delta + 1} \left[[T + (k_1 + k_2)r - k_2D]^{\delta+1} \right]_{|r|\max}^{r_1} , \quad (5.54a)$$

where $\quad r_1 =$ the distance of the boundary to the left of center I from the origin within center I, and

$$|r|_{\max} = T - k_2D/k_1 + k_2 \text{ from equation (5.22),}$$

is:

$$p_1 = \left[\frac{(k_1 + k_2)(\delta + 1)Y_1}{\mu[T + (k_1 + k_2)r_1 - k_2D]^{\delta+1}} \right]^{1-\beta} \quad (5.58)$$

Finally, following identical procedures, the maximum rent p_2 in the boundary of center II and to the right of that center is, from equation (5.55),

$$p_2 = \left[\frac{(k_1 + k_2)(\delta + 1)Y_2}{\mu[T - (k_1 + k_2)r_2 + k_2D]^{\delta+1}} \right]^{1-\beta}. \qquad (5.59)$$

Under the assumptions used, a consequence is that the rents are independent of the distribution of income in the area, and depend only on the aggregate income of each segment considered. It is also recognized that for fixed segment lengths dr the higher aggregate income of families suggests either that merely a few families of high individual income have clustered, or that families of low and/or medium income live in high residential concentrations. Obviously, the first case implies low density neighborhoods, while the second case is associated with higher density urban areas.

The distribution of rents obtained implies that the movement of households of different incomes does not affect the welfare of the urban area's residents. If, for instance, a high income household moves to a new neighborhood closer to a city center, it will cause lower income households to move to more distant locations. Consequently, it will force them to spend more time than previously commuting. The effect of the move, however, will not end here. In locations further from the city centers, rents are lower, and, consequently, the moving households will be compensated by having a larger quantity of housing space available. Thus, while the distribution of leisure and housing space may vary widely among income categories, the distribution of welfare remains unaltered.

Modification of Assumptions

1. The assumption of identical tastes and preferences for all of the city is obviously not a realistic one. However, it was very useful to simplify the computations of the initial model. It is now possible to relax this assumption by modifying the original utility function (equation 5.2) so that it distinguishes among income categories. Equation (5.7) then will become:

$$U = a_1 \log s + a_2 \log[T - (k_1 - k_2)r - k_2D] + a_3 \log(y(r) - p(r)s), \qquad (5.60)$$

and it is again the same for all households. While the mathematics of the model now become slightly more cumbersome, the procedure followed is identical, and the output of the model will stratify locational preferences on the basis of family income.

2. By a similar modification of the final equilibrium conditions, the way in which transportation costs enter the utility function is altered. This can be achieved if transportation cost is taken in terms of money rather than in

terms of time cost subtracted from leisure time as in the present model. This modifies the utility function of equation (5.2) to:

$$U = a_1 \log s + a_2 \log[T - (k_1 - k_2)r - k_2D] + a_3 \log(y - ps - gr), \quad (5.61)$$

where gr is the money cost of commuting per household, taken as proportional to distance r from the center I (or to distance $D - r$ from the center II). In this case again, the model will stratify household locations on the basis of family income, because income levels will determine the distance over which households of different income brackets will commute.

3. It is worth mentioning that the distribution of income within the urban area can be anything as long as equations (5.53) through (5.55) concerning the aggregate income hold true. In fact, the model remains just as valid if households of the same income levels congregate. The equations of the model do not change under these circumstances, but remain consistent with any and all types of distribution of income.

4. As in the case with most monocentric models, this model is not affected when the assumption of a concentration of employment solely in the centers of economic activity is altered. Indeed, if local employment opportunities and shopping places such as convenience stores are assumed to be evenly distributed throughout the urban area, and the labor market is assumed to remain competitive, the wages of workers employed outside the urban centers will simply be lower by an amount whose utility will be equal to the utility derived by the savings in terms of commuting time. Under such conditions the space-time trade-off still holds, and the equilibrium of the housing rents will not be altered. The difference between this situation and that of the original model (i.e., the existence of dispersed employment) is essentially the number of trips by households to the centers of the city. That is, now there will be either some workers employed outside these centers, or some households will do part of their shopping in the dispersed convenience stores. This change will actually alter the number of household trips to the centers, that is the k_1 and k_2 coefficients. However, it is still important that there are always a number of households which commute from each point within the urban area to the city centers for work, shopping and other business. As long as employment and other activities remain dispersed and do not aggregate to create a new center, the model remains valid.

6

Towards an Analysis of a Two-Dimensional City With Many Centers

Generalizing from the Linear Model—A Two-Center City

In the linear-city analysis, a set of demand functions for housing in a city with two centers but only one dimension—length—was produced. That is, the distribution of housing prices along the line ε connecting the two centers, was obtained. In figure 6-1, this distribution is shown for the case $a_2 > a_1$, that is, when the time element is more important to households that the space element.

In order to continue the analysis of two centers, center I will now be isolated but with a second dimension—width—taken into account. Then, an attempt will be made to construct a housing price function at each point within the urban area similar to the ones derived for the linear case. The product of this effort should be a mathematical description of the form of the iso-price curves in figure 6-2. The known facts to the left and right of center I are as follows (see figure 6-3):

1. The area covered by the center has a radius $= 1$ unit length;[a]
2. The highest price of housing to the left of the center (outlying area) is equal to p_1 (from equation 5.27);
3. The highest price of housing to the right of the center (i.e., the area between centers I and II) is equal to p_o (from equation 5.14);
4. It is expected that $p_o \geq p_1$;
5. The distribution of housing prices to the left of the center is given by:

$p(r)_L = p_1[T + (k_1 + k_2)r - k_2D]^{a_2/a_1}$, $r < 0$ (equation 5.27) and

6. The distribution of housing prices to the right of the center is given by:

$p(r)_R = p_o[T - (k_1 - k_2)r - k_2D]^{a_2/a_1}$, $r > 0$ (equation 5.14).

For a fixed price $\bar{p}$, the distances at which this price is found are, from equation (5.14):

$$r_o = \frac{T - k_2D - (\bar{p}/p_o)^{a_1/a_2}}{k_1 - k_2}, \tag{6.1}$$

---

[a] Thus, with radius $r = 1$, the circular boundary of center I is given by the equation:

$$x^2 + y^2 = 1,$$

where x is measured along the axis ε, and y is measured along the perpendicular to the ε axis of y's.

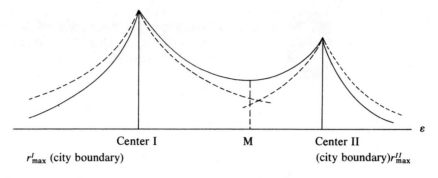

Center I M Center II

r^I_{max} (city boundary) (city boundary)r^{II}_{max}

Figure 6-1. Distribution of Housing Prices in a Two-Center Urban Area
With $a_2 > a_1$

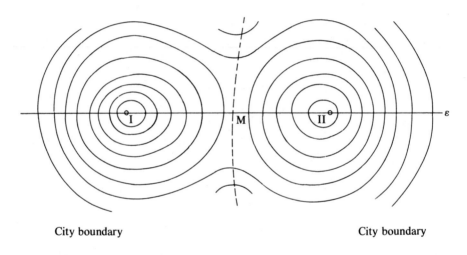

I

M II ε

City boundary City boundary

Figure 6-2. Iso-Price Housing Curves in the Two-Center Urban Area

and, from equation (5.27):

$$r_1 = \frac{T - k_2 D - (\bar{p}/p_1)^{a_1/a_2}}{k_1 + k_2}, \quad r > 0. \qquad (6.2)$$

In general, since $p_1 \leq p_o$, and $k_1 + k_2 \geq k_1 - k_2$, $(k_1, k_2 \geq 0)$, there will
always be

$$r_o \geq r_1. \qquad (6.3)$$

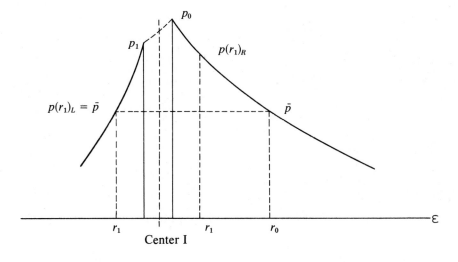

Figure 6-3. Housing Prices in the Vicinity of Center I

For a fixed distance $r = r_1$, the corresponding prices to the left and the right of the center are:

$$p(r_1)_L = p_1[T - (k_1 + k_2)|r_1| - k_2D]^{a_2/a_1},$$
$$p(r_1)_R = p_0[T - (k_1 - k_2)|r_1| - k_2D]^{a_2/a_1}.$$

But since $p_0 \geq p_1$, and

$$k_1 - k_2 \leq k_1 + k_2 \text{ or}$$
$$-(k_1 - k_2) \geq -(k_1 + k_2),$$

it will also be

$$p(r_1)_R \geq p(r_1)_L. \qquad (6.4)$$

In general, then, the prices indicated by the $p(r)_R$ gradient are higher than the prices indicated by the $p(r)_L$ gradient.

If viewed in a two-dimensional graph (plan), the price $p = p(r_1)$ of figure 6-3 has a contour like that of figure 6-4. Thus, the iso-price curve containing point A can be considered as the result of the clockwise *rotation* of the $p(r)_L$ curve until it coincides with curve $p(r)_R$. During this rotation r increases and $r_1 \leq r \leq r_0$. Two other changes that also occur cause the coincidence of the two curves:

1. The price p_1 at the left edge of the center I (figure 6-3) gradually increases until, after a rotation $\pi(= 180°)$, it becomes equal to p_0; and

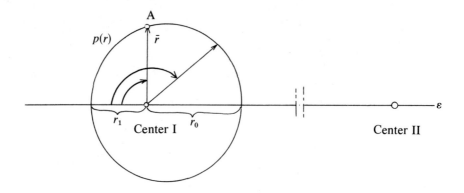

Figure 6-4. A Price Contour

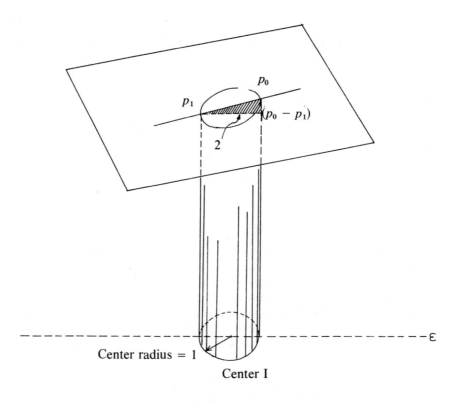

Figure 6-5. Intersection of a Cylinder With a Plane

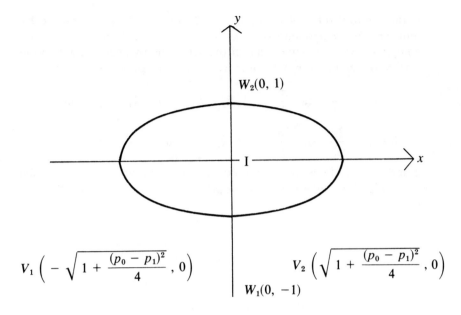

Figure 6-6. Ellipse Produced by the Intersection of Cylinder and Plane

2. The quantity $(k_1 + k_2)$ gradually changes to $(k_1 - k_2)$.

The two changes can be visualized as follows:

1. If center I has a circular form with a radius 1, the prices at the edge of the center can be represented by a cylinder of radius 1 cut by a plane along the section p_1, p_o (figures 6-4 and 6-5). According to analytical geometry, the shape of the intersection of a cylinder with a plane is an *ellipse*.[b]

---

[b] The standard form of an ellipse centered at the origin of the rectangular coordinates is given by the equation

$$\frac{x^2}{\alpha^2} + \frac{y^2}{\beta^2} = 1,$$

where x and y are the x and y coordinates of a point on the circumference of the ellipse, α is the length of the semi-major axis and β is the length of the semi-minor axis. For the ellipse in this case, the major axis has a length of 2α, and its square is equal to the sum of squares of the center diameter ($=2$) and the difference ($p_o - p_1$) of the two prices at the center boundary (figure 6-5). Thus,

$$(2\alpha)^2 = 2^2 + (p_o - p_1)^2, \text{ or}$$

$$\alpha = \sqrt{1 + \frac{(p_o - p_1)^2}{4}}, \text{ and}$$

$$\beta = 1,$$

so that the ellipse has the form shown in figure 6-6.

2. If the twofold form of equations (5.12) and (5.27) is generalized by replacing the components $(k_1 + k_2)$ and $(k_1 - k_2)$ with the more general component $(k_1 + k_2 \sin \phi)$, and if the set of the two centers within the system of reference x, y is taken as shown in figure 6-6 then:

$$\text{for } \phi = \frac{\pi}{2}, \; \sin \frac{\pi}{2} = 1, \; k_1 + k_2 \sin \phi = k_1 + k_2, \text{ and}$$

$$\text{for } \phi = \frac{3\pi}{2}, \; \sin \frac{3\pi}{2} = -1, \; k_1 + k_2 \sin \phi = k_1 - k_2.$$

For $\phi = \pi/2$, the prices described coincide with the curve $p(r)_L$, while for $\phi = 3\pi/2$ (difference $\pi = 180°$), the prices described coincide with curve $p(r)_R$.

Thus,

1. If $p_0 = p_1 = \bar{p}$, and center II is taken into account, the general form of the equation describing the prices in the area of center I is:

$$p(r) = \bar{p} \, [T - (k_1 + k_2 \sin \phi) - k_2 D]^{a_2/a_1}. \tag{6.5}$$

2. If $p_0 > p_1$, then $p_0 - p_1 = p'$, and $(dp'/ d(\pi/2 + \phi))$ is the increase of p_1 towards p_0 when the radius that includes point A in figure 6-4 turns counterclockwise by the angle ϕ. Then, the form of the equation of housing prices becomes:

$$p(r) = \left(p_1 + \frac{dp'}{d\left(\dfrac{\pi}{2} + \phi\right)}\right)[T - (k_1 + k_2 \sin \phi) - k_2 D]^{a_2/a_1}. \tag{6.6}$$

If these changes are incorporated into equations (6.1) and (6.2), then r changes as the price $\bar{p}$ (the constant), rotates around center I. The change (i.e., the increase of r) is then described by the term $\bar{p}/p_1$. This decreases as p_1 increases towards p_0. The denominator $(k_1 + k_2)$ also decreases as it follows the sine of angle ϕ, to $(k_1 - k_2)$.

This procedure describes the prices around center I and, similarly, those around center II. To the extent that a "boundary" can be specified, the locus of points M (figures 6-1 and 6-2) where households will be indifferent between the two centers is such a boundary between the two sub-areas. (Actually, as Chapter 4 illustrated, this boundary does not exist. It is mentioned here only for analytical purposes.) Its shape can be specified by equating the housing prices of centers I and II because the prices should be the same at the indifference point. For the special case of the two centers being equal, the housing prices at their boundaries are the same, and the price profiles originating at the two centers are identical. In

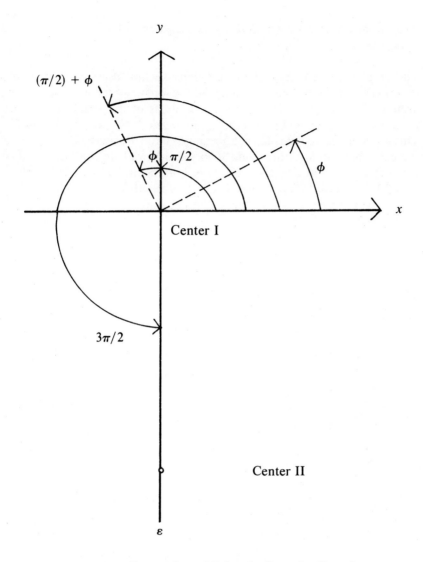

Figure 6-7. Generation of Price Surfaces by Rotation

such a case, the solution for the distances of the boundary from the centers I and II gives the relationship $2r = D$. That is, the "boundary" of the two perfectly symmetrical surfaces on the plain is a straight line perpendicular to the middle of the axis connecting centers I and II.[1]

Analysis of the Two-Center Case Using Trigonometric Functions

The graphic presentation of the previous section uses a trigonometric function to define the changing shape of the rent gradient at various points around centers I and II. In a formal analysis of the shape of surfaces generated by these gradients, the trigonometric form can be very useful. This is due to the dependence of households upon the two central locations (poles). Thus, an arbitrary point A in the urban plane can be described trigonometrically in reference to one or both central points. This is illustrated by figure 6-8, where the distance of point A from each center is expressed in terms of one distance and one angle.

From figure 6-8:

$$r_1 = r/\sin \phi, \text{ and}$$

$$r_2 = \sqrt{(r_1 \cos \phi)^2 + (D + r_1 \sin \phi)^2}, \tag{6.7}$$

where D is the distance between the two centers. The leisure time of the individual household is given by:

$$t = T - k_1r_1 - k_2r_2, \tag{6.8}$$

where T stands for the household's total disposable time and k_1, k_2 are as defined in Chapter 5. Following the procedure outlined in Chapter 5, the time and income constraints are incorporated into the utility function so that the household's utility can be maximized subject to the existing constraints. Thus:

$$U = a_1\log s + a_2\log (T - k_1r_1 - k_2r_2) + a_3\log (y - ps), \tag{6.9}$$

where $p = p (r_1, \phi)$.

In order to have a maximum, the partial derivatives with respect to s, r, and ϕ should be equal to zero. Assuming that the second derivatives will be negative:

$$\frac{\partial U}{\partial s} = \frac{a_1}{s} - \frac{a_3p}{y - ps} = 0, \tag{6.10}$$

$$\frac{\partial U}{\partial r_1} = -\frac{a_2\left[k_1 + \dfrac{k_2(r_1 + D\sin \phi)}{\sqrt{D^2 + r_1^2 + 2Dr_1 \sin \phi}} \right]}{T - k_1r_1 - k_2r_2} - \frac{a_3s}{y - ps}\frac{\partial p}{\partial r_1}$$

$$= 0, \tag{6.11}$$

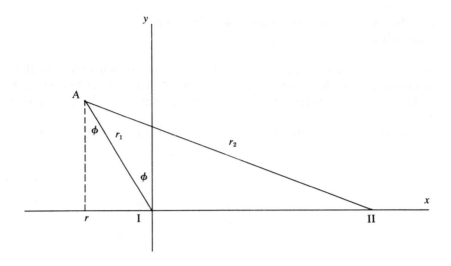

Figure 6-8. Trigonometric Determination of Points on the Plane

$$\frac{\partial U}{\partial \phi} = -\frac{a_2 k_2 r_1 D}{(T - k_1 r_1 - k_2 r_2)\sqrt{r_1^2 + D^2 + 2r_1 D \sin\phi}} - \frac{a_3 s}{y - ps}\frac{\partial p}{\partial \phi}$$
$$= 0. \tag{6.12}$$

Equation (6.10) again gives a demand function for housing identical to that of the linear case. That is:

$$s = \frac{a_1}{a_1 + a_3}\frac{y}{p}. \tag{6.13}$$

In order to obtain the schedule of housing prices in the urban area, equations (6.11) and (6.12) need to be solved simultaneously. There are only two unknowns (r_1 and the angle ϕ) in these equations because equation (6.7) gives r_2 as a function of these two variables. The solution of the two equations then gives the price a household of income y is willing to pay for housing at each distance r_1 and each angle ϕ between the axis connecting the two centers and the line connecting the particular point with center I, the primary pole. As Chapter 5 showed, from this point on, it is only a matter of routine algebra to determine the rent function and the final equilibrium solution.

**Solution of the Two-Center Case Using Cartesian
Coordinates**

If urban centers I and II are considered as points of a system of rectangular
coordinates, then any point A on the x, y plane can be determined by an
ordered pair (x_A, y_A) representing the point's coordinates. Figure 6-9 illus-
trates this.

The distances of point A from centers I and II is therefore given as:

$$r_1 = \sqrt{x_A^2 + y_A^2}, \text{ and}$$
$$r_2 = \sqrt{(D - x_A)^2 + y_A^2}, \tag{6.14}$$

where D is the distance between the two centers. Then, the time consumed
by household trips to center I equals $k_1 r_1$, and the time taken by trips to
center II is $k_2 r_2$. As was demonstrated previously, the leisure time available
to the household is given by:

$$t = T - k_1 r_1 - k_2 r_2, \tag{6.15}$$

where T again stands for the household's disposable time.

Therefore, the location of the household is fixed when r_1 and r_2 are
known, that is, when the coordinates (x_A, y_A) of the point are given. The
analysis of Chapter 5 and the previous section is applicable here again.
Consequently, the demand and housing price schedules which maximize
the household's satisfaction for housing and leisure time are obtained in
that manner. This rectangular coordinate approach may have an advantage
over the previous approach. Indeed, it is mathematically simpler in that
actual distances (airline distances or travel time distances) are easier to
measure in an urban area than are angles. Thus, empirical work could be
facilitated. Aside from this, however, the difference between the two
approaches is minimal.

The n-Center Urban Area

Analyzing the two-dimensional city with two centers of economic activity
was relatively simple, although the mathematics could be quite cumbersome. The selection of one system of coordinates or the other should
not make much difference aside from the measurement of the angle. Dealing with more than two centers, however, complicates things slightly. This
is where a model such as the one developed here could be of great use for
the simulation and study of urban household behavior.

Actually, an urban area with only two major centers is not a very
common phenomenon. Since most of the larger cities in the United States

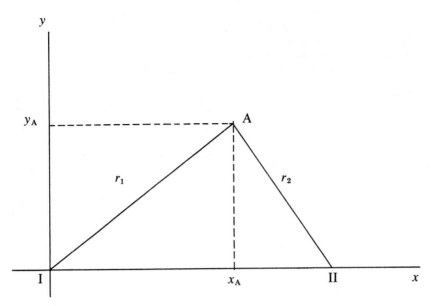

Figure 6-9. Determination of Points on the Plane Using Cartesian Coordinates

appeared during the eighteenth and nineteenth centuries, they are very often characterized by a major center, the CBD. As their development and expansion continued in all directions, a number of other nuclei gradually appeared. The presence of only two centers, then, could be explained if the city could expand in only one direction. In special cases, the presence of a second center might also be explained by other reasons, such as the existence of an earlier village center, or an industrial agglomeration or a company town, etc.

There is, of course, the possibility of an urban area developing along an axis connecting two preexisting separate cities. Here, the old cores of the two cities would constitute the economic activity centers, and the area in between would be offered for noneconomic uses. This model would be appropriate for the study of such an area. However, it would be a special case of urban development patterns.

To visualize the potential three-dimensional shape of the rent surfaces caused by a multi-center metropolitan area, the concept of "tents" suggested by J. Douglas Carroll could be used.[2] These tents directly relate to the concept of market areas and the exclusive influence of each center upon "its own" territory. But apart from this idea, which was criticized in previous sections, the description of the effect created by surface gradients fits this case very well. Carroll states:

Visualize a pole erected at each point on a map where a city is located. Each pole rises vertically a distance proportional to the size of the city it represents. These poles may be likened to tent poles from which are draped "tents of influence" representing the magnitude of each city's influence on populations located throughout the terrain. Each tent is independent of every other tent. That is, the existence of a neighboring city does not affect the shape of any city's tent. A plan view of this map can be made showing the area in which any one city's tent is highest. In this way it is possible to describe that area in which any particular city has a greater influence than competing cities.[3]

Carroll attempted to identify regional market boundaries. However, if instead the location of the poles represents the rent at the boundary of the center,[c] then the tent quite accurately represents the shape of the surfaces created by the rent gradients. This differs from Carroll in that it deals with *only one* continuous tent common to all centers. It exhibits peaks at the locations of the centers, and falls everywhere else with the steepness depending on the particular location. The tent only touches ground at the edge of the metropolitan area where urban rent vanishes (or rather becomes equal to "agricultural rent").[4]

How then would our rent surface for the two-center city change in the presence of a third center? It is obvious that the presence of a third center is contingent upon a proportional development of the whole urban area. In this way, the demand for housing services throughout the area will increase, and, consequently, prices will go up as well. Depending on the causes of growth, this shift can be gradual and continuous or be sudden and fluctuating in the short run. Whatever the causes of expansion, however, the two-center equilibrium will be disturbed.

In principle, the analysis of previous sections could again be employed. Using the method of polar coordinates, any point in the urban plane is determined uniquely by its distance from the pole and the angle of the two rays. The same, then, is true for the location of the third, fourth or any number of centers which are assumed to be fixed and exogenously determined. Then, the n-center case can be accommodated in the model by introducing the distances (r_3, r_4, etc.) of the particular point from each of the additional centers. Figure 6-10 shows the case of three such centers I, II, and III.

In figure 6-10, the location of center III is fixed in relation to centers I and II so that its distance D_1 from pole I is known. Its angle θ with the axis through I and II is also known. Any point A in the plane is determined equally by its distance r_1 to the pole and its angle ϕ. The distance r_2 of A can be expressed as a function of the length r_1 and the angle ϕ. And since point III is already uniquely determined, distance r_3 can also be expressed as a

---

[c] According to the analysis here, there is a range of such rents rather than a single rent at the boundary of each center. But for the moment, given the scale of the urban area, the rent differences at the boundary can be neglected without sacrificing reality.

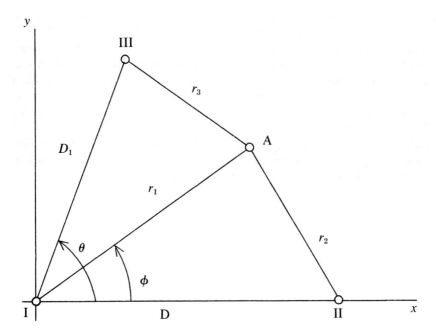

Figure 6-10. The Three Center City

function of r_1 and angles θ, ϕ. Thus, specifying the shape of the rent tent in the area between and around the three centers is not a conceptual problem. However, it becomes a problem each time a new unknown is introduced (in this case r_3) into the leisure equation, and, consequently, into the utility function. Aside from the algebraic complications this creates, it is also difficult to interpret the travel frequencies k_i.

This study does not complete the mathematical solution to the n-center problem. It describes it in principle and demonstrates its feasibility. The rest is largely a mathematical exercise. The difficulties of the calculations are recognized, as is the fact that no nice, closed formulas would be their final output. On the other hand, it is hoped that this model may be the starting point for more complete efforts through which other issues of concern will be considered.

One issue of great concern is the estimation of housing supply. The assumption of homogeneous housing stock not withstanding, the best work to date is the study by Quigley.[5] His empirical work and conclusions are excellent. But they are not incorporated in an equilibrium model such as that presented here. This is a major drawback which ought to be considered in the next phase of the research.

Since this is the first time the urban area has been treated as a whole rather than as an aggregate of sub-areas, the foregoing analysis can be used as a policy-exploring device. The perception of a city as a set of separate markets has been very harmful because it has denied the presence of interdependencies, a major characteristic of the city. By analyzing the city as a whole, this model also provides a tool for comparing the effects of various public actions. If its results are compared to those obtained by a monocentric model with exclusive urban sub-areas, the analysis of the differences between the two could reveal the effects of the interdependencies among the various parts of the city. It is also hoped that further improvements will make its usefulness even more apparent.

7   Summary and Conclusions

This study had two purposes: first, to trace the development of theories and models of residential location, to classify them in terms of common characteristics, and to discuss their fundamental assumptions and weaknesses; and second, to propose a model which would improve upon some of these weaknesses.

The study, then, is concerned with abstractions of the real-life phenomenon of households deciding on the location of their residences. Although the terms "theory" and "model" may appear to be used indiscriminantly on some occasions, they do not refer to the same thing. In general, "model" is used to suggest an operational concept. According to Britton Harris, it is "an experimental design based on a theory."[1] Thus, the analysis, evaluation, and criticism of each category discussed is directed at both the underlying theory and its operational forms.

Development of the Residential Location Theory

In chapters 2 through 4, the first purpose was addressed. The state of the art of residential modeling, from the simplest macrospatial models based on accessibility and density gradients to the more sophisticated theories were reviewed. These used microeconomic spatial equilibrium and made assumptions about the behavior of individual households as the unit of observation.

A problem with this section was the absence of clear-cut criteria to allow the classification of theories and models into distinct categories. Thus, a classification was based upon the nature of the fundamental assumptions and the analytical approach of each model. If, on the other hand, a typology based on the various dimensions characterizing models and their differences had been followed, it would have been necessary to classify each model into several groups;[2] and, therefore, it would have been possible to discuss only certain characteristics at a time. But since the purposes of the study were to present the models in their entirety and to discuss their effectiveness in simulating and planning for urban phenomena, the approach followed seemed more appropriate.

Difficulties were also encountered in the attempt to classify and present models according to their increasing sophistication and completeness. This occurred occasionally when a model dealt exhaustively with one factor or one issue, but was generally quite elementary or uninteresting. In such cases, it was determined that only the part of interest to this study would be discussed. This led, on the whole, to an "incremental" method of presentation in which each study or approach discussed improved upon the previous ones.

In summarizing the state of the art, it should be pointed out that the concepts of accessibility and its related transport costs are of primary concern throughout the residential location literature. However, more recently other issues of importance to households have been recognized. Of these, serious consideration was given to the size of the residential lot and the amount of housing services related to the household. But other considerations have also become more important in recent years. For instance, environmental quality, amenities, neighborhood characteristics, etc., have been considered more frequently, although often they are not formally incorporated into major modeling efforts. In addition, the effects of transportation land use, congestion, and the supply of housing have introduced more realism into the models. It should be kept in mind at this point that it cannot be expected that models will remain both elegant and simple when such considerations are introduced. Thus, large-scale models attempting to simulate the sub-systems of the urban environment are harder to comprehend, and cumbersome to manipulate and test. But this is the price that must be paid for more realism and accuracy in the model predictions. Life is not simple, and modeling technology is imperfect. Combining the two leaves many questions unanswered; but in tracing the recent developments in this field of knowledge, it is clear that this is the right track.

Four areas were identified for further effort by students of urban phenomena:

1. The recognition of the multi-nucleated character of our metropolitan areas, the simultaneous influence of those centers upon the shaping of our urban environment, and the possible problems caused by the interaction of the activities in these centers with the population in the rest of the urban area;

2. The permanent character of the housing stock in the city whose durability, heterogeneity and inflexibility make the modeling of the supply side very uncertain;

3. The presence of urban externalities which have taken the form of transportation, congestion, and pollution problems. Due to its very nature, the city is a generator of such externalities, the underestimation of which will greatly diminish the effectiveness of urban models as decision-making aids; and

4. The recognition of the imperfect character of the market which underlines the availability of sufficient information, the competitive conditions for urban land and housing, and the nonmonopolistic character of urban transactions.

These are all very important issues which require considerable research before complete models of urban residential structure become available and useful as policy tools. While attempts are already numerous, they have been scattered and disorganized. In addition, the time lag involved in the dissemination of scientific information and knowledge is a critical factor. In any event, the area which has attracted the least attention in urban studies is that of multiple nucleation since the standard monocentric model has provided a very convenient analytical tool whose deficiencies tend to be underestimated. For all these reasons, the second part of this study was concerned with the development of a model to explain the residential location decision process in metropolitan areas with many centers of economic activity.

The Proposed Model of Residential Location

Throughout the study, emphasis was placed on the need for recognition of the existence of a multi-center pattern in the contemporary metropolitan area, and of the simultaneous influence exercised by these urban centers upon the locating household. The first consequence of this recognition was the abandonment of the concept of market boundaries at the breaking points of each central influence. Therefore, a continuous surface of housing prices and rents in the urban area with peaks at the location of the centers of economic activities was adopted.

This conceptual form was then derived mathematically using the theory of microeconomic spatial equilibrium. Urban households attempted to maximize their utility, and urban firms tried to maximize their profits. In a linear city, the market equilibrium at each location was at centers of economic activity of varying magnitude located along one line. Due to the accessibility advantages in the area between the two centers, the final rent profiles show that the housing rents there will be higher than the rents in the outlying areas. In general, these rents are higher than those predicted by the monocentric model.

The model was then applied to a real-world, two-dimensional urban area in two stages. Initially only two centers were discussed and analytically derived. Then the model was modified to consider a theoretically infinite number of urban centers; and although the computations would definitely become cumbersome for a large number of urban centers, there appears to always be a solution.

The problems first encountered in developing the model had to do with the particular form of utility function adopted, the definition and assumptions concerning the various variables used, and problems encountered in the measurement of the variables. In addition, once the model was generalized for the two-dimensional case, problems arose in determining the supply of housing and in selecting the most appropriate system of coordinates for the model. Finally, as the number of centers of influence increased, the introduction of additional terms accounting for the travel time spent for each new center created the problem of allocation of trips by household. That is, the investigation of the properties and boundary conditions of the k_i becomes more complicated.

The model developed here does not claim either comprehensiveness or completeness. Its modest objective was to investigate the changes in the distribution of urban variables such as housing rent through the simultaneous consideration of several urban centers. The relationships developed are consistent with the assumptions employed, and seem to conform to the results of existing empirical studies. Hopefully, further work will show the extent to which the model can be used as a policy-making tool.

Several urban characteristics influence the applicability potential of the model. First of all is the size of the urban area. As was already discussed, the number of urban centers is a corollary of urban size, although the exact form of this correlation is not known. Nevertheless, the description of the growth process and the manner in which the physical form of cities is formed justifies the relationship between urban size and the number of centers. But how is urban size measured? Is population a good indicator, or is density? How could employment activities be used in building such an index? How one chooses from the very large range of answers determines the final relationship of size to number of centers. But unless this relationship is better defined, it is impossible to determine the threshold level for the urban size necessary to support two, three or more such centers.

Another major factor is the degree of specialization in the economic base of the city. Different activities have different distribution patterns which in turn affect the number, nature, and spacing of urban centers. In addition, the type of activity will determine the degree to which agglomeration economies are generated, and the number and type of complementary activities attracted. This is of major concern because the urban character of an area is a consequence of the types of activities located within its confines. Moreover, urban areas of different characteristics have different concentration patterns. Thus, cities of equal size but of different specializations will possibly have quite different patterns of urban center distribution. In addition, some basic characteristics of the population such as income distribution, educational levels, and travel patterns will also be different; and household behavior will deviate accordingly.

The degree of concentration or dispersion of the diverse activities in the city is a consequence of the nature of its activities. Thus, some metropolitan areas exhibit a high degree of polarization, while others have a rather diffused and dispersed pattern in which the various services occur at a variety of levels and few concentrations are obvious. In cases of this sort, many of the nonwork trips are scattered throughout the area, and application of this model will not be possible without modifications. Actually, the land throughout the area will be the object of competition between noncentral activities and households. In such locations, the rent surface will exhibit noncontinuities and unexpected changes in slope.

Despite the many obvious problems that a model such as this will have to overcome, it can be argued that it provides us with a more accurate picture of real phenomena than the monocentric models used thus far. Much empirical work is needed before this argument can be substantiated.

Conclusions

Static equilibrium models such as that developed in this study have two purposes. First, they attempt to describe and simulate the behavior of decision-making units (in this case the households), and substantiate empirically the theoretical results in order to provide decision makers with information regarding these units. Second, they seek to outline the optimal distribution of the variables of interest under the assumption of efficiency. Comparison of these distributions with observed patterns will identify cases of market imperfection and areas where governmental intervention is needed. The spatial character of the distribution is of particular importance because the most efficient management and the optimal allocation of this scarce resource is of major interest. To the extent that social welfare and economic development in the metropolis are predominent concerns, the spatial consideration of efficient distribution is an invaluable guide. There remains, of course, the question of equity and the degree to which models such as these help achieve it. However, the way in which the system operates does not provide for this. All one can really hope for is that policymakers will be sensitive enough to use models such as this in simulating the effects of their policies towards achieving this goal. If this model can serve such a function, its existence is justified.

Appendix A
Derivation of Consistency
Conditions for k_1 and k_2 of the
Linear City Model

The necessary condition for consistency of the time constraint is that

$$t_A \geq 0, \text{ or}$$

$$T - (k_1 - k_2)r - k_2D \geq 0. \tag{A.1}$$

There exist then three cases, depending on whether $k_1 \gtrless k_2$.

Case a. $k_1 > k_2$.
Relation (A.1) gives

$$\frac{T - k_2(D - r)}{r} \geq k_1 > k_2. \tag{A.2}$$

However, if (A.2) holds, then it will also hold that

$$\frac{T - k_1(D - r)}{r} \geq k_1$$

or

$$T - k_1D + k_1r \geq k_1r,$$

and finally,

$$k_1 \leq T/D. \tag{A.3}$$

Case b. $k_1 < k_2$.
Relation (A.1) gives

$$\frac{T - k_1r}{D - r} \geq k_2 > k_1, \tag{A.4}$$

and, then, even more

$$\frac{T - k_2r}{D - r} \geq k_2,$$

or

$$T - k_2r \geq k_2D - k_2r,$$

$$k_2 \leq T/D. \tag{A.5}$$

Case c. $k_1 = k_2$.

In this case, relation (A.1) becomes

$$T - k_2 D \geq 0,$$

and holds for

$$k_1 = k_2 \leq T/D. \tag{A.6}$$

Conditions (A.3), (A.5), and (A.6) are necessary for k_1 and k_2 to be consistent.

Notes

Notes to Chapter 1
Introduction

1. Walter Isard and Thomas A. Reiner, "Regional Science: Retrospect and Prospect," *Regional Science Association Papers* 16 (1966): p. 2.

2. Walter Isard, "Regional Science, the Concept of Region and Regional Structure," *Papers and Proceedings of the Regional Science Association* 2 (1956): p. 14.

3. In a study of sixteen cities with populations ranging between 5,000 and 300,000, Bartholomew found that single-family houses occupied 74.2 percent of the privately developed land, while two-family units used 4.28 percent and multi-family structures took up 2.23 percent, for a total of 80.71 percent. See Harland Bartholomew, *Urban Land Uses*, Harvard City Planning Studies, Vol. IV (Cambridge, Mass.: Harvard University Press, 1932), pp. 56-70 and 126 ff.
Similar residential land allocations are presented by Creighton, who estimates residential land use to be 40.3 percent of the total urban land in Chicago, 47 percent for Niagara Frontier, and 50.2 percent for Pittsburgh. See Roger L. Creighton, *Urban Transportation Planning* (Urbana: University of Illinois Press, 1970), pp. 63 ff.

4. The form and the growth patterns of a single center urban area are explained by Burgess' theory of concentric zones. E.W. Burgess, "The Growth of the City: An Introduction to a Research Project" in R.E. Park et al. (eds.), *The City* (Chicago, Ill.: The University of Chicago Press, 1925). Burgess' hypothesis states that any city tends to expand radially from the center so as to form a series of concentric circular zones, each of which is devoted primarily to one use. The growth of the urban area, then, is manifested physically by the invasion of each zone into the next outer ring. This follows a sequence known as "invasion-succession" which maintains the circular urban form. For more on the Burgess hypothesis, see Chapter 3.

5. The most notable examples of this type of analysis are the studies by Alonso and Muth. See, William Alonso, *Location and Land Use* (Cambridge, Mass.: Harvard University Press, 1964), pp. 134-142, and *ibid.*, "A Theory of the Urban Land Market," *Papers and Proceedings of the Regional Science Association* 6 (1960): 149-157, mainly the last two pages. Also, Richard E. Muth, *Cities and Housing* (Chicago, Ill.: The University of Chicago Press, 1969), pp. 86-90. For a discussion of the approaches followed by these modified models, see Chapter four on the analysis of the literature.

6. See Alonso, *Location and Land Use*.

7. Muth, *Cities and Housing*. In his fourth chapter, Muth attempts an analysis of the urban housing market in which his assumptions, including the one-center one, are relaxed. This modification is discussed in Chapter four of this work.

8. Relaxing the monocentric city assumption was one of the objectives of an excellent analysis of the housing market by Quigley. See, John M. Quigley, "Residential Location with Multiple Workplaces and a Heterogeneous Housing Stock," doctoral Dissertation, Harvard University, 1972.

9. William J. Reilly, *The Law of Retail Gravitation*. (New York: Reilly, 1931).

10. Brian J.L. Berry, *Geography of Market Centers and Retail Distribution* (Englewood Cliffs, N.J.: Prentice-Hall Inc., 1967), p. 41.

11. Arnold M. Rose, *Theory and Method in the Social Sciences* (Minneapolis, Minn.: The University of Minnesota Press, 1954), p. 3.

12. F. Stuart Chapin, *Experimental Designs in Sociological Research* (New York: Harper and Bros., 1955), pp. 52-43.

13. Harry S. Upshaw, "Attitude Measurement," in Hubert M. Blalock, Jr., and Ann B. Blalock (eds.), *Methodology in Social Research* (New York: McGraw-Hill Book Co., 1968), pp. 60-111.

14. Rose, *Theory and Method*, p. 3.

15. For a discussion of the use of the axiomatic method in decision theory see, William J. Baumol, *Economic Theory and Operations Analysis*, 3rd edition (Englewood Cliffs, N.J.: Prentice-Hall, Inc., 1972), pp. 586-591. Applications of this analytical framework are found in, among others, R. Duncan Luce, and Howard Raiffa, *Games and Decisions* (New York: John Wiley and Sons, Inc., 1958); R. Duncan Luce, *Individual Choice Behavior—A Theoretical Analysis* (New York: John Wiley and Sons, Inc., 1959); and Bernard S. Phillips, *Social Research—Strategy and Tactics*, 2nd edition (New York: The Macmillan Company, 1971).

16. Rose, (*Theory and Method* pp. 4-5), lists six major shortcomings in the use of theory:

a. Channeling the research along only limited lines:

b. Biasing observation due to the use of certain assumptions;

c. Reifying the necessary concepts;

d. Assuming consistency in empirical findings;

e. Overgeneralizing conclusions to areas outside their scope; and

f. Distorting simple facts only because of the existence of rival theories.

17. Stan Czamanski, "Regional Science and Regional Planning," *Plan, Journal of the Town Planning Institute of Canada* 9, 2 (July 1968): 55.

18. Jan Tinbergen, *Economic Policy: Principles and Design* (Amsterdam: North-Holland Publishing Co., 1956), pp. 3ff. His classification of variables was analyzed further in Karl A. Fox and Erik Thorbecke, "Specification of Structures and Data Requirements in Policy Models," in Bert G. Hickman (ed.), *Quantitative Planning of Economic Policy*. (Washington, D.C.: The Brookings Institution, 1965), pp. 43-44. The same classification, further refined, is adopted by Czamanski. See, Stan Czamanski, *Regional Science Techniques in Practice* (Lexington, Mass.: Lexington Books, D.C. Heath and Company, 1972), p. 280.

19. Various model classifications are used in the social sciences. The one presented here was adopted from Czamanski, *Regional Science Techniques*, pp. 281-283.

Notes to Chapter 2
Macro-Spatial Models of Residential Land Allocation

1. A very similar classification was proposed by Lowdon Wingo, Jr. (*Transportation and Urban Land*. Baltimore: The Johns Hopkins Press, 1961, pp. 11-18). Wingo classifies future distribution of household efforts into three categories, namely (a) ad hoc allocations, (b) gravity or potential models, and (c) economic models. While this is a meaningful classification, it omits the whole body of residential location literature produced by the human ecologists. With this one addition, then, his classification is adopted here.

2. For a thorough discussion of the relationship between land use and trip generation, see Roger I. Creighton, *Urban Transportation Planning* (Urbana, Ill.: University of Illinois Press, 1970), pp. 80-83.

3. For a complete analysis of the concept of holding capacity and its uses, see, F. Stuart Chapin, Jr., *Urban Land Use Planning*, 2nd edition (Urbana, Ill.: University of Illinois Press, 1972), pp. 431-440.

4. See, for example, John R. Hamburg, "Land Use Projections for Predicting Future Traffic," in Highway Research Board, *Bulletin*, No. 224 ("Trip Characteristics and Traffic Assignment"), 1959, pp. 72-84.

5. For a more detailed description of the Chicago land use forecasting process, see, John R. Hamburg and Robert H. Sharkey, *Land Use Forecast*, Document No. 32 (Chicago, Ill.: Chicago Area Transportation Study, 1961), and by the same authors, "Chicago's Changing Land Use and Population Structure", *Journal of the American Institute of Planners* 26, 4

(November 1960): 317-323. Also see, Chicago Area Transportation Study, *Final Report*, Vol. II (Chicago, Ill.: CATS, 1960) pp. 16-33; and John R. Hamburg, and Roger L. Creighton, "Predicting Chicago's Land Use Pattern," *Journal of the American Institute of Planners* 25, 2 (May 1959): 67-72.

6. Ernest H. Jurkat, "Land Use Analysis and Forecasting in Traffic Planning," *Traffic Quarterly* 11, 2 (April 1957): 151-63. Also, see Arthur Row and Ernest Jurkat, "The Economic Forces Shaping Land Use Patterns," *Journal of the American Institute of Planners* 25, 2 (May 1959): 77-81, where the same income-density combination is discussed.

7. Jurkat, "Land Use Analysis," p. 155.

8. Ibid., p. 158. Reprinted with permission.

9. Ibid., p. 161. Reprinted with permission.

10. Colin Clark, "Urban Population Densities," *Journal of the Royal Statistical Society*, Series A, Vol. 114 (1951): 490-496. See also his, "Urban Population Densities," *Bulletin d'Institut International de Statistique* 36, Part 4 (1958): 60-68.

11. For a complete survey and analysis of the literature on urban densities, see Brian J.L. Berry, James W. Simmons, and Robert J. Tennant, "Urban Population Densities: Structure and Change," *Geographical Review* 53 (July 1963): 389-405.

12. Ibid., pp. 391-395. A more sophisticated formula, providing for a "central crater" where residential densities fall in the areas adjacent to the center, was proposed by Newling. The formula has a quadratic form and lends itself to a dynamic model of urban growth in which the zone of peak density moves outward over time. See, Bruce E. Newling, "The Spatial Variation of Urban Population Densities," *Geographical Review* 59, 2 (April 1969): 242-252.

13. Hans Blumenfeld, "Are Land Use Patterns Predictable?", *Journal of the American Institute of Planners* 25, 2 (May 1959): 61-66. The same method of analysis was used in the Philadelphia metropolitan area. See, Hans Blumenfeld, "The Tidal Wave of Metropolitan Expansion," *Journal of the American Institute of Planners*, 20, 1 (February 1954): 3-14.

14. This problem is similar to the one faced in the CATS land use forecast (see related bibliography in note 5 of this chapter).

15. Blumenfeld, "Are Land Use Patterns Predictable?", pp. 63-64.

16. Kenneth E. Boulding, "Toward a General Theory of Growth," in J.J. Spengler and O.D. Duncan (eds.), *Population Theory and Policy* (Glencoe, Ill.: Free Press, 1956), pp. 109-124.

17. Richard F. Muth, "The Spatial Structure of the Housing Market," *Papers and Proceedings of the Regional Science Association* 7 (1961): 207-220.

18. Berry, Simmons, and Tennant, "Urban Population Densities," p. 398.

19. Gerald A.P. Carrothers, "An Historical Review of the Gravity and Potential Concepts of Human Interaction," *Journal of the American Institute of Planners* 22, 2 (May 1956): 94-102. Carrothers presents an excellent review of the literature based upon historical development. Isard, on the other hand, gives an in-depth treatment of the gravity concept from the technical and theoretical point of view. See, Walter Isard, *Methods of Regional Analysis: An Introduction to Regional Science* (New York: John Wiley & Sons, 1960), Chapter 11; and his, *Location and Space Economy* (Cambridge, Mass.: The MIT Press, 1956), Chapter 3.

20. Carrothers, "An Historical Review," p. 94.

21. These weights were proposed by Stewart to correct for differences in influence resulting from different characteristics of the populations, and they are equivalent to molecular weights in the physical analogy. See, J.Q. Stewart, "Potential of Population and its Relationship to Marketing," in Reavis Cox and Wroe Alderson (eds.), *Theory in Marketing* (Chicago, Ill.: Richard D. Irwin, 1950).

22. Gunnar Olsson, *Distance and Human Interaction*, Bibliography Series, No. 2. (Philadelphia, Penn.: Regional Science Research Institute, 1965), pp. 44-48.

23. The power to the population element was suggested by Anderson, and was generalized by Carrothers. See, Theodore R. Anderson, "Intermetropolitan Migration: A Comparison of the Hypotheses of Zipf and Stouffer," *American Sociological Review* 20, 3 (June 1955): 287-291, and "Potential Models and Spatial Distribution of Population," *Papers and Proceedings of the Regional Science Association* 2 (1956): 175-182. Also, Carrothers, "An Historical Review," p. 98.

24. It has generally been argued that the model only represents an empirical regularity for which a theoretical explanation has not yet been furnished. See, for example, William L. Garrison, Brian J.L. Berry, Duane F. Marble, John D. Nystuen, and Richard L. Morrill, *Studies of Highway Development and Geographic Change* (Seattle, Washington: University of Washington Press, 1959).

25. Walter C. Hansen, "How Accessibility Shapes Land Use," *Journal of the American Institute of Planners* 22, 2 (May 1959): 73-76.

26. Samuel A. Stouffer, "Intervening Opportunities: A Theory Relating Mobility and Distance," *American Sociological Review* 5 (December 1940): 845-867.

27. J. Douglas Carroll, Jr., "The Relation of Homes to Work Places and the Spatial Patterns of Cities," *Social Forces* 30 (March 1952): 278.

28. Hansen, "How Accessibility Shapes Land Use,"

29. Ibid., p. 73.

30. The empirical examination of the relationship between residential development and accessibility used accessibility to employment, population and shopping opportunities for seventy sub-areas in the Washington metropolitan area. When used to estimate residential growth for each of the zones, 40 percent of the estimates were within 30 percent of the actual growths, and 70 percent were within 60 percent of the actual zonal figures. See, Hansen, "How Accessibility Shapes Land Use," p. 75. Even larger variations were observed in the application of the model to the Hartford metropolitan area. Here a number of nonquantifiable factors, such as sewer-water service, zoning-subdivision controls, land costs, taxes, and prestige of the site were found to reduce considerably the observed variation. See, Hartford Area Traffic Study, *Report*, Vol. 1, "Hartford: The Study" (Hartford, Conn.: H.A.T.S., July 1961).

31. Stouffer, "Intervening Opportunities." In applying his model, Stouffer stratified the available residences by rent and race. Although this is an improvement over the completely aggregated model, it still does not allocate households realistically. Other characteristics like ethnic neighborhoods, etc., should also be considered.

32. Morton Schneider, "Gravity Models and Trip Distribution Theory," *Papers and Proceedings of the Regional Science Association* 5 (1959): 51-56.

33. George T. Lathrop and John R. Hamburg, "An Opportunity-Accessibility Model for Allocating Regional Growth," *Journal of the American Institute of Planners* 31, 2 (May 1965): 93-102.

34. Ira S. Lowry, *A Model of Metropolis* (Santa Monica, Calif.: The RAND Corporation, August 1964).

35. A time-phased version of the model was developed by CONSAD Research Corporation. See, John P. Crecine, "A Time Oriented Metropolitan Model for Spatial Location", *CRP Technical Bulletin*, No. 6 (Pittsburgh, Penn.: Department of City Planning, 1964).

36. In fact, recently there have been several efforts to derive the gravity formula within the framework of economic theory to provide a theoretical explanation of the "gravity law." An interesting derivation based on utility theory in terms of trips made by persons from a single origin to many destinations is suggested by Niedercorn and Bechdolt. See, J.H. Niedercorn and B.V. Bechdolt, Jr., "An Economic Derivation of the 'Gravity Law' of Spatial Interaction," *Journal of Regional Science* 9, 2 (1969): 273-282.

37. For a discussion of some improvements of the Lowry model, see, A.G. Wilson, "Developments of Some Elementary Residential Location Models," *Journal of Regional Science* 9, 3 (1969): 377-385. Wilson's position is that as long as behavioral models which are based on economic theory cannot become operational, it is worth developing further elementary models such as the gravity model which are applicable to empirical research. In listing weaknesses of the gravity formula, Wilson includes the following:

a. the specific form of the function $f(c_{ij})$ which is a decreasing function of the cost of travelling from i to j, c_{ij};
b. the inclusion of attractiveness characteristics of the residential zone itself;
c. the allowance by the model for some exogenously fixed populations;
d. the allowance for zonal capacity constraints; and
e. the utilization of the intervening opportunities and travel costs concepts.

Wilson proposes alternative gravity formulations which attempt to give an answer to these problems using an entropy maximizing methodology. While these constitute significant improvements to the gravity formulation, the basic descriptive character of the approach does not change. Wilson's own view on this question is that unless detailed information about preference structures and utility functions is known, any projects using such "elementary" models will be poor.

Similar work along the Wilson-suggested entropy maximizing approach was done by Karlqvist and Marksjo. They analyzed urban gravity models from the statistical point of view. Their derivation gives information on the maximum likelihood of parameter estimates as well as their actual distributions. Explicit methods for testing the models in both exact and assymptotic form are also suggested. See, A. Karlqvist and B. Marksjo, "Statistical Urban Models," *Environment and Planning* 3 (1971): 83-98.

38. The attacks against the importance of accessibility come from many directions. The main group of critics is the human ecologists, but there is also widespread consensus among economists and planners. Characteristic of them are Anderson and Stegman. See, T.R. Anderson, "Social and Economic Factors Affecting the Location of Residential Neighborhoods," *Papers and Proceedings of the Regional Science Association* 9 (1962): 161-170, and Michael A. Stegman, "Accessibility Models and Residential Location," *Journal of the American Institute of Planners* 35, 1 (January 1969): 22-29.

39. Lowry, *A Model of Metropolis*.

Notes to Chapter 3
Behavioral Theories of Residential Location—The
Macro-Approach

1. Neither Adam Smith nor John Stuart Mill gave more than passing attention to urban land. Adam Smith characterized it as "unproductive" and its landlord as a monopolist. Adam Smith, *The Wealth of Nations* (New York: Dutton, Everyman's Library Edition), Vol.I, p. 320, and Vol. II, p. 325. Similarly, J.S. Mill considered the urban land market as a situation in which supply is just absorbed by the existing demand. John Stuart Mill, *Principles of Political Economy* (New York: Longmans, Green), pp. 444-448, 649. Alfred Marshall, on the other hand, devoted a chapter to urban land values; but he discussed only profit-making uses, not residential land. In addition, he did not recognize the importance of lot size in determining site values. See Alfred Marshall, *Principles of Economics* (London: Macmillan, 7th edition, 1916), Book V, Chapter 11, pp. 445-450. For a discussion of the Marshallian contribution to today's theory of land values, see, William Alonso, *Location and Land Use* (Cambridge: Harvard University Press, 1964), pp. 4-5.

2. Richard M. Hurd can be considered as the pioneer in this area and his book, *Principles of City Land Values* (New York: The Record and Guide, 1903), as the first complete analysis of urban land values and, to a limited extent, urban location. Hurd's work is discussed in this section.

3. For a related discussion see Edwin S. Mills, "The Value of Urban Land," in Harvey S. Perloff (ed.), *The Quality of the Urban Environment* (Washington, D.C.: Resources for the Future, Inc., 1969), pp. 231-232.

4. Edwin S. Mills, *Urban Economics* (Glenview, Ill.: Scott, Foresman and Company, 1972), pp. 37-39. This discussion of land rent draws heavily from Mills' work in general and in particular, from Chapter three, pp. 37-52.

5. David Ricardo, *On the Principles of Political Economy and Taxation* (1817), and Piero Sraffa (ed.), *The Work and Correspondence of David Ricardo* (Cambridge, Mass.: Cambridge University Press, 1951), Vol. I.

6. Johann Heinrich von Thünen, *Der isolierte Staat in Beziehung auf Landwirtschaft und Nationalekonomie* (Hamburg: Fr. Derthes, 1826-1863). For the English translation see, Peter Hall, *Von Thünen's Isolated State* (London: Pergamon Press, 1966).

7. The von Thünen analysis was later fully developed by Dunn and Isard. See Edgar S. Dunn, Jr., *The Location of Agricultural Production* (Gainsville, Fla.: University of Florida Press, 1954), and Walter Isard, *Location and Space Economy* (Cambridge, Mass.: The MIT Press, 1956).

8. Philip H. Wicksteed, *An Essay on the Coordination of the Laws of Distribution* (London, 1894, reprinted by the London School of Economics and Political Science, London, 1932).

9. Kunt Wicksell, *Lectures on Political Economy,* Vol. I (London: Routlege, 1935).

10. For a complete discussion of the land rent issue and the state of the art, see Joseph S. Keiper, Ernest Kurnow, Clifford D. Clark, and Harvey H. Segal, *Theory and Measurement of Rent* (Philadelphia, Penn.: Chilton Company, 1961).

11. Richard M. Hurd, *Principles of City Land Values* (New York: The Record and Guide, 1903).

12. Ibid., p. 11.

13. Ibid., pp. 77-78.

14. Robert M. Haig, "Toward an Understanding of the Metropolis," *Quarterly Journal of Economics* 40, 1 (February 1926): 179-208, and No. 3 (May 1926): 402-434. The same article appeared a year later as the main chapter of the *Regional Survey of New York and its Environs*, Vol. I, "Major Economic Factors in Metropolitan Growth and Arrangement" (New York: The Regional Plan, 1927).

15. Ibid., p. 422.

16. Alonso, *Location and Land Use*, p. 7. The point was originally made by Ratcliff. See, Richard U. Ratcliff, *Urban Land Economics* (New York: McGraw-Hill Book Company, 1949).

17. Harry W. Richardson, *Regional Economics* (New York: Praeger Publishers, 1969), pp. 120-122.

18. Bartholomew's first such study was conducted in the early 1930s and surveyed twenty-two "typical" American cities with populations ranging from 5,000 to 300,000. See Harland Bartholomew, *Urban Land Uses— Amounts of Land Used and Needed for Various Purposes by Typical American Cities* (Cambridge, Mass.: Harvard University Press, 1932). Twenty years later, he presented a large compilation of urban land use data on ninety-seven American cities, fifty-three of which were central cities, thirty-three of which were satellite cities, and eleven of which were urban areas. See, Harland Bartholomew, *Land Uses in American Cities* (Cambridge, Mass.: Harvard University Press, 1955).

19. Homer Hoyt, *One Hundred Years of Land Values in Chicago* (Chicago: The University of Chicago Press, 1933).

20. Ratcliff, *Urban Land Economics*, p. 356.

21. Homer Hoyt, *The Structure and Growth of Residential Neighborhoods in American Cities* (Washington, D.C.: Federal Housing Administration, 1939).

22. Ratcliff, *Urban Land Economics,* pp. 396-397.

23. Ibid.

24. Ibid.

25. Albert Z. Guttenberg, "Urban Structure and Urban Growth," *Journal of the American Institute of Planners* 26, 2 (May 1960): 104-110.

26. According to James Quinn's definition, "human ecology centers on the study of relations between man and environment, where environment is taken to include the material and spatial aspects of the surrounding world," as well as the nonmaterial cultural environment. For a discussion of the various disciplines, see James A. Quinn, *Human Ecology* (Englewood Cliffs, N.J.: Prentice-Hall, Inc., 1950), pp. 3-11.

27. Robert E. Park, Ernest W. Burgess and Roderick D. McKenzie, *The City* (Chicago: The University of Chicago Press, 1925); Roderick D. McKenzie, *The Metropolitan Community* (New York: McGraw-Hill Book Company, 1933); D.J. Bogue, *The Structure of the Metropolitan Community* (Ann Arbor, Michigan: The University of Michigan Press, 1949); James A. Quinn, *Human Ecology;* Amos H. Hawley, *Human Ecology: A Theory of Community Structure* (New York: The Ronald Press Company, 1950).

28. Walter Firey, *Land Uses in Central Boston* (Cambridge: Harvard University Press, 1947).

29. Louis Wirth, "A Bibliography of the Urban Community," in Park et al., *The City*, p. 203.

30. Robert E. Park, "Sociology," in Wilson Gee (ed.), *Research in the Social Sciences* (New York: The MacMillan Company, 1929), p. 27.

31. Ernest W. Burgess, "The Growth of the City—An Introduction to a Research Project," in Park et al., *The City*, p. 61.

32. Quinn, *Human Ecology,* p. 448.

33. Ibid.

34. Ibid., pp. 282.

35. Ibid., pp. 285-286.

36. Hawley, *Human Ecology*, pp. 280-287.

37. See, for example, the discussion on slum areas in Egon E. Bergel, *Urban Sociology* (New York: McGraw-Hill Book Company, Inc., 1955), pp. 404-428. Also in Chester Rapkin, *The Real Estate Market in an Urban Renewal Area* (New York: The City Planning Commission, 1959), p. 120.

38. William Alonso, *Location and Land Use–Toward a General Theory of Land Rent* (Cambridge: Harvard University Press, 1964), pp. 10-11 and the discussion in Chapter 6. For more on Alonso's theory, see the next chapter of this study.

39. Burgess, *"The Growth of the City";* Homer Hoyt, *The Structure and Growth of Residential Neighborhoods in American Cities* (Washington D.C.: Federal Housing Administration, 1939); Chauncy D. Harris and

Edward L. Ullman, "The Nature of Cities," in *The Annals of the American Academy of Political and Social Sciences* 242 (November 1945): 7-17.

40. Maurice R. Davie, "The Patterns of Urban Growth," in G.P. Murdock (ed.), *Studies in the Science of Society* (New Haven: Yale University Press, 1937).

41. Ibid.

42. Harvey D. Zorbaugh, "The Natural Areas of the City," in E.W. Burgess (ed.), *The Urban Community* (Chicago: University Press, 1926); and Paul K. Hatt, "The Concept of the Natural Areas," in *American Sociological Review* 11, 4 (1946).

43. Zorbaugh, "Natural Areas," p. 233.

44. Firey, *Land Uses in Central Boston*.

45. For a detailed discussion of these and other criticisms, see Hawley, *Human Ecology*, pp. 282-285 and Bergel, *Urban Sociology*, pp. 105-113.

46. Robert S. Lynd and Helen M. Lynd, *Middletown* (New York: Harcourt and Brace, 1929); and, by the same authors, *Middletown in Transition* (New York: Harcourt and Brace, 1937).

47. Hoyt, *Structure and Growth of Residential Neighborhoods*.

48. Firey, *Land Uses in Central Boston*, pp. 326-327.

49. Burgess, *The Urban Community*.

50. Hoyt, *Structure and Growth of Residential Neighborhoods*.

51. Harris and Ullman, "The Nature of Cities."

52. Ibid., p. 48.

53. The economic approach to the concentric ring formation has been analyzed exhaustively, with particular emphasis given to residential land uses, in Alonso's *Location and Land Use*.

54. R.D. McKenzie, *The Metropolitan Community*. New York: McGraw Hill, 1933, p. 175; H. Hoyt, *op.cit.;* and Leslie Kish, "Differentiation in Metropolitan Areas," *American Sociological Review* 19, 4 (1954), 388-98.

55. Hoyt, *Structure and Growth of Residential Neighborhoods*.

56. Arthur W. Weimer and Homer Hoyt, *Principles of Real Estate* (New York: The Ronald Press Company, 1960), p. 351.

57. Hoyt, *Structure and Growth of Residential Neighborhoods*, p. 116.

58. Ibid., pp. 117-119.

59. A detailed critique of the sector theory was presented by Lloyd Rodwin. He summarized its defects as: (1) the ambiguous formulation and use of the sector concept; (2) an oversimplified version of class structure; (3) a distorted dependence on upper-class "attractions" as a basis for

interpreting shifts in residential location; (4) the inaccuracy of some of the empirical generalizations; (5) the potentially misleading reliance on nineteenth century free market residential trends; and (6) the narrow perspectives resulting from the essential purpose of the inquiry. See Lloyd Rodwin, "The Theory of Residential Growth and Structure," in *The Appraisal Journal* 18 (July 1950): 295-317.

60. For an attempt to combine the two theories, see Peter Mann's suggested structure of the typical medium-sized British city. Peter Mann, *An Approach to Urban Sociology* (London: Humanities Press, 1965).

61. Harris and Ullman, "The Nature of Cities." See also Ullman's later paper, "The Nature of Cities Reconsidered," in *Papers and Proceedings of the Regional Science Association* 9 (1962): 7-23.

62. Roderick D. McKenzie, *The Metropolitan Community* (New York: McGraw-Hill Book Company, 1933), pp. 197-198.

63. Harris and Ullman, "The Nature of Cities," pp. 14-15.

64. Guttenberg, "Urban Structure and Urban Growth."

Notes to Chapter 4
Behavioral Models of Residential Location

1. Paul F. Wendt, "Theory of Urban Land Values," *Journal of Land Economics* 33, 3 (August 1957): 228-240; also by the same author, "Urban Land Value Trends," *The Appraisal Journal* 26 (April 1958): 254-269, and "Economic Growth and Urban Land Values," *The Appraisal Journal* 26 (July 1958); 427-443. Of interest is a rejoinder to the first of the above papers by R. Ratcliff, "Commentary: On Wendt's Theory of Land Values," *Journal of Land Economics* 33, 4 (November 1957); 360-362.

2. Wendt, "Economic Growth and Urban Land Values," p. 427.

3. Linear programming was developed by George B. Dantzig in 1947 as a technique for planning the diversified activities of the U.S. Air Force. The original paper was published as "Maximization of a Linear Function of Variables Subject to Linear Inequalities'" in T.C. Koopmans (ed.), *Activity Analysis of Production and Allocation* (New York: John Wiley & Sons, Inc., 1951), pp. 339-347. The linear programming technique developed in two directions: as an aid to managerial planning, and as a tool to explore economic theory and its applications. It is in this latter context that linear programming was utilized in the Herbert-Stevens formulation.

Linear programming is the analysis of problems in which a linear function (objective function) of a number of variables is maximized (or minimized) when those variables are subject to a number of constraints expressed as linear inequalities. For an exhaustive analysis of linear programming and its economic applications, see, Robert Dorfman, Paul A. Samuelson and Robert M. Solow, *Linear Programming and Economic Analysis* (New York: McGraw-Hill Book Company, 1958).

4. Benjamin H. Stevens and Robert F. Coughlin, "A Note on Inter-Areal Linear Programming for a Metropolitan Area," *Journal of Regional Science* 1, 2 (Spring 1959): 75-83. The model's objective is to minimize the total number of services required to transport products to plants and distributors.

5. John D. Herbert, and Benjamin H. Stevens, "A Model for the Distribution of Residential Activity in Urban Areas," *Journal of Regional Science* 2, 2 (Fall 1960): 21-36.

6. Herbert and Stevens, "A Model for Distribution," pp. 26-27.

7. Britton Harris, *Linear Programming and the Projection of Land Uses*, Paper No. 20 (Philadelphia: Penn-Jersey Transportation Study, 1962).

8. A.G. Wilson, *Urban and Regional Models in Geography and Planning* (London: John Wiley & Sons, 1974), pp. 202-203.

9. M.L. Senior and A.G. Wilson, "Disaggregated Residential Location Models: Some Tests and Further Theoretical Developments", in E.L. Cripps, ed., *Space-Time Concepts in Urban and Regional Models* (London: Pion Publications, 1974).

10. Southeastern Wisconsin Regional Planning Commission, *Technical Record*, Vol. 2, No. 1 (Waukesha, Wisconsin: The Commission, 1964).

11. Kenneth J. Schlager, "A Land Use Plan Design Model," *Journal of the American Institute of Planners* 31, 2 (May 1965); 103-111.

12. Harris, *Linear Programming*, and, "Notes on an Approach to Metropolitan Housing Market Analysis," Philadelphia, Penn.: The University of Pennsylvania, Dept. of City and Regional Planning, 1966, (mimeo). The main exposition of the model is presented in Britton Harris, Josef Nathanson and Louis Rosenburg, *Research on an Equilibrium Model of Metropolitan Housing and Locational Choice* (Philadelphia, Penn.: University of Pennsylvania, Interim report, 1966).

13. For a detailed analysis of the derivation of this preference function from Alonso's equilibrium model, as well as for a discussion of the empirical work on Harris's model, see Michael A. Stegman, "An Analysis and Evaluation of Urban Residential Models and Their Potential Role in City Planning," Ph.D. dissertation, University of Pennsylvania, 1966.

14. Maisel and Winnick were unable to explain more than 23 percent of the variation of housing expenditure within very finely stratified and sufficiently homogeneous groups of people. See Sherman J. Maisel and Louis Winnick, "Family Housing Expenditures: Elusive Laws and Intrusive

Variances," *Proceedings of the Conference on Consumption and Savings*, 1 (Philadelphia: University of Pennsylvania,1960). Similar results have been reported by other researchers. See, for example, Nelson W. Foote et al., *Housing Choices and Housing Constraints* (New York: McGraw-Hill, 1960); and Chester Rapkin and William G. Grigsby, *Residential Renewal in the Urban Core* (Philadelphia: University of Pennsylvania, 1960).

15. A good example of such a regional model is the empiric model constructed for the Boston region by the Traffic Research Corporation. The model uses a number of equations interrelated through variables which are dependent in one equation and independent in others. This type of simultaneous equations model requires more sophisticated techniques of estimation than those of simple regression analysis. For a description and discussion of the model, see Donald M. Hill, "A Growth Allocation Model for the Boston Region," *Journal of the American Institute of Planners* 31, 2 (May 1965): 111-120; and Donald H. Hill, Daniel Brand and Willard B. Hansen, "Prototype Development of a Statistical Land Use Prediction Model for the Greater Boston Region," *Highway Research Record*, No. 114 (1965): 51-70. Other models of major significance dealing with regional economies and the location of economic activities and employment are the Connecticut model constructed by Alan M. Voorhees and Associates, and the Pittsburgh model, developed by CONSAD. For a description of these efforts, see T.R. Lakshmanan, "A Model for Allocating Urban Activities in a State," *Socioeconomic Planning Sciences* 1, 3 (1968): 283-295; and S.H. Putman, "Intra-urban Industrial Location Model Design and Implementation," *Papers, Regional Science Association* 19 (1967): 199-214.

16. D.R. Seidman, *The Construction of an Urban Growth Model*, Plan Report No. 1, Technical Supplement, Vol. A (Philadelphia, Penn.: Delaware Valley Regional Planning Commission, 1969).

17. Wilson, *Urban and Regional Models*, pp. 243-256.

18. For a presentation of the complete model, see Seidman, *Construction of an Urban Growth Model*.

19. William Alonso, *Location and Land Use* (Cambridge, Mass.: Harvard University Press, 1964). Alonso's equilibrium location theory is discussed towards the end of this chapter.

20. John F. Kain, *A Multiple Equation Model of Household Locational and Tripmaking Behavior*, Memorandum RM-3086-FF (Santa Monica, Calif.: The RAND Corporation, April 1962). The model follows the same general approach outlined in J.F. Kain and J.R. Meyer, *A First Approximation to a RAND Model for Study of Urban Transportation*, Memorandum RM-2878-FF (Santa Monica, Calif.: The RAND Corporation, 1961).

21. See Kain, *Multiple Equation Model*, pp. 9-10.

22. Martin J. Beckmann, "On the Distribution of Rent and Residential Density in Cities," paper presented at the Inter-departmental Seminar on Mathematical Applications in the Social Sciences, at Yale University, February 1957. Beckmann refined and elaborated further the basic concepts of his papers—"On the Distribution of Urban Rent and Residential Density," *Journal of Economic Theory* 1, 1 (June 1969): 60-67, and "Spatial Equilibrium in the Housing Market," *Journal of Urban Economics* 1, 1 (January 1974): 99-107. The multi-center linear model developed in the next chapter of this study is largely based on the model developed in the latter article.

23. The original formulation of the Alonso theory appeared in his Ph.D. dissertation at the University of Pennsylvania. See William Alonso, "A Model of the Urban Land Market: Location and Densities of Dwellings and Businesses," University of Pennsylvania, 1960. Subsequently, the same work was revised and published as *Location and Land Use: Toward a Theory of Land Rent* (Cambridge, Mass.: Harvard University Press, 1964).

24. Lowdon Wingo, Jr., *Transportation and Urban Land* (Baltimore, Md.: The Johns Hopkins Press, 1961).

25. Kain's model also appeared first as a Ph.D. dissertation. See John F. Kain, "The Journey to Work as a Determinant of Residential Location," Ph.D. dissertation, University of California, 1961. A reexamination and revision of the model was published with the same title in the *Papers and Proceedings of the Regional Science Association* 9 (1962): 137-60.

26. Richard F. Muth, *Cities and Housing* (Chicago, Ill.: The University of Chicago Press, 1969).

27. T.R. Anderson, "Social and Economic Factors Affecting the Location of Residential Neighborhoods," *Papers and Proceedings of the Regional Science Association* 9 (1962): 161-170.

28. R.H. Ellis, "Modeling of Household Location: A Statistical Approach," *Highway Research Record*, No. 207 (1967): 42-51.

29. Michael A. Stegman, "Accessibility Models and Residential Location," *Journal of the American Institute of Planners* 35, 1 (January 1969): 22-29.

30. Harry W. Richardson, *Urban Economics* (Baltimore, Md.: Penguin Books, 1971), pp. 24-28.

31. Martin J. Beckmann, "On the Distribution of Rent and Residential Density in the Cities."

32. Martin J. Beckmann, "On the Distribution of Urban Rent and Residential Density," *Journal of Economic Theory* 1, 1 (June 1969): 60-67.

33. The Beckmann solution was seriously challenged in a paper by Montesano. Essentially, he proved Beckmann's solution to be wrong; and

he also showed that even in certain restrictive cases, the urban monocentric pattern suggested by Beckmann is incompletely analyzed. Thus, it is shown that while only households of the same income live at a given distance from the CBD, not *all* households of a given income live at the same distance. That is, Beckmann's solution only holds for income as a monotonically increasing function of distance from the city center. For the detailed exposition and solution of the model, see Aldo Montesano, "A Restatement of Beckmann's Model on the Distribution of Urban Rent and Residential Density," *Journal of Economic Theory* 4, 2 (April 1972): 329-54.

34. William Alonso, *Location and Land Use*.

35. Johan H. von Thünen, *Der isolierte Staat in Beziehung auf Landwirtschaft und Nationalekonomie*. (Hamburg, 1826), translated as Peter Hall (ed.), *von Thünen's Isolated State* (Oxford: Pergamon Press, 1966). von Thünen's model was formally developed by Dunn and Isard. See Edgar S. Dunn, *The Location of Agricultural Production* (Gainsville, Fla.: The University of Florida Press, 1954); and Walter Isard, *Location and Space-Economy* (Cambridge, Mass.: The M.I.T. Press, 1956).

36. Wingo, *Transportation and Urban Land*.

37. This complementarity was suggested originally by R.M. Haig. It is described in Chapter 2 of this study. See Richard M. Haig, "Toward an Understanding of the Metropolis," *Quarterly Journal of Economics* 40, 1 (February 1926): 179-208, and No. 3 (May 1926): 402-434.

38. For a detailed discussion of the elasticity of demand and its restricted value, see Edwin S. Mills, *Studies in the Structure of the Urban Economy* (Baltimore, Md.: The Johns Hopkins Press, 1972), pp. 63-65. Also see, Harry W. Richardson, *Regional Economics* (New York: Praeger Publishers, 1969), pp. 143-144.

39. See particularly, Muth, *Cities and Housing*, whose analysis is discussed in the next section of this chapter.

40. Kain, "The Journey-to-Work."

41. Kain, "The Journey-to-Work," p. 143.

42. Muth, *Cities and Housing*. A number of other papers document and elaborate specific topics related to this major work. See Richard F. Muth, "The Demand for Non-farm Housing," in Arnold C. Harberger (ed.), *The Demand for Durable Goods* (Chicago, Ill.: The University of Chicago Press, 1960), pp. 29-96. See also Muth's "Economic Change and Rural-Urban Land Conversions," *Econometrica* 29, 1 (January 1961): 1-23; "The Spatial Structure of the Housing Market," *Papers and Proceedings of the Regional Science Association* 7 (1961): 207-220; "The Variation of Population Density and its Components in South Chicago," *Papers of the Re-*

gional Science Association 15 (1965): 173-183; "The Distribution of Population within Urban Areas," in Robert Ferber (ed.), *Determinant of Investment Behavior* ((New York: National Bureau of Economic Research, 1967), pp. 271-299.

43. Muth justifies this assumption as necessary to understand the effects on urban land use of factors such as durability and heterogeneity. These are introduced as departures from the assumptions once the theoretical model is developed. See, Muth, *Cities and Housing*, pp. 46-47.

44. The mathematical derivation of the density function is given by E. Mills in his *Studies in the Structure of the Urban Economy* (Baltimore, Md., The Johns Hopkins Press, 1972), pp. 76-77.

45. Von Thünen, *Der isolierte Staat*.

46. See John F. Meyer, John F. Kain and Martin Wohl, *The Urban Transportation Problem* (Cambridge, Mass.: Harvard University Press, 1966).

47. See John F. Kain, "The Distribution and Movement of Jobs and Industry," in James Q. Wilson (ed.), *The Metropolitan Enigma* (Cambridge, Mass.: Harvard University Press, 1968), pp. 1-33.

48. Mayer, Kain and Wohl, *The Urban Transportation Problem,* pp. 25-30.

49. Edwin S. Mills, "An Aggregative Model of Resource Allocation in a Metropolitan Area," *American Economic Review* 57, 2 (May 1967): 197-210.

50. Edwin S. Mills, "The Value of Urban Land," in Harvey S. Perloff (ed.), *The Quality of the Urban Environment* (Baltimore, Md.: The Johns Hopkins Press, 1969), pp. 231-253.

51. Julius Margolis, "Discussion" on Edwin S. Mills "An Aggregative Model of Resource Allocation in a Metropolitan Area," *American Economic Review* 57, 2 (May 1967): 235-237.

52. Robert M. Solow and William S. Vickery, "Land Use in a Long Narrow City," *Journal of Economic Theory* 3, 4 (December 1971): 430-447.

53. Robert M. Solow, "Congestion, Density and the Use of Land in Transportation," *Swedish Journal of Economics* 74, 1 (March 1972): 161-173. See also his "On Equilibrium Models of Urban Location," in Michael Parkin (ed.), *Essays in Modern Economics* (London: Longmans, 1973), pp. 2-16, and "Congestion Cost and the Use of Land for Streets," *Bell Journal of Economics and Management Science*. 4, 2 (Autumn 1973): 602-18.

54. Since width was neglected, Solow and Vickery developed their model for a "long narrow city" with a single dimension, length. The analysis was carried further by Marvin Kraus. He applied the same analyti-

cal principles to a circular city thereby making the Solow-Vickery model comparable to the two-dimensional, monocentric city of the general equilibrium models. Furthermore, in addition to using the radial pattern of earlier models, the Kraus model introduced the circumferential travel pattern. See Marvin Kraus, "Land Use in a Circular City," *Journal of Economic Theory* 8, 4 (August 1974): 440-457.

55. Solow, "Congestion, Density and the Use of Land."

56. Ibid., p. 169. Also see his "Congestion Cost and the Use of Land for Streets."

57. Chauncy D. Harris and Edward L. Ullman, "The Nature of Cities," *The Annals of the American Academy of Political and Social Sciences* 242 (November 1954): 7-17.

58. On this subject, see Brian J.L. Berry, *Geography of Market Centers and Retail Distribution* (Englewood Cliffs, N.J.: Prentice-Hall, Inc., 1967); and T.R. Lakshmanan and Walter G. Hansen, "A Retail Market Potential Model," *Journal of the American Institute of Planners* 31, 2 (May 1965): 134-143.

59. See, for example, Berry, *Geography of Market Centers*, and George J. Papageorgiou and Emilio Casetti, "Spatial Equilibrium Residential Land Values in a Multicenter Setting," *Journal of Regional Science* 11, 3 (1971); 385-389.

60. Alonso, *Location and Land Use*, pp. 134-142.

61. Muth, *Cities and Housing*, pp. 86-90.

62. Wilhelm Launhardt, *Mathematische Befrundung der Volkswirtschaftslehre* (Leipsig: B.G. Teumner, 1885).

63. John M. Quigley, "Residential Location With Multiple Workplaces and a Heterogeneous Housing Stock," Ph.D. dissertation, Harvard University, 1972, pp. 17-18.

64. Lakshmanan, and Hansen, "Retail Market Potential Model," p. 135.

65. Berry refers to William J. Reilly's breaking point equation as part of his "laws of retail gravitation." These summarize market area patterns. This equation states that the trade area boundary between two towns A and B is, in miles from B, equal to;

$$\frac{d_{AB}}{1 + \sqrt{\frac{m_A}{m_B}}}$$

where d_{AB} = distance between A and B

m_A = size of A; and

m_B = size of B.

See William J. Reilly, *The Law of Retail Gravitation* (New York: Reilly, 1931).

66. Berry, *Geography of Market Centers,* p. 41. For more on the concept see David L. Huff, *Determination of Intra-Urban Retail Trade Areas* (Los Angeles, Calif.: University of California, Real Estate Research Program, 1962). Also see Huff's "A Probabilistic Analysis of Shopping Center Trading Areas," *Land Economics* 53, 1 (February 1963), pp. 81-90.

67. See, for example, the work by J.B. Lansing and E. Mueller, *Residential Location and Urban Mobility* (Ann Arbor, Michigan: The University of Michigan, Survey Research Center, 1964); and J.B. Lansing, *Residential Location and Urban Mobility: The Second Wave of Interviews* (Ann Arbor, Mich.: The University of Michigan, Survey Research Center, 1966).

68. Theodore T. Anderson, "Social and Economic Factors Affecting the Location of Residential Neighborhoods," *Papers and Proceedings of the Regional Science Association* 9 (1962): 161-170.

69. Britton Harris, "Quantitative Models of Urban Development: Their Role in Metropolitan Policy-Making," in Harvey S. Perloff and Lowdon Wingo, Jr. (eds.), *Issues in Urban Economics* (Baltimore, Md.: The Johns Hopkins Press, 1968), pp. 363-412.

70. Ibid., p. 393.

71. Michael A. Stegman, "Accessibility Models and Residential Location," *Journal of the American Institute of Planners* 35, 1 (January 1969): 22-29.

72. Ibid., p. 22.

73. Jay Siegel, *Intrametropolitan Migration of White and Minority Group Households* (Stanford, Calif.: Stanford University Press, 1970).

74. See, for example the discussion in Mark D. Menchik, *"Residential Environmental Preferences and Choice: Some Preliminary Empirical Results Relevant to Urban Form*, RSRI Discussion Paper No. 46 (Philadelphia, Penn.: Regional Science Research Institute, March 1971).

75. Quigley, "Residential Location," pp. 18-22.

76. Ibid., p. 20.

77. See Quigley for a similar and more exhaustive discussion of the housing market. This includes empirical evidence that invalidates the monocentric assumption for a homogeneous housing stock. Quigley, "Residential Location," pp. 22-38.

78. Harry W. Richardson, *Urban Economics* (Baltimore, Md.: Penguin Books, 1971), pp. 24-28.

Notes to Chapter 5
A Model of Residential Location for a Linear Multi-Center City

1. The characteristics and features of the homogeneous plain are spelled out in Johann Heinrich von Thünen, *Der isolierte Staat in Beziehung auf Landwirtschaft und Nationalekonomie* (Hamburg: 1st volume, 1826; 3rd volume and new edition, 1863); translated as, Peter Hall (ed.), *von Thünen's Isolated State* (Oxford: Pergamon Press, 1966). The assumption is further refined in: Walter Isard, *Location and Space Economy* (Cambridge, Mass.: The M.I.T. Press, 1956).

2. This assumption was recently tested by Brown and Kain in an analysis of job changes in San Francisco. H. James Brown and John F. Kain, "Moving Behavior of San Francisco's Households," in John F. Kain (ed.), *The NBR (National Bureau of Economic Research) Urban Simulation Model*, Ch. 6. This study follows the movements of a cross-section of employed households. It indicates that when tenure type and age were held constant, the incidence of residential change was substantially higher for those households which had changed job locations within the metropolitan area during the previous eighteen months. Change was even higher for households that had moved their employment locations longer distances. The general conclusion of the study is that relocation decisions of households occur in response to exogenous changes in the location of employment.

3. This form of the supply function is adopted here because of its widespread acceptance. There is no empirical evidence, however, that the housing supply does indeed follow a Cobb-Douglas function. For a more detailed discussion of the function, see William Baumol, *Economic Theory and Operations Analysis*, 3rd edition (Englewood Cliffs, N.J.: Prentice-Hall, Inc., 1972), pp. 426-427.

4. This multi-center model is based on Martin Beckmann's monocentric model developed in 1973 while he was a consultant with the Department of Transportation and Urban Analysis at the General Motors Research Laboratories. The original paper was presented at a faculty seminar of the Department of Economics at the University of Wisconsin-Milwaukee. It was published later under the title "Spatial Equilibrium in the Housing Market," in the *Journal of Urban Economics* 1, 1 (January 1974): 99-107.

5. See, for example, Richard F. Muth, *Cities and Housing* (Chicago: The University of Chicago Press, 1969), p. 21 ff; and also the related discussion in Robert M. Solow, "Congestion, Density and the Use of Land in Transportation," *The Swedish Journal of Economics* 74, 1 (March 1972): 162.

6. An advantage of using an explicit utility function is that it allows demand functions of specific forms to be derived. See, for example, Martin J. Beckmann, "On the Distribution of Urban Rent and Residential Density," *Journal of Economic Theory* 1, 1 (June 1969); 60-67.

7. Studies by Richard F. Muth, Margaret G. Reid, John R. Malone and others do indeed suggest that the consumption of housing is strongly related to the household's income, and that it tends to rise at least in proportion to it. See Richard F. Muth, "The Demand for Non-Farm Housing," in Arnold C. Harberger (ed.), *The Demand for Durable Goods* (Chicago: The University of Chicago Press, 1960), pp. 29-96; Margaret G. Reid, *Housing and Income* (Chicago: The University of Chicago Press, 1962); and John R. Malone, "A Statistical Comparison of Recent New and Used Home Buyers," Ph.D. dissertation, University of Chicago, Graduate School of Business, 1963.

8. Beckmann, "Spatial Equilibrium in the Housing Market."

9. R.G.D. Allen, *Mathematical Analysis for Economists* (New York: St. Martin's Press, 1968), pp. 340-343.

Notes to Chapter 6
Towards an Analysis of a Two-Dimensional City With Many Centers

1. The special case where the two centers are equal can be analyzed according to Launhardt's study. This considered the shape of two markets when the two sellers are surrounded by many buyers, and both prices and transport rates are the same. See Wilhelm Launhardt, *Mathematische Begründung der Volkswirtschaftslehre* (Leipzig: B.G. Teubner, 1885).

2. J. Douglas Carroll, Jr., "Spatial Interaction and the Urban-Metropolitan Regional Description," *Papers and Proceedings of the Regional Science Association* 1 (1955): D-2 to D-14.

3. Ibid., p. D-3.

4. Such an edge does not really exist. This issue is similar to that of the "breaking point" between markets. Here, the boundary of an urban area is a zone of transition where continuous rural-urban land conversion takes place. Depending upon the particular urban area and its dynamics, the degree and forms of sprawl and the existence of suburban economic activity, etc., this zone can be very wide in places. For a discussion of this concept, see A. Allan Schmid, *Converting Land From Rural to Urban Uses* (Baltimore, Maryland: The Johns Hopkins Press, 1968).

5. John M. Quigley, "Residential Location with Multiple Workplaces and a Heterogeneous Housing Stock," Ph.D. dissertation, Harvard University, 1972.

Notes to Chapter 7
Summary and Conclusions

1. Britton Harris, "The Use of Theory in the Simulation of Urban Phenomena," *Journal of the American Institute of Planners* 32, 5 (September 1966): 258-273.

2. Harris, for instance, distinguishes six such dimensions:
   1. descriptive versus analytic models,
   2. holistic versus partial,
   3. macro versus micro,
   4. static versus dynamic,
   5. deterministic versus probabilistic,
   6. simultaneous versus sequential.

See, Britton Harris, "Quantitative Models of Urban Development: Their Role in Metropolitan Policy-Making," in Harvey S. Perloff and Lowdon Wingo, Jr. (eds.), *Issues in Urban Economics* (Baltimore: The Johns Hopkins Press, 1968), pp. 363-410.

Bibliography

Books and Monographs

Ackoff, R.L. *Scientific Method-Optimizing Applied Research Decisions*. New York: John Wiley & Sons, 1961.

Allen, R.G.P. *Mathematical Analysis for Economists*. New York: St. Martin's Press, 1968.

Alonso, William. *Location and Land Use: Toward a General Theory of Land Rent*. Cambridge, Mass.: Harvard University Press, 1964.

Bartholomew, Harland. *Land Uses in American Cities*. Cambridge, Mass.: Harvard University Press, 1955.

_____. *Urban Land Uses*. Cambridge, Mass.: Harvard University Press, 1932.

Baumol, William J. *Economic Theory and Operations Analysis*, 3rd edition. Englewood Cliffs, N.J.: Prentice-Hall, Inc., 1972.

Beckmann, Martin. *Location Theory*. New York: Random House, 1968.

Bergel, Egon. *Urban Sociology*. New York: McGraw-Hill Book Company, Inc., 1955.

Berry, Brian J.L. *Commercial Structure and Commercial Blight*. Research Paper No. 85. Chicago, Ill.: University of Chicago, Department of Geography, 1963.

_____. *Geography of Market Centers and Retail Distribution*. Englewood, Cliffs, N.J.: Prentice-Hall, Inc., 1967.

_____ and Frank E. Horton. *Geographic Perspectives on Urban Systems*. Englewood Cliffs, N.J.: Prentice-Hall, Inc., 1970

Birch, David L. *The Economic Future of City and Suburb*. CED Supplementary Paper No. 30. New York: Committee for Economic Development, 1970.

Blalock, H.M. Jr. *Theory Construction*, Englewood Cliffs, N.J.: Prentice-Hall, 1969.

Board, Christopher, Richard J. Chorley, Peter Haggett and David R. Stoddart, eds. *Progress in Geography: International Reviews of Current Research*, Vol. 4. New York: St. Martin's Press, 1972.

Bogue, D.J. *The Structure of the Metropolitan Communities*. Ann Arbor, Michigan: The University of Michigan Press, 1949.

Boyce, David E., Bruce Allen, Richard R. Mudge, Paul B. Slater and Andrew M. Isserman. *Impact of Rapid Transit of Sub-Urban Residential Property Values and Land Development: Analysis of the Philadelphia-Lindenwold High-Speed Line*. Philadelphia, Penn.: University of Pennsylvania, Department of Regional Science, 1972.

Brigham, Eugene F. *A Model of Residential Land Values*. Memorandum RM-4043-RC. Santa Monica, Calif.: the RAND Corporation, August 1964.

_____. *Some Pitfalls in the Analysis of Residential Location Preferences*. Paper P-280. Santa Monica, Calif.: the RAND Corporation, October 1963.

Brown, H. James, J.R. Ginn, F.J. James, J.F. Kain and M.R. Straszheim. *Empirical Models of Urban Land Use: Suggestions on Research Objectives and Organization*. New York: Columbia University Press, (for the National Bureau of Economic Research), 1972.

Burgess, Ernest, W., ed. *The Urban Community*. Chicago, Ill.: The University of Chicago Press, 1926.

Chapin, F. Stuart Jr. *Experimental Designs in Sociological Research*. New York: Harber & Bros., 1947, (revised 1955).

_____. *Urban Land Use Planning*, 2nd edition. Urbana, Ill.: University of Illinois Press, 1972.

_____ and Shirley F. Weiss. *Factors Influencing Land Development*. Chapel Hill, N.C.: University of North Carolina, Center for Urban and Regional Studies, August 1962.

_____. *Some Input Refinements for a Residential Model*. Chapel Hill, N.C.: University of North Carolina, Institute for Research in Social Science, Center for Urban and Regional Studies, July 1965.

_____, eds. *Urban Growth Dynamics in a Regional Cluster of Cities*. New York: John Wiley & Sons, 1962.

Chicago Area Transportation Study. *Final Report*. Chicago, Ill.: CATS, 1960.

Chorley, Richard J. and Peter Haggett. *Models in Geography*. London: Methuen & Co., 1971.

Crecine, John P. "A Time Oriented Metropolitan Model for Spatial Location." *CRP Technical Bulletin*, No. 6. Pittsburgh: Department of City Planning, 1964.

Creighton, Robert L. *Urban Transportation Planning*. Urbana, Ill.: University of Illinois Press, 1970.

Cripps, E.L., ed. *Space-Time Concepts in Urban and Regional Models*. London: Pion Publishers, 1974.

Czamanski, Stan. *Regional Science Techniques in Practice*. Lexington, Mass.: Lexington Books, D.C. Heath and Company, 1972.

David, Martin H. *Household Composition and Consumption*. Amsterdam: North-Holland Publishing Company, 1962.

de Leeuw, Frank. *The Distribution of Housing Services*. Paper 208-6. Washington, D.C.: The Urban Institute, 1972.

Donnelly, Thomas G., F. Stuart Chapin, Jr. and Shirley F. Weiss. *A Probabilistic Model for Residential Growth*. Chapel Hill: Center for Urban and Regional Studies, University of North Carolina, May 1964.

Dorfman, Robert, Paul A. Samuelson and Robert M. Solow. *Linear Programming and Economic Analysis*. New York: McGraw-Hill, 1958.

Downs, Anthony. *Urban Problems and Prospects*. Chicago, Ill.: Markham Publishing Company, 1973.

Dunn, Edgar S. *The Location of Agricultural Production*. Gainsville, Fla.: University of Florida Press, 1954.

Evans, Alan W. *The Economics of Residential Location*. London: The MacMillan Press, 1973.

Fellmeth, Robert C., ed. *Politics of Land—Ralph Nader's Study Group Report on Land Use in California*. New York: Grossman Publishers, 1973.

Firey, Walter. *Land Use in Central Boston*. Cambridge, Mass.: Harvard University Press, 1947.

Foote, Nelson W., et al. *Housing Choices and Housing Constraints*. New York: McGraw-Hill, 1960.

Forrester, Jay W. *Urban Dynamics*. Cambridge, Mass.: The M.I.T. Press, 1969.

Garrison, William L., Brian J.L. Berry, Duane F. Marble, John D. Nystuen and Richard L. Morril. *Studies of Highway Development and Geographic Change*. Seattle: University of Washington Press, 1959.

Gillies, James, ed. *Essays in Urban Land Economics*. Los Angeles: University of California Press, Real Estate Research Program, 1966.

Goldner, W. *Projective Land Use Model (PLUM): A Model for the Spatial Allocation of Activities and Land Uses in a Metropolitan Region*. Technical Report 219. Berkeley: Bay Area Transportation Study Commission, September 1968.

Goodal, Brian. *The Economics of Urban Areas*. New York: Pergamon Press, 1972.

Gottman, Jean. *Megalopolis*. Cambridge, Mass.: The M.I.T. Press, 1961.

Graybeal, R.S. *A Simulation Model of Residential Development*. Berkeley: University of California Press, 1966.

Grebler, Leo, David M. Blank and Louis Winnick. *Capital Formation in Residential Real Estate: Trends and Prospects*. Princeton, N.J.: Princeton University Press, 1956.

Green, Robert N. *An Analysis of Household Locational and Tripmaking Behavior*. Washington D.C.: Urban Mass Transportation Administration, 1971.

Greenhut, M.L. *Microeconomics and the Space Economy*. Chicago: Scott Foresman and Company, 1963.

Grigsby, William G. *Housing Markets and Public Policy*. Philadelphia, Penn.: University of Pennsylvania Press, 1963.

Haggett, Peter. *Locational Analysis in Human Geography*. London: Edward Arnold Ltd., 1967.

Haig, Robert M. *Regional Survey of New York and Its Environs*. New York: New York City Plan Commission, 1927.

Hall, Peter. *von Thünen's Isolated State*. Oxford: Pergamon Press, 1966.

Hamburg, John R. and Robert H. Sharkey. *Land Use Forecast*. Document No. 32. Chicago, Ill.: Chicago Area Transportation Study, 1961.

Harberger, Arnold C., ed. *The Demand for Durable Goods*. Chicago, Ill.: The University of Chicago Press, 1960.

Harris, Britton. *Linear Programming and the Projection of Land Uses*. Paper No. 20. Philadelphia: Penn-Jersey Transportation Study, 1962.

_____, Joseph Nathanson and Louis Rosenberg. *Research on an Equilibrium Model of Metropolitan Housing and Locational Choice*. Interim Report. Philadelphia: University of Pennsylvania, 1966.

Harrison, David and John F. Kain. *An Historical Model of Urban Form*. Discussion paper No. 63. Cambridge, Mass.: Harvard University, Program on Regional and Urban Economics, September 1970.

Hauser, Philip M. and Leo F. Schnore, eds. *The Study of Urbanization*. New York: John Wiley & Sons, 1965.

Hawley, Amos H. *Human Ecology: A Theory of Community Structure*. New York: The Ronald Press Company, 1950.

_____. *Urban Society—An Ecological Approach*. New York: The Ronald Press Company, 1971.

Hirsch, Werner. *Urban Economic Analysis*. New York: McGraw-Hill, 1973.

Hoover, Edgar M. *An Introduction to Regional Economics*. New York: Alfred A. Knopf, 1971.

_____ and Raymond Vernon. *Anatomy of a Metropolis*. Garden City, N.J.: Anchor Books, Doubleday and Company, 1962.

Hoyt, Homer. *One Hundred Years of Land Values in Chicago*. Chicago: University of Chicago Press, 1933.

_____. *The Structure and Growth of Residential Neighborhoods in American Cities*. Washington D.C.: Federal Housing Administration, 1939.

_____. *Where the Rich and the Poor People Live*. Technical Bulletin No. 55. Washington D.C.: Urban Land Institute, 1966.

Huff, David L. *Determination of Intraurban Retail Trade Areas*. Los Angeles: University of California, Real Estate Research Program, 1962.

Hurd, R.M. *Principles of City Land Values*. New York: The Record and Guide, 1903.

Ingram, Gregory K., John F. Kain and J. Royce Ginn. *The Detroit Prototype of the NBER Urban Simulation Model*. New York: National Bureau of Economic Research, 1973.

Isard, Walter. *Location and Space Economy*. Cambridge, Mass.: The M.I.T. Press, 1956.

_____. *Methods of Regional Analysis: An Introduction to Regional Science*. New York: John Wiley & Sons, 1960.

James, Franklin J., ed. *Models of Employment and Residence Location*. New Brunswick: Rutgers University, Center for Urban Policy Research, 1974.

_____ and James W. Hughes. *Economic Growth and Residential Patterns*. New Brunswick: Rutgers University Center for Urban Policy Research, 1972.

Johnson, James H. *Urban Geography*. New York: Pergamon Press, 1967.

_____. *Urban Residential Patterns*. New York: Praeger, 1971.

Kain, John F. *The Journey-to-Work as a Determinant of Residential Location*. Paper P-2489. Santa Monica, California: The RAND Corporation, December 1961.

_____. *A Multiple Equation Model of Household Locational and Tripmaking Behavior*. Memorandum RM-3086-FF. Santa Monica, California: The RAND Corporation, April, 1962.

_____. *Theories of Residential Location and Realities of Race*. Discussion Paper No. 47. Cambridge Mass.: Harvard University Program on Regional and Urban Economics, 1969.

_____ and J.R. Meyer. *A First Approximation to a RAND Model for Study of Urban Transportation*. Memorandum RM-2878-FF. Santa Monica: The RAND Corporation, 1961.

Kaiser, Edward J. *A Producer Model for Residential Growth Analyzing and Predicting the Location of Residential Subdivisions*. Chapel Hill: University of North Carolina, Institute of Research in Social Science, Center for Urban and Regional Studies, November 1968.

Keiper, J.A., E. Kurnow, C.D. Clark and H.H. Segal. *Theory and Mea-*

170

surement of Rent. Philadelphia, Penn.: Chilton Company, 1961.

Lansing, John B. *Residential Location and Urban Mobility: The Second Wave of Interviews*. Ann Arbor: University of Michigan, Institute for Social Research, Survey Research Center, January 1966.

_____ and Gary Hendricks. *Automobile Ownership and Residential Density*. Ann Arbor: The University of Michigan, Survey Research Center, Institute for Social Research, 1967.

_____ and Eva Mueller. *Residential Location and Urban Mobility*. Ann Arbor: The University of Michigan, Institute for Social Research, Survey Research Center, June 1964.

Launhardt, Wilhelm. *Mathematische Begrundung Der Volkswirtschaftslehre*. Leipzig: B.G. Teubner, 1885.

Lefeber, Louis. *Allocation in Space*. Amsterdam: North-Holland Publishing Company, 1958.

Loewenstein, Louis K. *The Location of Residences and Work Places in Urban Areas*. New York: Scarecrow Press, 1965.

Lowry, Ira S. *A Model of Metropolis*. Memorandum RM-4035-RC. Santa Monica, California: The RAND Corporation, August 1964.

Luce, R. Duncan. *Individual Choice Behavior—A Theoretical Analysis*. New York: John Wiley & Sons, 1959.

_____ and Howard Raiffa. *Games and Decisions*. New York: John Wiley & Sons, Inc., 1958.

Lynd, Robert S. and Helen M. Lynd. *Middletown*. New York: Harcourt and Brace, 1929.

_____ and Helen M. Lynd. *Middletown in Transition*. New York: Harcourt and Brace, 1937.

Mann, Peter H. *An Approach to Urban Sociology*. London: Humanities Press, 1965.

Marshall, Alfred. *Principles of Economics*. London: MacMillan, 7th edition, 1916.

Martin, Leslie and Lionel March, eds. *Urban Space and Structures*. Cambridge: Cambridge University Press, 1972.

McKenzie, Roderick D. *The Metropolitan Community*. New York: McGraw-Hill Book Company, 1933.

Medvedkov, Yuri. *Space Consumption as a Specific Viewpoint of Geography in Forecasting Skills*. Coulston Research Society Papers. Bristol: Symposium on Regional Forecasting, April 1970.

Menchik, Mark D. *Residential Environmental Preferences and Choice: Some Preliminary Empirical Results Relevant to Urban Form*. RSRI Discussion Paper Series No. 46, Philadelphia: Regional Science Research Institute, March 1971.

Meyer, John R. and Mahlon R. Straszheim. *Pricing and Project Evaluation*. Washington D.C.: The Brookings Institution, 1971.

______, John F. Kain and Martin Wohl. *The Urban Transportation Problem*. Cambridge, Mass.: Harvard University Press, 1966.

Meyerson, Martin, Barbara Terrett and W.L.C. Whearon. *Housing, People and Cities*. New York: McGraw-Hill Book Company, 1962.

Mill, John Stuart. *Principles of Political Economy*. New York: Longmans, Green, 1929.

Mills, Edwin S. *Studies in the Structure of the Urban Economy*. Baltimore: Johns Hopkins Press, 1972.

______. *Urban Economics*. Glenview, Ill.: Scott, Foresman and Company, 1972.

Mogridge, M.J.H. *A Discussion of Some of the Factors Influencing the Income Distribution of Households Within a City Region*. Working Paper CES-WP-7. London, N.W.1: Centre for Environmental Studies, July 1968.

Moore, Eric. *Models of Residential Location and Relocation in the City*. Paper No. 20, Evanston, Ill.: Northwestern University, Studies in Geography, 1973.

Muth, Richard F. *Cities and Housing: The Spatial Pattern of Urban Residential Land Use*. Chicago: The University of Chicago Press, 1969.

Netzer, Dick. *Economics and Urban Problems*. New York: Basic Books, 1970.

Niedercorn, John. *An Econometric Model of Metropolitan Employment and Population Growth*. Report RM-3758-RC. Santa Monica, California: RAND Corporation, October 1963.

Norborg, Knut. *Proceedings of the IGU Symposium in Urban Geography*. Lund, Sweden: C.W.K. Gleerup Publishers, 1960.

Page, Alfred N. and Warren R. Seyfried, eds. *Urban Analysis*. Glenview, Ill.: Scott, Foresman and Co., 1970.

Papandreou, Andreas G. *Economics as a Science*. Chicago: J.B. Lippincott Company, 1958.

Park, Robert E., Ernest W. Burgess, and Roderick D. McKenzie. *The City*. Chicago: The University of Chicago Press, 1925.

Phillips, Bernard S. *Social Research-Stragegy and Tactics*, 2nd Editon. New York: The MacMillan Co., 1971.

Quinn, James. *Human Ecology*. Englewood Cliffs, N.J.: Prentice-Hall, Inc., 1950.

Rapkin, Chester. *The Real Estate Market in an Urban Renewal Area*. New

York: The City Planning Commission, 1959.

_____ and William G. Grigsby. *Residential Renewal in the Urban Core*. Philadelphia: University of Pennsylvania Press, 1960.

Ratcliff, Richard U. *Urban Land Economics*. New York: McGraw-Hill Book Company, 1949.

Reid, Benjamin. *Models in Urban and Regional Planning*. New York: Intertext Educational Publishers, 1973.

Reid, Margaret G. *Housing and Income*. Chicago: The University of Chicago Press, 1962.

Reilly, William J. *The Law of Retail Gravitation*. New York: Reilly, 1931.

Ricardo, David. *On the Principles of Political Economy and Taxation*. Georgetown, Washington D.C.: J. Milligan, 1819.

Richardson, Harry W. *Regional Economics*. New York: Praeger Publishers, 1969.

_____. *Urban Economics*. Baltimore, Md.: Pergamon Books, Inc., 1971.

Rickert, John E. *The Present and Potential Role of State and Local Taxation in the Preservation or Development of Open Space in Urban Fringe Areas*. Washington D.C.: Urban Land Institute, December 1965.

Rose, Arnold M. *Theory and Method in the Social Sciences*. Minneapolis: The University of Minnesota Press, 1954.

Rose, Harold. *Social Processes in the City: Race and Residential Choice*. Association of American Geographers, Resource Paper No. 6. Washington D.C.: Commission on College Geography, 1969.

Rose, Jerome. *Landlords and Tenants: A Complete Guide to the Residential Rental Relationship*. New Brunswick: Rutgers University, Center for Urban Policy Research, 1973.

Rothenberg, Jerome. *Economic Evaluation of Urban Renewal*. Washington D.C.: The Brookings Institution, 1967.

Schafer, Robert. *The Suburbanization of Multi-Family Housing*. Lexington, Mass.: Lexington Books, D.C. Heath and Company, 1974.

Schmid, A. Allan. *Converting Land from Rural to Urban Uses*. Baltimore, Maryland: The Johns Hopkins Press, 1968.

Schwirian, Kent P. *Comparative Urban Structure: Studies in the Ecology of Cities*. Lexington, Mass.: Lexington Books, D.C. Heath and Company, 1974.

Scientific American. *Cities*. New York: Alfred A. Knopf, 1966.

Seidman, David R. *The Construction of an Urban Growth Model*. DVRPC Plan Report No. 1, Technical Supplement, Vol. A. Philadelphia: Delaware Valley Regional Planning Commission, 1969.

Seigel, Jay. *Intrametropolitan Migration of White and Minority Group Households*. Stanford, California: Stanford University Press, 1970.

173

Smith, Adam. *The Wealth of Nations*. New York: Dutton, Everyman's Library Edition, Vol. I and II, 1910.

Smith, Wallace F. *Filtering and Neighborhood Change*. Research Report 24. Berkeley: University of California, Center for Real Estate and Urban Economics, 1964.

_____. *Housing*. Berkeley: The University of California Press, 1971.

Southeastern Wisconsin Regional Planning Commission. *Technical Record*, Vol. II, No. 1. Waukesha, Wisconsin: The Commission, 1964.

Spengler, J.J. and O.D. Duncan, eds. *Population Theory and Policy*. Glencoe, Ill.: Free Press, 1956.

Sraffa, Piero, ed. *The Works and Correspondence of David Ricardo*. Vol. I—Principles. Cambridge: The University Press, 1951.

Straszheim, Mahlon. *The Demand for Residential Housing Service.* Discussion Paper No. 192. Cambridge, Mass.: Harvard University, Harvard Institute for Economic Research, June 1971.

Sweet, David C. *Models of Urban Structure*. Lexington, Mass.: Lexington Books, D.C. Heath and Company, 1972.

Thompson, Wilbur R. *A Preface to Urban Economics*. Baltimore: The John Hopkins Press, 1968.

Tinbergen, Jan. *Economic Policy: Principles and Design*. Amsterdam: North-Holland Publishing Company, 1956.

von Thünen, J.H. *Der isolierte Staat in Beziehung auf Landwirtschaft und Nationalekonomie*. Hamburg: Fr. Perthes, 1826.

Voorhees, Alan M., G.B. Sharpe and J.T. Stegmaier. *Shopping Habits and Travel Patterns*. Special Report No. 11-B. Washington D.C.: Highway Research Board, 1955.

Webber, Michael J. *Impact of Uncertainty on Location*. Cambridge: The M.I.T. Press, 1972.

Weimer, Arthur M. and Homer Hoyt. *Principles of Real Estate*. New York: The Ronald Press Company, 1960.

Wickseel, Kunt. *Leisure on Political Economy,* Vol. I. London: Routlege, 1935.

Wicksteed, Philip H. *An Essay on the Coordination of the Laws of Distribution*. London: 1894. (Reprinted by the London School of Economics and Political Science, London, 1932).

Wilson, A.G. *Urban and Regional Models in Geography and Planning*. London: John Wiley and Sons, Ltd., 1974.

Wingo, Lowdon, Jr. *Transportation and Urban Land*. Baltimore: Johns Hopkins Press, 1961.

Zoller, Henry G. *Localisation Résidentielle: Décision des Ménages et Développement Suburbain*. Bruxelles: Les Editions Vie Ouvrière, 1972.

Articles

Adams, F. Gerald, Grace Milgram, Edward W. Green and Christine Mans-
field. "Undeveloped Land Prices During Urbanization: A Micro-
empirical Study Over Time." *The Review of Economics and Statistics*
50, 2 (May 1968): 248-258.

Alonso, William. "Equilibrium of the Household." Alfred N. Page and
Warren R. Seyfried, eds. *Urban Analysis*, Glenview, Ill.: Scott, Foresman and Company, 1970, pp. 168-177.

_____. "A Reformulation of Classical Location Theory, and Its Relation
to Rent Theory." *Regional Science Association Papers* 19 (1967): 23-44.

_____. "A Theory of the Urban Land Market." *Papers and Proceedings
of the Regional Science Association* 6 (1960): 149-157.

Amson, J.C. "Equilibrium and Catastrophic Modes of Urban Growth."
E.L. Cripps, ed. *Space-Time Concepts in Urban and Regional Models*.
London: Pion Publishers, 1974.

Anas, A. "A Dynamic Disequilibrium Model of Residential Location."
Environment and Planning 5, 5 (1975): 633-647.

Anderson, Theodore R. "Intermetropolitan Migration: A Comparison of
the Hypotheses of Zipf and Stouffer." *American Sociological Review*
20, 3 (June 1955): 287-291.

_____. "Potential Models and Spatial Distribution of Population." *Pa-
pers, Regional Science Association* 2 (1956): 175-182.

_____. "Social and Economic Factors Affecting the Location of Residen-
tial Neighborhoods." *Papers and Proceedings of the Regional Science
Association* 9 (1962): 161-170.

Angel, Shlomo and Geoffrey Hyman. "Urban Transport Expenditures."
Papers of the Regional Science Association 29 (1972): 105-123.

Apps, Patricia F. "An Approach to Urban Modeling and Evaluation—A
Residential Model: 1. Theory." *Environment and Planning* 5, 5 (1973):
619-632.

_____. "An Approach to Urban Modelling and Evaluation—A Residen-
tial Model: 2. Implicit Prices for Housing Services." *Environment and
Planning* 5, 6 (1973): 705-717.

_____. "An Approach to Urban Modelling and Evaluation—A Residen-
tial Model: 3. Demand Equations for Housing Services." *Environment
and Planning A* 6, 1 (1974): 11-31.

Bahl, Roy W. "A Land Speculation Model: The Role of the Property Tax
as a Constraint to Urban Sprawl." *Journal of Regional Science* 8, 2
(1968): 199-208.

Batty, M., R. Bourke, P. Cormodey, and M. Anderson-Nicholls. "Experiments in Urban Modelling for County Structure Planning: The Area 8 Pilot Model." *Environment and Planning A* 6, 4 (1974): 455-478.

Beckmann, Martin J. "On the Distribution of Urban Rent and Residential Density." *Journal of Economic Theory* 1, 1(June 1969): 60-67.

_____. "Spatial Cournot Oligopoly." *Papers, The Regional Science Association* 28 (1972): 37-47.

_____. "Spatial Equilibrium in the Housing Market." *Journal of Urban Economics* 1, 1 (January 1974): 99-107.

_____. "Von Thünen Revisited: A Neoclassical Land Use Model." *The Swedish Journal of Economics* 74, 1 (March 1972): 1-7.

Berry, Brian J.L. "Cities as Systems within Systems of Cities." *Papers of the Regional Science Association* 13 (1964): 147-163.

_____, James W. Simmons, and Robert J. Tennant. "Urban Population Densities: Structure and Change." *Geographical Review* 53, 3 (July 1963): 389-405.

Blumenfeld, Hans. "Are Land Use Patterns Predictable?" *Journal of the American Institute of Planners* 25, 2 (May 1959): 61-66.

_____. "The Tidal Wave of Metropolitan Expansion." *Journal of the American Institute of Planners* 20, 1 (February 1954): 3-14.

Boulding, Kenneth E. "Toward a General Theory of Growth." J.J. Spengler and O.D. Duncan, eds. *Population Theory and Policy*. Glencoe, Ill.: Free Press, 1956, pp. 109-124.

Bourne, L.S. "Apartment Location and the Housing Market." Larry S. Bourne, ed. *Internal Structure of the City*. New York: Oxford University Press, 1971, pp. 321-328.

Boyce, Ronald R. "Residential Mobility and Its Implications for Urban Spatial Change." Larry S. Bourne, ed. *Internal Structure of the City*. New York: Oxford University Press, 1971, pp. 338-343.

Boyes, William J. and Dennis E. Peseau. "On Optimization in Models of Urban Land Use Densities: A Comment." *Journal of Regional Science* 13, 1 (1973): 129-133.

Brigham, Eugene F. "The Determinants of Residential Land Values." *Land Economics* 41, 4 (November 1965): 325-334.

Burgess, Ernest W. "The Determination of Gradients in the Growth of the City.: *The American Sociological Society, Papers and Proceedings* 21 (1926): 178-184.

_____. "The Growth of the City." *American Sociological Society– Papers and Proceedings* 18 (1923): 85-99.

Carey, George W. "The Regional Interpretation of Manhattan Population and Housing Patterns Through Factor Analysis." *Geographical Review* 56, 4 (Oct. 1966): 551-569.

Carroll, J. Douglas, Jr. "The Relation of Homes to Work Places and the Spatial Patterns of Cities." *Social Forces* 30, 3 (March 1952): 271-282.

_____. "Spatial Interaction and the Urban-Metropolitan Description." *Papers and Proceedings of the Regional Science Association* 1 (1955): D-1 to DD-14.

Carrothers, Gerald A.P. "An Historical Review of the Gravity and Potential Concepts of Human Interaction." *Journal of the American Institute of Planners* 22, 2 (Spring 1956): 94-102.

Casetti, Emilio. "Equilibrium Land Values and Population Densities in an Urban Setting." *Economic Geography* 47, 1 (January 1971): 16-20.

_____. "On the Derivation of Spatial Equilibrium Urban Land Value Functions." David C. Sweet, ed. *Models of Urban Structure.* Lexington, Mass.: Lexington Books, D.C. Heath and Company, 1972, pp.123-133.

Chapin, F. Stuart. "A Model for Stimulating Residential Development." *Journal of the American Institute of Planners* 31, 2 (May 1965): 120-125.

_____, and H.C. Hightower. "Household Activity Patterns and Land Use." *Journal of the American Institute of Planners* 31, 3 (August 1965): 222-231.

_____, and Shirley F. Weiss. "Land Development Patterns and Growth Alternatives." *Urban Growth Dynamics in a Regional Cluster of Cities.* New York: John Wiley & Sons, Inc., 1962, pp. 425-458.

Clark, Colin. "Urban Population Densities." *Bulletin d'Institut International de Statistique* 36, part 4 (1958): 60-68.

_____. "Urban Population Densities." *Journal of the Royal Statistical Society–Series A* 114, Part 4 (1951): 490-496.

Clark, W.A.V. and Martin Cadwallader. "Locational Stress and Residential Mobility." *Environment and Behavior* 5, 1 (March 1973): 29-41.

Coughlin, Robert F. "A Note on Intra-Areal Linear Programming for a Metropolitan Area." *Journal of Regional Science* 1, 2 (Spring 1959): 75-83.

Czamanski, Stan. "A Model of Urban Land Allocation." *Growth and Change* 4, 1 (Jan. 1973): 43-48.

_____. "The Effects of Public Investments on Urban Land Values." *Journal of the American Institute of Planners* 32, 4 (July 1966): 204-217.

_____. "Regional Science and Regional Planning." *Plan, Journal of the Town Planning Institute of Canada* 9, 2 (July 1968): 52-66.

Dacey, Michael. "Some Comments on Population Density Models, Tractable and Otherwise." *The Regional Science Association Papers* 27 (1971): 119-133.

Dantzig, George B. "Maximization of a Linear Function of Variables subject to Linear Inequalities." T.C. Koopmans, ed. *Activity Analysis of Production and Allocation.* New York: John Wiley & Sons, Inc., 1951, pp. 339-347.

Davie, Maurice R. "The Patterns of Urban Growth." G.P. Murdock, ed. *Studies in the Science of Society.* New Haven: Yale University Press, 1937.

Dixit, Avinash. "The Optimum Factory Town." *The Bell Journal of Economics and Management Science* 4, 2 (Autumn 1973): 637-651.

Downing, Paul B. "Estimating Residential Land Value by Multivariate Analysis." D.M. Holland, ed. *The Assessment of Land Value.* Madison, Wisconsin: The University of Wisconsin Press, 1970, pp. 101-123.

Duncan, Beverly and Otis Dudley Duncan. "The Measurement of Intracity Locational and Residential Patterns." *Journal of Regional Science* 2, 2 (1960): 37-54.

Duncan Otis D. and Beverly Duncan. "Residential Distribution and Occupational Stratification." *American Journal of Sociology* 60, 5 (March 1955): 493-503.

Echenique, M., A. Feo, R. Herrera and J. Riquezes. "A Disaggregated Model of Urban Spatial Structure: Theoretical Framework." *Environment and Planning A* 6, 1 (1974): 33-63.

Ellis, R.H. "Modeling of Household Location: A Statistical Approach." *Highway Research Record*, No. 207, 1967, pp. 42-51.

Fales, Raymond L. and Leon N. Moses. "Land-Use Theory and the Spatial Structure of the Nineteenth-Century City." *Papers, The Regional Science Association* 28 (1972): 49-80.

Fisch, Oscar. "Impact Analysis on Optimal Urban Densities and Optimal City Size." *Journal of Regional Science* 14, 2 (1974): 233-246.

Fox, Karl A. and Erik Thorbecke. "Specification of Structures and Data Requirements in Policy Models." Bert G. Hickman, ed. *Quantitative Planning of Economic Policy.* Washington D.C.: The Brookings Institution, 1965, pp. 279+.

Frieden, Bernard J. "Locational Preferences in the Urban Housing Market." *Journal of the American Institute of Planners* 27, 4 (Nov. 1961): 316-324.

Gaffney, M. "Land Rent, Taxation and Public Policy." *Papers, Regional Science Association* 23 (1969): 141-153.

178

Gans, Herbert J. "The Balanced Community: Homogeneity or Heterogeneity in Residential Areas." *Journal of the American Institute of Planners* 27, 3 (Aug. 1961): 176-184.

Garrison, William Louis. "Urban Transportation Planning Models in 1975." *Journal of the American Institute of Planners* 31, 2 (1965): 156-158.

––––––. "Verification of a Location Model." *Northwestern University Studies in Geography*, No. 2 (1957): 133-140.

Goldberg, M.A. "An Economic Model of Intrametropolitan Industrial Location." *Journal of Regional Science* 10, 1 (April 1970): 75-80.

Goldman, S.M. and H. Uzawa. "A Note on Separability in Demand Analysis." *Econometrica* 32, 3 (July 1964): 387-398.

Gordon, Peter and William K. MacReynolds. "Optimal Urban Forms." *Journal of Regional Science* 14, 2 (1974): 217-231.

Gorman, W.M. "Separable Utility and Aggregation." *Econometrica* 23, 3 (1959): 469-481.

Gottlieb, Manuel, "Influences on Value in Urban Land Markets, U.S.A., 1956-1961." *Journal of Regional Science* 6, 1 (1965): 1-16.

Guttenbert, Albert Z. "Urban Structure and Urban Growth." *Journal of the American Institute of Planners* 26, 2 (May 1960): 104-110.

Haig, Robert M. "Toward an Understanding of the Metropolis." *Quarterly Journal of Economics* 40, 1 (Feb. 1926): 179-208; and No. 3 (May 1926): 402-434.

Hale, C.W. "Impact of Technological Change on Urban Market Areas, Land Values, and Land Uses." *Land Economics* 43, 3 (August 1973): 351-356.

Hamburg, John R. "Land Use Projection and Predicting Future Traffic." Highway Research Board. *Bulletin*, No. 224, "Trip Characteristics and Traffic Assignment," 1959, pp. 72-84.

–––––– and Roger L. Creighton. "Predicting Chicago's Land Use Pattern," *Journal of the American Institute of Planners* 25, 2 (May 1959): 67-72.

–––––– and Robert H. Sharkey. "Chicago's Changing Land Use and Population Structures." *Journal of the American Institute of Planners* 26, 4 (November 1960): 317-323.

Hansen, Walter. "How Accessibility Shapes Land Use." *Journal of the American Institute of Planners* 25, 2 (May 1959): 73-76.

Hansen, Willard B. "An Approach to the Analysis of Metropolitan Residential Extension." Alfred N. Page and Warren R. Seyfried, eds. *Urban Analysis.* Glenview, Ill.: Scott, Foresman and Co., 1970, pp. 226-243.

Harris, Britton. "Conference Summary and Recommendations." Highway Research Board: *Urban Development Models*. Special Report No. 97 (Proceedings of the Dartmouth Conference). Washington D.C.: Highway Research Board, 1968, pp. 3-17.

_____. "A Note on the Probability of Interaction at a Distance." *Journal of Regional Science* 5, 2 (1964): 31-35.

_____. "Quantitative Models of Urban Development: Their Role in Metropolitan Policy-Making." Harvey S. Perloff and Lowdon Wingo, Jr., eds. *Issues in Urban Economics*. Baltimore: The Johns Hopkins Press, 1968, pp. 363-431.

Harris, Chauncy D. and E.L. Ullman. "The Nature of Cities." *The Annals of the American Academy of Political and Social Sciences* 242 (Nov. 1945): 7-17.

Harris, Curtis C., Jr. "A Stochastic Process Model of Residential Development." *Journal of Regional Science* 8, 1 (1968): 29-39.

Harris, R.N.S., G.S. Tolley, and C. Harrell. "The Residence Site Choice." *The Review of Economics and Statistics* 50, 2 (May 1968): 241-247.

Harvey, Robert O. and W.A.V. Clark. "The Nature and Economics of Urban Sprawl." Larry S. Bourne, ed. *Internal Structure of the City*. New York: Oxford University Press, 1971, pp. 475-482.

Hatt, Paul. "The Concept of Natural Area." *American Sociological Review* 11, 4 (1946): 423-427.

Herbert, John D. and Benjamin H. Stevens. "A Model for the Distriburion of Residential Activity in Urban Areas." *Journal of Regional Science* 2, 2 (1960): 21-36.

Hicks, J.R. "Direct and Indirect Additivity." *Econometrica* 37, 2 (April 1969): 353-354.

Hill, Donald M. "A Growth Allocation Model for the Boston Region." *Journal of the American Institute of Planners* 31, 2 (May 1965): 111-120.

_____, Daniel Brand and Willard B. Hansen. "Prototype Development of a Statistical Land Use Prediction Model for the Greater Boston Region." *Highway Research Record*, No. 114 (1965): 51-70.

Hoch, Irving. "The Three-dimensional City: Contained Urban Space." Harvey S. Perloff, ed. *The Quality of the Urban Environment*. Washington D.C.: Resources for the Future, 1962, pp. 75-135.

Hoover, Edgar M. "The Evolving Form and Organization of the Metropolis." Harvey S. Perloff and Lowdon Wingo, Jr., eds. *Issues in Urban Economics*. Baltimore: Johns Hopkins Press, 1968, pp. 237-284.

Houthakker, H.S. "A Note on Self-Dual Preferences." *Econometrica* 33, 4 (October 1965): 797-801.

Huff, David L. "A Probabilistic Analysis of Shopping Center Trading Areas." *Land Economics* 53, 1 (February 1963): 81-90.

Irwin, N.A. "Review of Existing Land-Use Forecasting Techniques." *Highway Research Record,* No. 88, 1965, pp. 182-216.

Isard, Walter. "Regional Science, the Concept of Region and Regional Structure." *Papers and Proceedings of the Regional Science Association* 2 (1956): 1-13.

_____ and Thomas A. Reiner. "Regional Science: Retrospect and Prospect." *Regional Science Association Papers* 16 (1966): 1-16.

Johnston, M. Bruce. "Travel Time and the Price of Leisure." *Western Economic Journal* 4, 2 (Spring 1966): 135-145.

Jurkat, Ernest H. "Land Use in Traffic Planning." *Traffic Quarterly* 11, 2 (1957): 151-163.

Kain, John F. "The Distribution and Movement of Jobs and Industry." James Q. Wilson, ed. *The Metropolitan Enigma*. Cambridge, Mass.: Harvard University Press, 1968, pp. 1-33.

_____. "The Journey-to-Work as a Determinant of Residential Location." *Papers and Proceedings of the Regional Science Association* 9 (1962): 137-160.

_____. "Postwar Metropolitan Development: Housing Preferences and Auto Ownership." *American Economic Review* 57, 2 (May 1967): 223-234.

_____ and John M. Quigley. "Evaluating the Quality of the Residential Environment." *Environment and Planning* 2, 1 (1970): 23-32.

_____. "Measuring the Value of Housing Quality." *Journal of the American Statistical Association* 65, 330 (June 1970): 532-548.

Kaiser, Edward J. :Decision Agent Models: An Alternative Modeling Approach for Urban Residential Growth." David C. Sweet, ed. *Models of Urban Structure*. Lexington, Mass.: Lexington Books, D.C. Heath and Company, 1972, pp. 109-122.

_____ and Shirley F. Weiss. "Decision Agent Models of the Residential Development Process—A Review of Recent Research." *Traffic Quarterly* 23, 4 (October 1969): 597-632.

Karlqvist, A. and B. Marksjö. "Statistical Urban Models." *Environment and Planning* 3, 1 (1971): 83-98.

Kashuba, Edward N. "Land Use Models." Anthony Catanese, ed. *New Perspectives in Urban Transportation Research*. Lexington, Mass.: Lexington Books, D.C. Heath and Company, 1972, pp. 27-61.

Kish, Leslie. "Differentiation in Metropolitan Areas." *American Sociological Review* 19, 4, (August 1954): 388-398.

Kraus, Marvin. "Land Use in a Circular City." *Journal of Economic Theory* 8, 4 (August 1974): 440-457.

Lakshmanan, T.R. "A Model for Allocating Urban Activities in a State." *Socioeconomic Planning Sciences* 1, 3 (July 1968): 283-295.

_____, and Walter G. Hansen. "A Retail Market Potential Model." *Journal of the American Institute of Planners* 21, 2 (May 1965): 134-143.

Lancaster, K.J. "A New Approach to Consumer Theory." *Journal of Political Economy* 74, 2 (April 1966): 132-157.

Lansing, John B. and G. Hendricks. "How People Perceive the Cost of the Journey to Work." *Highway Research Record*, No. 197 (1967): 44-55.

Lathrop, George T. and John R. Hamburg. "An Opportunity-Accessibility Model for Allocating Regional Growth." *Journal of the American Institute of Planners* 31, 2 (May 1965): 95-103.

Lau, Lawrence J. "Duality and the Structure of Utility Functions." *Journal of Economic Theory* 1, 4 (December 1970): 374-396.

Lave, Lester B. "Congestion and Urban Location." *Papers and Proceedings of the Regional Science Association* 25 (1970): 133-150.

Lee, Tong Hung. "Housing and Permanent Income: Tests Based on a Three-Year Reinterview Survey." *The Review of Economics and Statistics* 50, 4 (Nov. 1968): 480-490.

_____. "The Stock Demand Elasticities of Non-Farm Housing." *The Review of Economics and Statistics* 46, 1 (February 1964): 82-89.

Leven, Charles L. "Determinants of the Size and Spatial Form of Urban Areas." *Regional Science Association Papers* 22 (1968): 7-28.

Liepmann, K. "Land Use, Location and Transport." *Manchester School of Economic and Social Studies* 23, 1 (Jan. 1955): 77-93.

Lombardini, Siro. "Urban Planning and the Housing Market." *Regional Science Association Papers* 29 (1972): 179-185.

Lowry, Ira S. "Seven Models of Urban Development: A Structural Comparison." Highway Research Board: *Urban Development Models,* Special Report No. 97 (Proceedings of the Dartmouth Conference), Washington D.C.: Highway Research Board, 1968, pp. 121-146.

Ludlow, William H. "Measurement and Control of Population Densities." Jack P. Gibbs, ed. *Urban Research Methods*. Princeton, New Jersey: D. Van Nostrand Company, Inc., 1961, pp. 86-99.

Lundqvist, Lars. "Integrated Location Transportation Analysis: A Decomposition Approach." *Regional and Urban Economics* 3, 3 (February 1973) 233-262.

MacPherson, I.C. "High Densities." *Journal of the Town Planning Institute* 49, 10 (December 1964): 446-449.

Marble, Duane F. "Highways and Urban Residential Land Use." William L. Garrison et al. *Studies of Highway Development and Geographic Change*. Seattle: University of Washington Press, 1959, pp. 141-177.

Margolis, Julius. "Discussion on Edwin S. Mills, An Aggregative Model of Resource Allocation in a Metropolitan Area." *American Economic Review* 57, 2 (May 1967): 235-237.

McKean, R.N. "An Outsider Looks at Urban Economics." *Urban Studies* 10, 1 (Feb. 1973): 19-37.

Medvedkov, Yuri. "Internal Structure of a City: An Ecological Assessment." *The Regional Science Association Papers* 27 (1971): 95-117.

Mertz, William L. and Lamelle B. Hamner. "A Study of Factors Related to Urban Travel." *Public Roads* 29 (1957): 170-174.

Michelson, William. "Most People Don't Want What Architects Want." *Trans-Action* 5, 6 (July-August 1968): 37-42.

Miller, A.J. "The Intervening-Opportunities Model Applied to Residential Land Use in a Uniform City." *Transportation Research* 4, 2 (July 1970): 145-149.

Mills, Edwin S. "An Aggregative Model of Resource Allocation in a Metropolitan Area." *American Economic Review* 57, 2 (1967): 197-241.

_____. "The Efficiency of Spatial Competition." *The Regional Science Association Papers* 25 (1970): 71-82.

_____. "Urban Density Functions." *Urban Studies* 7, 1 (Feb. 1970): 5-20.

_____. "The Value of Urban Land." Harvey S. Perloff, ed. *The Quality of the Urban Environment*. Baltimore: The Johns Hopkins Press, 1969, pp. 231-253.

_____ and James Mackinnon. "Notes on the New Urban Economics." *The Bell Journal of Economics and Management Science* 4, 2 (Autumn 1973): 593-601.

Mirrlees, J.A. "The Optimum Town." *The Swedish Journal of Economics* 74, 1 (March 1972): 114-135.

Mohring, H. "Land Values and the Measurement of Highway Benefits." *Journal of Political Economy* 69, 3 (June 1961): 236-249.

Montesano, Aldo. "A Restatement of Beckmann's Model on the Distribution of Urban Rent and Residential Density." *Journal of Economic Theory* 4, 2 (April 1972): 329-354.

Mooney, J.D. "Housing Segregation, Negro Employment and Metropolitan Decentralization: An Alternative Perspective." *Quarterly Journal of Economics* 83, 2 (May 1969): 299-311.

Morrill, Richard L. "Expansion of the Urban Fringe: A Simulation Experiment." *Papers of the Regional Science Association* 15, (1965): 185-199.

Muth, Richard. "The Demand for Non-Farm Housing." A.C. Harberger, ed. *The Demand of Durable Goods*. Chicago: The University of Chicago Press, 1960, pp. 29-96.

———. "The Distribution of Population Within Urban Areas." Robert Ferber, ed. *Determinants of Investment Behavior*. New York: National Bureau of Economic Research, 1967, pp. 271-299.

———. "Economic Change and Rural-Urban Land Conversions." *Econometrica* 29, 1 (1961): 1-23.

———. "Slums and Poverty." Adela Adam Nevitt, ed. *The Economic Problems of Housing*. New York: St. Martin's Press, 1967, pp. 12-26.

———. "The Spatial Structure of the Housing Market." *Papers and Proceedings of the Regional Science Association* 7 (1961): 207-220.

———. "Urban Residential Land and Housing Markets." H. Perloff and L. Wingo, eds. *Issues in Urban Economics*. Baltimore: Johns Hopkins Press, 1968, pp. 285-333.

———. "The Variation of Population Density and its Components in South Chicago." *Papers of the Regional Science Association* 15 (1965): 173-183.

———. "A Vintage Model of the Housing Stock." *The Regional Science Association Papers* 30 (1973): 141-156.

Nelson, R.H. "Accessibility and Rent: Applying Becker's 'Time Price' Concept to the Theory of Residential Location." *Urban Studies* 10, 1 (February 1973): 83-86.

Newling, Bruce E. "The Spatial Variation of Urban Population Densities." *Geographical Review* 59, 2 (April 1969): 242-252.

———. "Urban Growth and Spatial Structure: Mathematical Models and Empirical Evidence." *Geographical Review* 56, 2 (April 1966): 213-225.

Niedercorn, John H. "A Negative Exponential Model of Urban Land Use Densities and its Implications for Metropolitan Development." *Journal of Regional Science* 11, 3 (December 1971): 317-326.

———. "Reply." *Journal of Regional Science* 13, 1 (1973): 139-140.

——— and B.V. Bechdolt, Jr. "An Economic Derivation of the 'Gravity Law' of Spatial Interaction." *Journal of Regional Science* 9, 2 (1969): 273-282.

Olsen, Edgar O. "A Competitive Theory of the Housing Market." *American Economic Review* 59, 4, Part I, (September 1969): 612-622.

Oron, Yitzhak, David Pines and Eytan Sheshinski. "Optimum vs. Equilibrium Land Use Pattern and Congestion Toll." *The Bell Journal of Economics and Management Science* 4, 2 (Autumn 1973): 619-636.

Pahl, R.E. "Sociological Models in Geography." R.J. Chorley, and P.

Hagget eds. *Models in Geography*. London: Methuen and Co., Ltd., 1967, pp. 217-242.

Papageorgiou, George J. "A Generalization of the Population Density Gradient Concept." *Geographical Analysis* 3, 2 (1971): 121-127.

_____. "A Theoretical Evaluation of the Existing Population Density Gradient Functions." *Economic Geography* 47, 1 (January 1971): 21-26.

_____ and Emilio Casetti. "Spatial Equilibrium Rei Residential Land Values in a Multi-Center Setting." *Journal of Regional Science* 11, 3 (1971): 385-389.

Park, Robert E. "Sociology." Wilson Gee, ed., *Research in the Social Sciences*. New York: The Macmillan Company, 1926, pp. 3-49.

Peterson, George L. "A Model of Preference: Quantitative Analysis of the Perception of the Visual Appearance of Residential Neighborhoods." *Journal of Regional Science* 7, 1 (1967): 19-31.

Pollard, Leon. The Interrelationships of Selected Measures of Residential Density." *Journal of the American Institute of Planners* 20, 2 (Spring 1954): 87-94.

Putman, Stephen H. "Intraurban Industrial Location Model Design and Implementation." *The Regional Science Association Papers* 19 (1967): 199-214.

Ratcliff, R.M. "Commentary: On Wendt's Theory of Land Values." *Journal of Land Economics* 33, 4 (November 1957): 360-362.

Ratford, Bruce E. "A Note of Niedercorn's Negative Exponential Model of Urban Land Use." *Journal of Regional Science* 13, 1 (1973): 135-138.

Ridker, Ronald G. and John A. Henning. "The Determinants of Residential Property Values with Special Reference to Air Pollution." *The Review of Economics and Statistics* 49, 2 (May 1967): 246-257.

Ripper, N. and P. Varaiya. "An Optimizing Model of Urban Development." *Environment and Planning A* 6, 2 (1974): 149-168.

Robinson, Ira M., Harry B. Wolfe and Robert L. Barringer. "A Simulation Model For Renewal Programming." *Journal of the American Institute of Planners* 31, 2 (May 1965): 126-134.

Rodwin, Lloyd. "The Theory of Residential Growth and Structure." *The Appraisal Journal* 18, 3 (July 1950): 295-317.

Rothenberg, Jerome. "Consumers' Sovereignty Revisited and the Hospitality of Freedom of Choice." *American Economic Review* 52, 2 (May 1962): 269-283.

Row, Arthur, and Ernest Jurkat. "The Economic Forces Shaping Land Use Patterns." *Journal of the American Institute of Planners* 25, 2 (May 1959): 77-81.

185

Samuelson, Paul A. "Corrected Formulation of Direct and Indirect Additivity." *Econometrica* 37, 2 (April 1969): 355-359.

_____. "Using Full Duality to Show that Simultaneously Additive Direct and Indirect Utilities Implies Unitary Price Elasticity of Demand." *Econometrica* 33, 4 (October 1965): 781-796.

Schlager, Kenneth J. "A Land Use Plan Design Model." *Journal of the American Institute of Planners* 31, 2 (May 1965): 103-111.

Schneider, Morton. "Access and Land Development." George C. Hemmens, ed. *Urban Development Models*. Washington, D.C.: Highway Research Board, Special Report No. 97, 1968, pp. 164-177.

_____. "Gravity Models and Trip Distribution Theory." *Papers and Proceedings of the Regional Science Association* 5 (1969): 51-56.

Schnore, Leo F. and Hall H. Windsborough. "Functional Classification and the Residential Location of Social Classes." B.J.L. Berry, ed. *City Classification Handbook: Methods and Applications*. New York: Wiley-Interscience, 1972, pp. 124-151.

Schuler, Richard E. "The Interaction Between Local Government and Urban Residential Location." *The American Economic Review* 64, 4 (September 1974): 682-696.

Scitovsky, Tibor. "On the Principle of Consumers' Sovereignty." *American Economic Review* 52, 2 (May 1962): 262-268.

Senior, M.L. "Approaches to Residential Location Modeling 1: Urban Ecological and Spatial Interaction Models (A Review)." *Environment and Planning* 5, 2 (1973): 165-197.

_____. "Approaches to Residential Location Modeling 2: Urban Economic Models and Some Recent Developments (A Review)." *Environment and Planning A* 6, 9 (1974): 369-409.

_____. "A Further Note on Two Disaggregated Models of Residential Location." *Environment and Planning A* 6, 3 (1974): 355-357.

_____ and A.G. Wilson. "Disaggregated Residential Location Models; Some Tests and Further Theoretical Development." E.L.Cripps, ed. *Space-Time Concepts in Urban and Regional Models*. London: Pion Publishers, 1974.

Seyfried, Warren R. "The Centrality of Urban Land Values." *Land Economics* 39, 3 (August 1963): 275-284.

Sherman, J. Maisel and Louis Winnick. "Family Housing Expenditures: Elusive Laws and Intrusive Variances." Irwin Friend and Robert Jones, eds. *Study of Consumer Expenditures, Incomes and Savings*. (Proceedings of the Conference on Consumption and Savings, Vol. I). Philadelphia: University of Pennsylvania, 1960, pp. 359-435.

Simmons, James W. "Changing Residence in the City—A Review of Intraurban Mobility." *Geographical Review* 58, 4 (Oct. 1968): 622-651.

Solow, Robert M. "Congestion Cost and the Use of Land for Streets." *The Bell Journal of Economics and Management Science* 4, 2 (Autumn 1973): 602-618.

_____. "Congestion, Density and the Use of Land in Transportation." *The Swedish Journal of Economics* 74, 1 (March 1972): 161-173.

_____. "On Equilibrium Models of Urban Location." Michael Parkin, ed. *Essays in Modern Economics*. London: Longmans, 1973, pp. 1-16.

_____ and William S. Vickrey. "Land Use in a Long Narrow City." *Journal of Economic Theory* 3, 4 (December 1971): 430-447.

Steger, Wilbur A. "Review of Analytic Techniques for the CRP. *Journal of the American Institute of Planners* 31, 2 (May 1965): 166-172.

Stegman, Michael A. "Accessibility Models and Residential Location." *Journal of the American Institute of Planners* 35, 1 (January 1969): 22-29.

Steinnes, Donald N. and Walter D. Fisher. "An Econometric Model of Intraurban Location." *Journal of Regional Science* 14, 1 (1974): 65-80.

Sternlieb, George, Robert W. Burchell, James A. Hughes and Franklin J. James. "Housing Abandonment in the Urban Core." *Journal of the American Institute of Planners* 40, 5 (September 1974): 321-332.

Stewart, John Q. "Potential of Population and Its Relationship to Marketing." Reavis Cox and Wroe Anderson, eds. *Theory in Marketing*. Chicago: Richard D. Irwin, 1950, pp. 19-40.

_____ and William Warntz. "Physics of Population Distribution." *Journal of Regional Science* 1, 1 (1958): 99-123.

Stigler, George J. "The Development of Utility Theory." *The Journal of Political Economy*, Part I, 58, 4 (August 1950): 307-327; Part II, 58, 5 (October 1950): 373-396.

Stouffer, Samuel A. "Intervening Opportunities: A Theory Relating Mobility and Distance." *American Sociological Review* 5, 6 (December 1940): 845-867.

Strotz, Robert H. "The Utility Tree—A Correction and Further Appraisal." *Econometrica* 27, 3 (July 1959): 482-488.

Stull, William J. "A Note on Residential Bid Price Curves." *Journal of Regional Science* 13, 1 (1973): 107-113.

Swerdloff, C.N. and J.R. Stowers, "Test of Some First Generation Residential Land Use Models." *Public Roads* 34, 5 (Dec. 1966): 101-109.

Tiebout, Charles M. "Intraurban Location Problems: An Evaluation." Alfred N. Page and Warren R. Seyfried, eds. *Urban Analysis*. Glenview, Ill.: Scott, Foresman and Co., 1970, pp. 256-261.

Ullman, Edward L. "The Nature of Cities Reconsidered." *Papers and Proceedings of the Regional Science Association* 9 (1962): 7-23.

Upshaw, Harry S. "Attitude Measurement." Hubert M. Blalock, Jr. and Ann B. Blalock, eds. *Methodology in Social Research*. New York: McGraw-Hill Book Co., 1968.

Vernon, Raymond and Edgar M. Hoover. "Economic Aspects of Urban Research." Philip M. Hauser and Leo F. Schnore, eds. *The Study of Urbanization*. New York: John Wiley & Sons, 1965, pp. 191-207.

Walsh, Brian F. and Sigurd Grava. "A Dynamic Land Use Allocation Model." *Papers of the Association for Computer Machinery*—4th Annual Symposium on the Application of Computers to the Problems of Urban Society, New York, October 1969, pp. 62-118.

Weiss, Shirley F. and Thomas G. Donnelly. "Short-Range Residential Forecasts for Testing Public Policy." *Traffic Quarterly* 20, 3 (1966): 384-392.

Wendt, Paul F. "Economic Growth and Urban Land Values." *The Appraisal Journal* 26, 3 (July 1958): 427-443.

_____. "Theory of Urban Land Values." *Journal of Land Economics* 33, 3 (August 1967): 288-240.

_____. "Urban Land Value Trends." *The Appraisal Journal* 26, 2 (April 1958): 254-269.

_____ and William Goldner. "Land Values and the Dynamics of Residential Location." James Gillies, ed. *Essays in Urban Land Economics*. Los Angeles: University of California, Real Estate Research Program, 1966, pp. 188-213.

Wheeler, James O. "Residential Location by Occupational Status." Larry S. Bourne, ed. *Internal Structure of the City*. New York: Oxford University Press, 1971, pp. 309-315.

Wieand, Kenneth, F. "Air Pollution and Property Values: A Study of the St. Louis Area.: *Journal of Regional Science* 13, 1 (1973): 91-95.

_____ and Richard F. Muth. "A Note on the Variation of Land Values with Distance from the CBD in St. Louis." *Journal of Regional Science* 12, 3 (1972): 469-473.

Wilson, A.G. "Developments of Some Elementary Residential Location Models." *Journal of Regional Science* 9, 3 (1969): 377-385.

_____. "A Statistical Theory of Spatial Distribution Models." *Transportation Research* 1, 3 (November 1967): 253-269.

Wingo, Lowdon, Jr. "An Economic Model of the Utilization of Urban Land for Residential Purposes." *Papers and Proceedings of the Regional Science Association* 7 (1961): 191-205.

Winsborough, Hal. H. "City Growth and City Structure." *Journal of*

Regional Science 4, 2 (1962): 35-49.

Wirth, Louis. "A Bibliography of the Urban Community." R.E. Park, E.W. Burgess and R.D. Mckenzie, eds. *The City*. Chicago: The University of Chicago Press, 1925, pp. 161-228.

Yamada, Hiroyuki. "On the Theory of Residential Location: Accessibility, Space, Leisure, and Environmental Quality." *Papers of the Regional Science Association* 29 (1972): 125-135.

Zorbaugh, Harvey D. "The Natural Areas of the City.: E.W. Burgess, ed. *The Urban Community*. Chicago: The University of Chicago Press, 1926, pp. 219-229.

Bibliographies

Bartholomew, Robert. *Residential Environments and Human Behavior*. Exchange Bibliography No. 51. Monticello, Ill.: Council of Planning Librarians, 1973.

Bolan, Lewis. *The Role of Urban Planning in the Residential Integration of Middle Class Negroes and Whites*. Exchange Bibliography No. 41. Monticello, Ill.: Council of Planning Librarians, 1968.

Daniel, Robert E. *Local Residential Mobility: A Selected and Annotated Bibliography*. Exchange Bibliography No. 104. Monticello, Ill.: Council of Planning Librarians, November 1969.

Glance, Richard and Eric C. Freund. *The Urban Environment and Residential Satisfaction with an Emphasis on New Towns—An Annotated Bibliography*. Exchange Bibliography No. 429. Monticello, Ill.: Council of Planning Librarians, July 1973.

Hoggart, Keith. *Transportation Accessibility: Some References*. Exchange Bibliography No. 482. Monticello, Ill.: Council of Planning Librarians, 1973.

Northwestern University, Transportation Center. *The Journey to Work*. Selected References 1960-67. Exchange Bibliography No. 40. Monticello, Ill.: Council of Planning Librarians. 1968.

Olsson, Gunnar. *Distance and Human Interaction: A Review and Bibliography*. Philadelphia: University of Pennsylvania, Regional Science Research Institute, 1969.

Quigley, John M. *Residential Location with Multiple Workplaces and a Heterogeneous Housing Stock*. Exchange Bibliography No. 388. Monticello, Ill.: Council of Planning Librarians, April 1973.

Ronningen, Johan. *Residential Densities*. Exchange Bibliography No. 416. Monticello, Ill.: Council of Planning Librarians, June 1973.

Sternlieb, George, Robert W. Burchell and Virginia Paulus. *Residential Abandonment: The Environment of Decay.* Exchange Bibliography No. 342. Monticello, Ill.: Council of Planning Librarians, 1972.

Stutz, Frederick P. *Research on Intra-Urban Social Travel: Introduction and Bibliography.* Exchange Bibliography No. 173. Monticello, Ill.: Council of Planning Librarians, 1971.

Wheeler, James O. *Research on the Journey to Work: Introduction and Bibliography.* Exchange Bibliography No. 65. Monticello, Ill.: Council of Planning Librarians, 1969.

Theses and Dissertations

Alonso, William. "A Model of the Urban Land Market: Locations and Densities of Dwellings and Business." Ph.D. dissertation, University of Pennsylvania, 1960.

Hamburg, John R. "Some Social and Economic Factors Related to Intra-City Movement." M.A. thesis, Wayne State University, 1957.

Ingram, Gregory K. "A Simulation Model of Metropolitan Housing Market." Ph.D. dissertation, Harvard University, 1971.

Jones, Barclay Gibbs. "The Theory of the Urban Economy: Origins and Development with Emphasis on Intraurban Distribution of Population and Economic Activity." Ph.D. dissertation, University of North Carolina, 1960.

Kain, John Forest. "The Journey to Work as a Determinant of Residential Location." Ph.D. dissertation, University of California, Berkeley, 1962.

Kaiser, Edward John. "Toward a Model of Residential Developer Locational Behavior." Ph.D. dissertation, University of North Carolina, 1966.

Lee, Douglas Boardman, Jr. "Urban Models and Household Disaggregation—An Empirical Problem in Urban Research." Ph.D. dissertation, Cornell University, 1968.

Lisco, Thomas E. "The Value of Commuter's Travel Time: A Study in Labor Transportation." Ph.D. dissertation, University of Chicago, 1967.

Loewenstein, Louis Klee. "The Spatial Distribution of Residences and Workplaces in Urban Areas." Ph.D. dissertation, University of Pennsylvania, 1962.

Lowry, Ira South. "Residential Location in Urban Areas." Ph.D. dissertation, University of California, 1960.

Malone, John R. "A Statistical Comparison of Recent New and Used Home Buyers." Ph.D. dissertation, University of Chicago, 1963.

Massie, Ronald Wayne. "A System of Linked Models for Forecasting Urban Residential Growth." Master thesis, University of North Carolina, 1969.

Mayo, Stephen K. "An Econometric Model of Residential Location." Ph.D. dissertation, Harvard University, 1972.

Nelson, Robert Henry. "The Theory of Residential Location." Ph.D. dissertation, Princeton University, 1971.

Pendleton, William C. "The Value of Highway Accessibility." Ph.D. dissertation, University of Chicago, 1963.

Quigley, John M. "Residential Location with Multiple Workplaces and a Heterogeneous Housing Stock." Ph.D. dissertation, Harvard University, 1972.

Stegman, Michael A. "An Analysis and Evaluation of Urban Residential Models and their Potential Role in City Planning." Ph.D. dissertation, University of Pennsylvania, 1966.

Unpublished Material

Beckmann, Martin J. "The Optimum Density Distribution in a City." Work supported by N.S.F. Grant No. 3280, April 1972.

Bradbury, Katherine, Robert Engle, Owen Irvine and Jerome Rothenberg. "Simultaneous Estimation of the Supply and Demand for Household Location in a Multizoned Metropolitan Area." Paper presented at Econometric Society Meetings, San Francisco, Dec. 27-30, 1974.

Brown, James and John F. Kain. "Moving Behavior of San Francisco's Households." John F. Kain, ed. The NBER (National Bureau of Economic Research) Urban Simulation Model.

Burns, Leland S. "The Intra-Urban Income Distribution." Presented at the British Section of the Regional Science Association Annual Conference, London, Aug. 1968.

Drennan, Matthew P. "Estimating Commuters' Marginal Value of Travel Time." (mimeo).

Gordon, Josephine G. "Is the Land Tax Really a Neutral Tax?" Presented at the Regional Science Association Meetings, Chicago, November 1974.

Guthrie, Harold W. "Differences Among Consumers Attributable to Locations." (mimeo).

Harris, Britton. "A Model of Locational Equilibrium for Retail Trade." Penn Jersey Transportation Study, Oct. 15, 1964. (mimeo).

_____. "Notes on an Approach to Metropolitan Housing Market Analysis." University, 1966. (mimeo).

Kanemoto, Yoshitsugu. "Congestion and Cost-Benefit Analysis in Cities." 1974. (mimeo).

_____. "Optimum, Market and Second Best Land Use Patterns in a Von Thünen City with Congestion." Paper prepared for the Rokko Econometric Conference, Japan, 1973.

Pollakowski, Henry. "Effects of Local Public Services on Residential Location Decisions." Prepared for the Regional Science Association Meetings, Chicago, Nov. 7-10, 1974.

Quigley, John M. "Towards a Synthesis of Theories of Residence Site Choice." Prepared for the Regional Science Association Meetings, Chicago, November 7-10, 1974.

Index

Index

196

Households, income of, 93
Housing: consumption of, 95; demand for, 73, 95, 99; heterogeneous stock of, 163; homogeneous stock of, 87, 133, 136; market analysis of, 144n, 155n; market equilibrium of, 8; price of, 6, 9, 71, 75, 93, 101-103, 107, 109-110, 121-123, 129; quality of, 86; quantity of, 93; supply of, 87, 95, 111, 133
Hoyt, H., 40, 44, 45, 46, 49, 50, 51, 151n, 152n, 153n
Huff, D.L., 161n
Human ecological approach, 31, 42-46
Hurd, R., 37, 38, 40, 150n, 151n

Invasion-succession process, 47, 143n
Isard, W., 4, 143n, 147n, 150n, 158n, 162n

Journey-to-work, 5, 28, 67, 79, 84; as an explanatory variable, 69
Jurkat, E., 19, 146n

Kain, J., 67-68, 69, 71, 73, 74, 79, 156n, 157n, 158n, 159n, 162n
Karlquist, A., 149n
Keiper, J.S., 151n
Kish, L., 49
Kraus, M., 159n
Kurnow, E., 151n

Lakshmanan, T.R., 84, 156n, 160n
Land: agricultural use of, 33; agricultural value of, 31; economics of, 31-32, 42; patterns of use, 44; price of, 43; rent of, 32-37, 41, 44, 70, 77, 80, 81, 87, 88-89, 93, 114-118, 151n; rent bid prices of, 71; rent as negative transport cost, 47; rent as a residual of, 32; value of, 31, 32, 42, 43, 45, 102-103, 107
Lansing, J.B., 161n
Lathrop, G.T., 24, 148n
Launhardt, W., 82, 160n, 163n
Least resistance, lines of, 49
Leisure time, 94, 101, 128, 130
Linear multiple regression, 57
Linear programming, 57-67, 154n, 155n; critique of, 63-64
Linearity, assumption of, 63
Lowry, I.S., 25, 26, 27, 28, 148n, 149n
Luce, R.D., 144n
Lynd, H.M., 153n
Lynd, R.S., 45, 153n

McKenzie, R., 42, 49, 51, 152n, 153n, 154n
Maisel, S.J., 155n
Malone, J.R., 163n
Mann, P., 154n

Marble, F., 147n
Margolis, J., 81, 159n
Market area, 8; boundary of, 7-8, 84, 126-127, 137, 163n; delimitation of, 82-84
Marksjo, B., 149n
Marshall, A., 150n
Menchick, M.D., 161n
Metropolitan region, 8, 43, 139
Meyer, J., 79, 156n, 159n
Mill, J.S., 150n
Mills, E.S., 72, 79, 80, 150n, 158n, 159n
Models: behavioral, of residential location, 15, 55-90, 149n; classification of, 12, 135, 145n; definition of, 11, 135; of density, 20; econometric, 64-68; equilibrium of residential location, 56, 69, 70-137, 139; gravity, 148n, 149n; gravity-potential, 15; linear programming, 57-67; mathematical, 53; microeconomic, 8; monocentric, 5, 8, 20, 87, 139; operational, of residential location, 56-57, 68-69; of opportunity-accessibility, 24; relationship to theory, 11; types of, 71
Monocentric city, 29, 72
Monocentricity, assumption of, 5, 8, 33, 47, 49, 50, 71, 75, 78, 79, 80, 81, 88
Montesano, A., 158n
Morrill, R.L., 147n
Mueller, E., 161n
Multi-center city, 6, 49, 52, 84, 93-119, 121-134, 136-137
Multi-nuclei, 41; comparison with monocentric city, 9; concept, 46, 51; hypothesis, 44, 47, 82
Murdock, G.P., 153n
Muth, R., 5, 8, 69, 71, 75-78, 80, 82, 143n, 144n, 146n, 157n-160n, 162n, 163n

Nathanson, J., 155n
Natural area, concept of, 45
Newling, B.E., 146n
Niedercorn, J.H., 148n
Nystuen, J.D., 147n

Olsson, G., 147n
Operational models of residential location. See models

Papageorgiou, G., 160n
Pareto income distribution, 70, 94n
Park, R., 42, 43, 152n
Penn-Jersey Transportation Study, 58, 64-67
Phillips, B.S., 144n
Putman, S.H., 156n

Quigley, J.M., 84, 87, 133, 144n, 160n, 161n, 163n

About the Author

Michael C. Romanos was born in 1941 on the Greek island of Crete. He earned a diploma in architectural engineering from the Athens National Technical University, a master of science degree in urban and regional planning from the Florida State University, and a Ph.D. in regional science from Cornell University.

Before coming to the United States as a Fulbright Scholar, he spent several years working in the Greek Ministry of Coordination and Planning. Between 1973 and 1975 he taught at Cornell University, and he is presently an assistant professor of urban and regional planning at the University of Illinois, Urbana.

A member of several professional associations and honor societies, Professor Romanos is also the author of several papers and monographs on regional economic development and urban spatial structure.